CW01022540

I Think
I'm on the
Guest List

Gary Shail

TO LEE

Best wishes

Gary Shail

I Think I'm on the Guest List

First Edition
Published 2015
NEW HAVEN PUBLISHING LTD
www.newhavenpublishingltd.com
newhavenpublishing@gmail.com

Editor Katrina Sisowath

Cover design © Pete Cunliffe
pcunliffe@blueyonder.co.uk

Copyright © 2015 Gary Shail
All rights reserved
ISBN:
ISBN: 978-1-910705-04-9

Foreword

I am sure that a few people mentioned in this book may well disagree with some of my recollections and stories. To those I say, write your own fucking book then!

-   Gary Shail

Dear Reader,

When I was asked to write an introduction and foreword for Gary Shail's new book I was, to say the least, extremely flattered. When the phone call came from Gary saying 'please be kind', I was petrified.

How on earth does one be true to that particular request when it concerns one of our well know celebrated BAD boys? Then I read the book…

As with Peter O'Toole, Richard Wymark, Ronnie Fraser, Richard Burton, Richard Harris and Jimmy Villiars, there were in fact so many so called bad boys in the sixties and seventies that to mention them all would be longer than a Keith moon drum solo. Let's face it, to be seen with a drink in your hand at the wrong time, in the wrong place, put you on the slaying block, and didn't the press love it?

Gary Shail, the late seventies, eighties and nineties scream with your explosive interviews and minstrel activities. I am in awe of your honesty as you lay down the facts of many of these exploits in exact and factual detail. You have bared your soul as none other could, and have put yourself in the firing-line through that honesty, many a stronger being would be scared to admit to.

My dear Gary, you have my admiration for writing a recollection of a time that so many miss and life experiences that few survived. The photos are priceless and your memories are, without doubt, something that had to be told.

With the greatest of respect

ROBIN STEWART
Actor and Author of
Being Mike Abbot and
A Life in the Wild – Toads Abode series

This book is dedicated to my Mum and Dad

Yankee Candle International, Ltd.

A subsidiary of Jarden Corporation (NYSE:JAH)
Cabot Park, Poplar Way East, Avonmouth,
Bristol, BS11 0YH, UK
008 008 658 8466
yankeecandle.co.uk

1

"Childhood is like being drunk — everyone remembers what you did —except you."

Summers were jelly and ice cream, winters' jam roly-poly and custard, and that is how I remember my early childhood.

In the seemingly endless summer holidays, I was allowed (after my Ready Brek) out of the house and left to my own devices. As long as I was back in time for tea, (around 4.30-ish) that would be the last my parents would see of me for the rest of the day. Everyone in my street knew where the man with the grubby raincoat lived, and so did the local policeman. I also had 'surrogate mothers' all over the place, so when I eventually arrived home after a hard days' exploring, Mum would always know where I'd been, and who I'd talked to. It was a small but safe world that I inhabited, where rules were adhered to, and punishments, although never administered, were deadly! It was 1970, I was 11yrs old, and Jimmy Hendrix was number 1 in the charts with 'Voodoo Child'.

Music played a huge part in our everyday family life. Dad played guitar and the banjo and Mum sang, so it was never questioned when I showed an interest in music and how it was made. I joined the local Boys' Brigade, which had a marching band, and decided that I would be a drummer. This would mean attending the local Baptist Church every Sunday but a small price to pay if it meant that I would get my hands on one of those sparkly side drums that were loaned out to the very best. Dad bought me a Premier snare drum with a stand and I practiced whenever possible, or until Mum bribed me with a jam sandwich to stop.

Within a year, I was the lead drummer of the 2nd Hendon Boys' Brigade, regularly marching on a Sunday morning through the leafy streets of North London whilst crowds of people (probably only a few) looked on with admiration (probably not). I had found something that I was good at and had been noticed. I decided that I would forever more be noticed.

Getting noticed at Hendon Junior High School was proving to be harder than I thought. I was not exactly a bad pupil, but by the age of 11 it was clear to everyone and anyone who could be arsed, that I was not university material. In fact, I don't think I had actually met anyone, or knew anyone who knew anyone who'd been to university, until I was in my late teens. However, every parent harbours the vain hope that they have spawned the next Einstein, don't they? Well, it certainly wasn't me. What I was good at though, was showing off!

I was now taking piano lessons with a local teacher called Angela Brownage. Mum and Dad had bought the family a splendid rosewood upright piano, which now stood pride of place in our back room overlooking the garden. Dad played me a record by Jerry Lee Lewis called "Chantilly Lace", and that was it. I would now play the piano.

Angela, who lived only five houses away, was absolutely gorgeous. Think 'Morticia' from The Addams Family, but much sexier, and you get the picture. Angela was (and still is) a renowned concert pianist who travelled the world playing the classics to thousands, but I just wanted her to teach me to play songs that people knew, and look down her cleavage.

Mum or Dad would play me something, and I would learn it. It was simple but brilliant, and my parents' taste in music was impeccable. Elvis, Bacharach, Herb Albert, Sinatra, The Beach Boys, Glenn Campbell and Neil Sedaka…they had all written songs that everyone knew, and now I knew them. It was great fun to learn the piano this way and even now, when I am asked to teach, I use this approach.

I was learning television theme tunes, pop songs, country & western, ballads and basically anything that took my fancy. Sundays, when my grandparents came over, was especially great, as inevitably after tea Dad would get his guitar out and we would play through my most recent repertoire. I loved my music lessons at school too. It was the one subject where I was top of the class. The Head of Music at Hendon High was the formidable Trevor Easterfield.

Mr Easterfield was unlike any other teacher at the school. He was a strange and mysterious man with a wry smile and sense of humour that I am sure was wasted on some of his colleagues in the staff room. Mr Easterfield, I think, recognised me as a fellow musician and not just a pupil, and I looked forward to his lessons eagerly, and tried not to piss him off. One day, he changed my life forever.

With the approval of my parents, Mr Easterfield asked me if I'd like to play drums at some gigs that he'd been asked to play for. They were only private party shows, but as far as I was concerned they might as well have been at Wembley Stadium. Plus, I would be getting paid. Mr Easterfield now became Trevor, and I became a professional musician.

Discipline at Hendon High was strict, and positively barbaric by today's standards. But the regime did teach you extremely useful basic skills, such as evasion techniques, deniability, interrogation endurance, and pain resistance. You would only get one warning for any breach of the rules and then, depending on the mood of the enforcing teacher, you would be punished. Detentions were the norm, but in extreme cases, Mr Thompson (Headmaster) would invite you to his office, where he would whack you with a swish cane, normally onto your outstretched open hands, whilst you tried to look hard and uncaring.

One wet Wednesday afternoon whilst on a detention, I met the man who would alter my destiny. I had been charged, and convicted, of wearing non-standard colourful socks on school property. A misdemeanour that had now placed me in the drill hall in front of a member of staff who usually wasted this time marking. On this occasion though, my detention officer was the drama teacher Marcus Kimber. Instead of making me stand motionless with my hands clasped behind my back as usual, he asked me if I could read something in an American accent. I didn't know it at the time, but I was auditioning for the lead role in Marcus Kimber's adaptation of Mark Twain's Tom Sawyer. Marcus was a real force of nature and changed the daily dynamics of my life completely. I threw myself into the role of Tom and relished the new attention that it gave me.

Tom Sawyer changed everything. Girls started talking to me, and I now had a social life. I even got to snog Usha Goswami who was the hottest girl in my year (she will deny this of course, as she is now a renowned doctor of physics and will probably put it down to misplaced adolescent hormones). I think she was just starstruck.

My best friend was Milton Jaghai who lived three streets away in Dartmouth Road. He had come over from Jamaica with his elder brother Dalton and his parents Fredrick and Avis in the early sixties. Fred was a bus driver and Avis was a nurse. She was also a fantastic cook. Some days I would get my dinner twice: sausage, egg and chips at home, and then 'round to Milton's for stewed chicken with rice and peas. If I was really lucky, I might even get a fried dumpling thrown in, although this was a rarity as dumplings were extremely popular in the Jaghai household. It didn't matter what time you arrived at the Jaghais', there was always something in the pot. Only recently I popped over to say hello, and within minutes I was eating.

Just like in my own home, music was prevalent. Fredrick loved Ska and Bluebeat, and the boys loved Reggae. It was the summer of 1971, and a song by Dave and Ansell Collins had topped the U.K charts with a song called 'Double Barrel'. It was regarded by the press at the time as a bit of a novelty record, but to me it marked the beginning of a musical journey that bordered on obsession. I started to delve deeply into the history of Reggae and the people who made it. This was music you didn't just listen to, you could actually feel it. Milt's brother Dalton had built a speaker cabinet out of an old wardrobe in his bedroom with 4 bass bins and a host of tweeters that, if stood next to, could induce vomiting when turned up to the max.

To get hold of this music wasn't easy, and the records usually had to be imported. There was a little shop just off Oxford Street called Daddy Cool that sold pre-releases from Jamaica, and on Saturdays, once I'd earned some money washing Dad's car, we would hop on the 113 bus down to Oxford Circus hoping that all the best tunes hadn't yet been sold. Sometimes there would only be two or three copies of a record for sale, so you had to be quick.

Gary and Milton 1971

If you got the tune you wanted, it was better than sex! Not that I knew anything about sex... not yet. I had found my musical identity at last, but now the piano just seemed a tad tame. I didn't want to be Jerry Lee anymore. I wanted to be Aston Family Man Barrett.*

Persuading Mum and Dad to let me buy a bass guitar was not difficult. They had seen that I was prepared to learn and practice, I had already achieved grade 3 on the piano, and I was earning money from playing drums, so guitar seemed like a logical progression.

Dad agreed, as I knew he would, so that weekend we took the short drive to Cricklewood where I purchased my first, but certainly not my last, bass guitar. It was a Gibson SG, only a copy, but I cherished it, and kept it beside the bed so that it was the first thing I saw in the morning.

Marcus Kimber had started an after-school drama club called Nucleus, which I was invited to join. I didn't need a lot of persuading, as my triumphant debut as Tom Sawyer had given me the self-confidence to raise my head from the trenches. Trouble is: there's always someone ready to take a pot-shot when you do. I certainly wasn't bullied at school, but the playground mafia certainly had me in their sights, and quite often I was subjected to random acts of violence. Mum's advice was to hit them back harder, and if they were too big, stand on a chair; and if necessary, hit them with the chair. This meant I would have to carry a chair around with me at all times, but I knew what she meant. Dad's advice was far more practical, learn to fight properly.

Our next door neighbour at that time was a guy called Albert Wong who was the manager of our local Chinese restaurant The Bamboo House. He was a lovely, quiet, and gentle man who would often invite us to the restaurant for a free dinner. This personable demeanour hid a side that few people ever saw of him, though. He was a master of the martial arts. I had done a bit of Judo at school, but nothing could have prepared me for this. Albert's philosophy was, if you know you can beat your opponent, then why bother fighting? He was a hard taskmaster, but slowly and surely my brain and body started to react to the training. I could run faster, jump higher and punch harder.

I don't know what it was that changed about me, but no one ever dead-legged me in the playground ever again, and I never had to use anything that I'd learned, except for one time in a night club called Stringfellows more than a decade later.

*Aston was one of the Barrett brothers (the other being Carlton "Carly" Barrett) who played with Bob Marley and The Wailers, The Hippy Boys, and Lee Perry's The Upsetters. It has been stated that Aston was the 'leader' of the backing band and responsible for many, if not all, bass lines on Bob Marley's greatest hits, as well as having been active in co-producing Marley's albums and responsible for most overall song arrangements. He was the mentor of Robbie Shakespeare of the duo Sly & Robbie, and is considered one of the elder statesmen of reggae bass guitar playing

Nucleus was a real success and quite revolutionary for its time. We were school kids but worked and behaved like a professional company. Marcus taught us about all aspects of the theatre, including stage management, lighting, and stage design, as well as movement and mime. He also invited professional actors in to talk about their careers. One such actor was a very young Philip Martin Brown*, I seem to remember.

Our first production was *Zigger Zagger* by Peter Terson, where I played the leading role of Harry Philton. In the second show I played a dung collecting beetle in Joseph Capek's *The Insect Play*, which we even performed at a drama festival in France. Unfortunately, on the drive home, Marcus misjudged the height of a bridge and ripped the roof off of the mini bus that we were travelling in. But apart from that we were having the time of our lives.

My after-school activities were completely taking over. Every evening was catered for. Something had to give. I gave up The Boys' Brigade, as I could now play military drums and the uniform just didn't do it for me anymore. I also gave up doing homework.

Quite often I would have to get up at the crack of dawn to finish something that I should've done the night before, and this didn't go unnoticed. There are only so many excuses one can make. 'The dog ate my homework' is an urban myth, I tell thee.

Lucky for me then, that Marcus Kimber noticed too and called a meeting with my parents.

The Arts Educational School originated from two schools, one founded in 1919 by Grace Cone, and one in 1922 by Olive Ripman. These two women were educational pioneers, who believed passionately in the value of combining a general academic education with a specialised training in dance, drama, music, and art, preparing young men and women for professional careers in, or connected with, the theatre. The Cone Ripman School became known as the Arts Educational School in 1939. The school was first based in premises at Stratford Place in London, but following the outbreak of World War II, the school was relocated to Tring, Hertfordshire, where it shared premises with the Rothschild Bank in the mansion at Tring Park.

---

*Brown has appeared in over 130 episodes of *Waterloo Road*. He has also worked on *The Professionals, The Bill*, where he appeared in 10 episodes as Seth Mercer, and has made appearances on many other British dramas, including *Heartbeat, Midsomer Murders, Hetty Wainthropp Investigates, New Tricks* and *Doctors*. His most prominent role in a drama before *Waterloo Road* was his portrayal of Eddie Vincent in *Casualty*, where he starred in 17 episodes between 2002 and 2003. He played John Adams in the film *The Bounty* and appeared in *Sharpes Justice* in 1995. He played a detective in series 1 episode 2 of ITV drama *Rosemary & Thyme*. He also appeared in a *Skins* Online Episode in 2012, playing a drug-dealer. Philip bowed out of *Waterloo Road* as Grantly Budgen during the Autumn Term of Series 9.

In 1941 the school reopened its premises at Stratford Place, with a second school continuing to operate in Tring, and in 1947 both schools were renamed the Arts Educational Schools (London/Tring Park). Since it was reopened the London school has been based in various locations, but in 1973 the address was no.1, The Golden Lane Theatre, The Barbican, City of London, W1.

This was a private school that was too good to be true. Could I really be good enough to get into a place like this? It was a mad idea and it was expensive! But it was being discussed seriously by Marcus Kimber and my parents. There would have to be radical economic changes made, even with a government grant. Also, I would have to say farewell to the Hendon Junior High School and the Dead-Legging Mafia. FUCK YES, OF COURSE I WANTED TO GO!

I had to prepare two theatrical pieces (speeches) and a dance...DANCE! What did they mean? I could do The Hustle and Jive with my mum, but at this school they took their dancing seriously. I would also have to play something on the piano. Now that I could do! For my pieces Marcus chose an excerpt from Zigger Zagger and Jacques's, act 11, scene V11, speech from Shakespeare's *As You Like It*. You know the one.

All the world's a stage,
And all the men and women merely players.
They have their exits and their entrances,
And one man in his time plays many parts,
His acts being seven ages...etc.

For the music, I would play the Rodgers and Hart classic 'Blue Moon' (my mum's favourite) and a medley of 50's rock n roll songs, just in case anyone on the auditioning committee was younger than 50. As for the dance, well, I would have to blag that, but I was confidant I could pull it off.

On the day of the audition, (a Saturday), Dad and I took the Northern Line tube from Hendon Central to Moorgate. We then made the short walk through the deserted streets of the city to the Barbican.

The Golden Lane Theatre was like a little oasis in a concrete desert. The Barbican was, and still is, a prominent example of 1960's/70's British brutalist architecture, and in 2011 actually achieved Grade 11 status. In 1973 it looked like something out of Fritz Lang's Metropolis. But right smack in the middle of this concrete and steel nightmare stood this beautiful little theatre, and hopefully my future school.

What happened next is a complete mystery. To this day I cannot remember one moment of my audition—not one thing! And this wouldn't be the last time that I would block out complete performances from my memory.

Over the next few weeks I tried to concentrate on all my other activities. Piano lessons, bass practice, Albert Wong randomly attacking me like 'Cato' from the Pink Panther Movies, all helped to stop me thinking about the future. I am like that even now. As long as I am busy doing something today, I don't worry too much about tomorrow. But give me too much time to think, and I am fucked! No news was good news right? Milton and his family knew and so did a few family friends, but apart from that I kept my aspirations to myself. And then one day, all of a sudden, a letter appeared addressed to me. I was in!

The list of stuff I was required to have was as remarkable as it was long. Some of the items we had never heard of, such as court shoes and Jazz pants. We would have to buy these items at a specialist dance-wear shop in town, as well as stage makeup, text books, tap shoes and a completely new uniform. I enjoyed the shopping in town immensely though, and on one of these shopping expeditions (to acquire stage makeup) we had to venture into Covent Garden, to a beautiful little theatrical shop just off Long Acre called The Theatre Zoo.

The shop was owned and run by an elderly bloke (probably only 50) called Bert. As soon as we gave him the list of our requirements he laughed, "So you are about to become an Arts Ed boy eh?" said Bert. "Yes," I replied. "Well…I will be seeing you next term then, as I am going to be teaching you how to use all this stuff that you have just bought."

Back then, in my naivety, I thought that this was just a lovely coincidence, but of course Bert's shop was on the list. He was the supplier! It would only be a few weeks after starting that we realised that I actually didn't need half of this stuff, but by then it was too late, and the money had been spent.

The 1973 school summer holidays at Hendon were much longer for me than for the rest of my friends that year. I wouldn't be starting at The Arts for about six weeks after everyone else had gone back to school. I felt like the luckiest boy on earth!

The Arts Educational School

14

2

I don't remember feeling nervous at all on my first day at Arts Ed. I was as prepared as any 13year old boy about to enter a completely alien world could be. It didn't actually feel like I was going to school, more like a day out really. Sitting on the train and watching the grey faces of my fellow commuters on that first day as they headed off to their boring office jobs just reinforced my belief that I was never going to be like them.

The walk from Moorgate station to the Barbican was completely different this time around. The City Of London is like another world during weekdays, and the hustle and bustle took me completely by surprise. It took me a while to get my bearings. It would also take me two weeks to find out that The Barbican actually had its own station, and I didn't have to walk from Moorgate at all.

As I eventually reached the main entrance to the school, I was confronted by a sea of green-clad females chatting enthusiastically on the steps. They were all wearing straw boaters and little white gloves. This really was St Trinians! I took a deep breath before edging my way around them all and into the building that would be my seat of learning for the next three years.

I had to report my presence to Miss Bose the school secretary, a bird-like creature who peered at me over her half-rimmed spectacles like I was an insect about to be devoured. "Ahh yes…Shail- the new boy, stand over there with Lelliott and Boweres, and Matron will see you presently." I had no idea why a Matron would need to see me, but at this point it seemed logical to just go with the flow. I nodded politely and headed over to where Lelliott and Boweres were standing. They were the only other boys in reception.

Keith Lelliott was about my age but quite a bit shorter. He had a 70's mullet haircut and flared trousers to match. He was also wearing platform shoes. Paul Boweres, on the other hand, was dressed in a 50's style black drape jacket with brothel creeper shoes to match his quiffed slick-backed hair (so much for the new school uniform that my parents had spent a small fortune on, eh). Paul and Keith were ballet students. Suddenly I heard my name being called.

Matron was about 103, dressed in starch, and smelled of TCP. She had probably trained Florence Nightingale and had performed amputations in the trenches with a nail file.

"Follow me," Matron commanded.

At my audition I had only seen the ground floor rooms, but now I was being led by an unfeasibly speedy octogenarian through the bowels of the building towards Matron's lair. Once there, I was weighed, measured, had my temperature and blood pressure taken, and basically given a complete once-over. At this school fitness and health were paramount. If I had any health problems Matron wanted to know about them sooner rather than later, and if I thought my Kung Fu training with Albert Wong had been strenuous, I had another think coming.

After my examination had been completed, I was led back upstairs to the large mirrored room that I'd had my original audition in for assembly. It was full of girls, about 200 of them. I tried my hardest to look cool, and nonchalantly glanced around the room to find the other boys. There they were, stood behind the girls in a row, all 15 of them. I sauntered over and casually asked the tallest, a lad called Adrian, "Where's all the other boys?"

"This Is It," he said.

Adrian Hall was the head boy of the school. He had been a child star and had acted alongside Dick Van Dyke in a film called *Chitty Chitty Bang Bang*. He was a very good-looking male specimen and didn't he fucking know it! He also played the guitar and sang. We got on immediately. There was also a young lad called Dave Williams who, like me, also came from North London. I later found out that Dave played the drums and had also been in the Boys' Brigade, so already I was making friends with lots in common. In fact, I had never felt so comfortable around new people. I was also becoming very comfortable in the company of scantily clad girls.

After the morning academic classes and lunch which, if you were a ballet student, usually consisted of an apple and piece of cheese, we would change into the appropriate attire for the afternoon dance, music, or drama sessions. Bare feet and Lycra were the norm, and no one that I can remember ever wore jazz pants or court shoes ever! (Another expenditure that my parents could've done without.) In the professional theatre environment that we were being trained to inhabit, shyness was literally a waste of time. If you ever have to quick-change backstage, then no one has the time to ogle tits. Not that any of my female fellow students had anything to be shy about. The first couple of weeks had been difficult though.

At Hendon High just getting a brief glimpse of knicker-elastic was enough to give a 13yr old lad a stiffy, so being surrounded by perfectly formed dancers with only a millimetre of Lycra separating you from flesh was obviously the reason why all the boys wore Jock Straps. It was the one thing on the school list that wasn't a waste of money.

My attitude to homosexuality has never changed. The reason for this is because I don't have one. I am sure that some of my fellow students were gay, but the subject just never came up. I have never been interested in anyone's love life but my own, but the common misapprehension that all ballet dancers were queer was very far from the truth.

I think my old Hendon mates had been dubious about my new friends, but when Keith Lelliott came back to my house for the weekend, he ended up snogging the face off my old school friend Jacquie Wood. In fact, I have known many male dancers over the years, and believe me; a lot of them still use the Gay Card to get into a woman's underwear.

I only had two girlfriends whilst at The Arts School and both of them were called Debbie. I would've liked to have written a lot more about the adolescence heartache, and that first apprehensive kiss before moving in for the bra-strap kind of thing, but they are both now in their 50's and have grown up lives with children and husbands who I'm sure wouldn't want to read about their wives' early love life adventures. I will say this though...I lost my virginity to one of them.

The Arts also had an agency, and one day I was asked if I'd audition for a new TV series called *Holding On*, to be produced by London Weekend Television. The part of Young Ted required a young actor who could convincingly portray an East End docker's son in the 1920's. As soon as I'd met the Producer (Paul Knight) and the Directors (Ray Menmuir & Gerry Mill) I knew I was in with a chance. My London accent got me the job.

Holding On was a joy to do. It had been my first professional job as an actor, and I was only just 14. I learnt so much from the other cast members, especially from the young brilliant actor playing my dad, Michael Elphick. He was only 27, but over the course of six episodes would have to age 50 yrs., whilst my character's part would be replaced by an older actor in the third episode. His name was Kenneth Cranham. I was having the best time ever! I loved school passionately, I was learning, earning and my loins were burning. With my very first TV pay check, I bought a brand new stereo system. I think it cost about £75, a lot of money in 1974.

Very soon after *Holding On* I was hired to play a Victorian street urchin in a TV drama for the BBC starring Polly James, called *Never 'eard of Paradise*. Seems like I was getting good at playing rough and tough little bleeders. My academic life wasn't bad either. I had been used to 30 kids to a class at Hendon High, but at The Arts ten in a class was a big class. I could no longer hide at the back, or gaze out of the window daydreaming. I became far more focussed, but would only concentrate on the subjects I thought I would need. History, English Literature, Art, Music, Greek Mythology and Religious Education were the subjects I chose. I always knew that one day we'd have Google Earth, so why bother with geography. No, geography time was spent on the back stairs snogging a Debbie!

Also, the teaching methods were completely different. In English Literature, for example, if we were discussing a piece of Shakespeare or poetry, we were encouraged to act it out, and not just read it from the book. I passed O Levels in all these subjects, which pleased my parents no end. Mum and Dad had been working flat out to keep me at this school. Mum even started working from home, making everything from wedding veils to puncture repair outfits. For a while our house constantly smelled of rubber. Everything was running smoothly, and then I got arrested!

I have no doubts at all, that I have been the only child ever, to be arrested from The Arts Educational School. But it was worth it, and my parents thought so too.

One evening, I had a late music class with Miss Rose, our resident piano teacher. I had about half an hour to wait, so I sauntered around the mezzanine kicking my heels. I could hear a piano being plonked in one of the other music rooms, so decided to investigate. All of a sudden I saw the caretaker, clearly agitated and annoyed, run into the room shouting and screaming like a madman. No one liked this new caretaker! He was a South African and thought he was a prison officer. I heard him shout "No one plays piano unsupervised," and with that

I heard the lid of the piano slam shut. I ran to the room to find him towering over a terrified little new girl clutching her hands close to her chest. I couldn't believe what I was witnessing. Had this total arsehole really slammed a piano lid down onto this little girl's fingers? It didn't matter if he had missed; the poor girl was shaking like a leaf.

With that he barged past me and out of the room. I followed him out on to the landing and threw him head first down the stairs. He must've landed heavily; because by the time I reached him, he was clutching his shoulder and moaning like a girl. Suddenly there were people everywhere, and he was screaming for the police. Miss Bose was first on the scene, and looked stunned. I told her to do what he had said, and phone the police, and then after that, phone an ambulance, then after that, phone my dad.

The police and ambulance turned up at the same time. Twat Face was carted off to casualty, and I was carted off by The City of London Police. As I was only 15, I couldn't be questioned without a parent present, and my dad was brilliant. After I'd explained to him what had happened, he went into overdrive. How could such a man be allowed to be around children etc.? My son must've been provoked (which I thought I had been) etc. Miss Bose also gave a statement as to the character of the caretaker, and so after about an hour, I was released without charge. We never saw that caretaker again.

One of the total joys of attending a school like The Arts was watching my fellow pupils grow into professional performers. Keith Lelliott was an amazing dancer who would eventually join the Houston Ballet Company, and others in my class would be as equally as successful. Maria Friedman* was an amazing singer, as was Sarah Brightman*, who would go on to become a million-album-selling artist and the wife of a Lord less than a decade later. They were also the naughtiest kids in the school.

*Maria Friedman is an English actress of stage and screen, best known for her work in musical theatre. She is a seven-time Olivier Award nominee, winning three. Her first win was for her 1994 one-woman show, *By Special Arrangement*. She has also twice won Best Actress in a Musical for the original London productions of *Passion and Ragtime*.

*Sarah Brightman (born 14 August 1960) is an English classical crossover soprano, actress, songwriter and dancer. She has sung in many languages, including English, Spanish, French, Latin, German, Italian, Russian, Mandarin Chinese, Japanese and Catalan. Brightman began her career as a member of the dance troupe *Hot Gossip* and released several disco singles as a solo performer. In 1981, she made her West End musical theatre debut in *Cats* and met composer Andrew Lloyd Webber, whom she married. She went on to star in several West End and Broadway musicals, including *The Phantom of the Opera*, where she originated the role of Christine Daaé. The Original London Cast Album of the musical was released in CD format in 1987 and sold 40 million copies worldwide, making it the biggest-selling cast album of all time.

The other great thing about being here was that bad behaviour was treated, not punished. If anyone got stressed or upset, it was classed as Artistic Temperament, and the worse that would happen is that you would be made to lie down in Matron's room for an hour.

Sarah Brightman was this little fire-bomb, with wiry red hair and braces on her teeth when I first met her. She was always being caught bunking off (usually with me) but there was never any doubting her ambition to become a superstar. I remember watching Top of the Pops in 1978 and couldn't believe that the gorgeous girl singing "I Lost My Heart to a Star Ship Trooper" was Sarah Brightman.

In my final year of school, it was discussed at home whether or not I should leave or stay on to do the two year drama course. As I had already been at the school, it meant that I wouldn't have to re-audition for a place. Plus it would give me a qualification of sorts, so we decided that I would do it. I had loved being a stage school kid, but how would I like being a Drama Student? Only time would tell.

Even though I'd now started using the Barbican station, sometimes, if the trains were especially busy, I'd still travel straight through to Moorgate. On Friday, 28th of February 1975, the decision not to probably saved my life.

The Northern Line tube was split into two lines, one traveling south from High Barnet and the other from Edgware. To get to Moorgate directly meant getting the Bank train, so if the train I was on was the Charing Cross train, it would mean a change at Camden Town. On the day in question, I had decided to stay on the train until Kings Cross and then change to the Circle Line for the Barbican. For some reason I had been running late that morning, so when I eventually arrived at school, I was surprised that everyone seemed relieved to see me. What I didn't know was that the southbound train had failed to stop at the Moorgate terminus, and crashed into the wall at the end of the tunnel. 43 people died as a result of the crash, and a further 74 were injured. The greatest loss of life during peacetime on the London Underground.

London in the mid 70's was a precarious place to live anyway. Today we are constantly told that we are under threat from terrorism. But the I.R.A made the Islamic fundamentalists that we face today look like choirboys. Bombs were going off all over London.

17 June 1974: A bomb exploded at the Houses of Parliament in London, causing extensive damage and injuring 11 people.

17 July 1974: An explosion in the Tower of London left one person dead and 41 injured. This was the second bomb in London on this day. At 04:30 there was an explosion at government buildings in Balham, South London. Nobody was injured in the morning blast but there was substantial damage to surrounding buildings.

22 October 1974: A 5-pound bomb exploded in the Brooks Club, London, injuring three members of staff.

7 November 1974: An off-duty soldier and a civilian were killed when a bomb was thrown through the window of the Kings Arms pub in Woolwich, and 28 people were injured.

19 December 1974: The I.R.A. carried out a bomb attack on Selfridge's Department Store in Oxford Street, London. A time bomb had been placed in a car which was then parked outside the store. Three telephone warnings were given and the area was evacuated. The explosion was later estimated to have caused £1.5 million worth of damage.

21 December 1974: A bomb was defused in Harrods Department Store in Knightsbridge, London. A second bomb was defused in the King's Arms public house in Warminster, Wiltshire.

22 December 1974: A 2-pound bomb exploded at Edward Heath's home in Victoria, London. Heath was not at home at the time, but arrived 10 minutes later. Minor damage. No injuries.

28 August 1975: Seven people were injured when a bomb exploded in Oxford Street, London, outside the south-east corner of Selfridge's Sore. A telephone warning was issued to The Sun newspaper five minutes before the explosion.

5 September 1975: Two people were killed and 63 injured when an IRA bomb exploded in the lobby of the Hilton Hotel in London.

9 October 1975: A bomb detonated at a bus stop outside Green Park tube station, killing a 23 year old man and injuring at least 20 people — two of them children.

3 November 1975: Several people injured by a car bomb in Connaught Square, London W2.

27 November 1975: Ross McWhirter was shot at his home on Village Road, Bush Hill Park, Enfield, Middlesex, by two IRA volunteers, and died soon after in hospital.

You get the picture! I certainly won't be letting any Islamic Jihadist converts from Cardiff dictate to me when and where I can travel.

Moorgate crash 1975

3

The 1976 United Kingdom heat wave led to the hottest summer average temperature in the UK since records began. It really was hot enough to fry an egg on the hood of a car. I know, because I tried it on my dad's. This would be my final summer holiday before I would become a full time drama student, and so theoretically start to take things seriously. But before that... It was Carnival time.

Since 1966, Carnival had been held on the streets of Notting Hill, and had steadily, over the years, become one of the largest street parties in the world. My friends and I had been going since we were 13, and loved the fact that it was relatively local. Held over three days, it was a celebration of West Indian culture in Great Britain, and was one of the highlights of the year.

We would all meet up at my friend Vernon's house in West Hendon, and plan the day.

This was the place to be if you wanted to hear reggae music played at its best (Fucking Loud!) and the Sound Systems that played it had become legendary. King Tubby and Sir Lloyd Coxsone were as famous, if not more so, than the artists on the records that they played.

The food was excellent too. Jerk Chicken, Jamaican Patties, Dumplings, all were available from street vendors, as was Red Stripe beer. On the Sunday it was children's day.

The local communities spent all year creating the most beautiful costumes to parade in, and the vibe was joyful as usual. It was getting on for evening when suddenly the atmosphere changed.

We had definitely noticed a stronger police presence that day than in previous years. Race relations between young black youths and the police were at the time at an all-time low, due mainly to the over use of the 'sus' law, under which anybody could be stopped, searched and held, even if only suspected of a crime. Anticipating trouble, 3,000 police officers turned up. Whatever set it off; police officers were soon dodging a hail of bottles, bricks and a surging crowd. Windows were smashed, fires were lit, and ill-equipped police officers picked up dustbin lids and milk crates to combat the rioters.

My friends and I decided to try and get out of the area as quickly and quietly as possible. The cops were just throwing people into the backs of vans for no apparent reason. Luckily we knew the area well, so managed to detour the trouble. When we eventually got home, it had been all over the national news. It had been a truly frightening experience. More than 100 police officers and 60 other people were taken to hospital. Seventeen youths were eventually charged, but only two were convicted, after a case costing £250,000, a record at the time.

I should never have decided to go to college. I had been spoilt by stage school completely. Whereas at school I had been surrounded by students who were undoubtedly talented, at college 'normal' people were now allowed to play at being actors. I definitely had a misguided superiority complex, which I am sure didn't go down too well with my fellow students, but at just 17 I thought I knew it all. What's more, one of the new students had also been a pupil at Hendon High, I remembered him well.

Jon Caplan had been one of the most popular kids at Hendon High. Flash, good-looking, and Jewish. We hadn't really ever spoken to each other at all whilst I was there, but somehow he had managed to get an audition, and now he was here. Actually, Jon ended up being my closest friend for many years, but at the time I don't remember being too happy about it. The other thing I wasn't too happy about was that I would no longer be studying at Golden Lane, but at an annex in Kings Cross. I had got used to theatrical surroundings, but now I was forced to attend classes in a building that looked like a Victorian Prison.

The drama course was run by a husband and wife team called Brian and Yvette Cook, and on the first day they outlined how the next two years of my life was going to pan out. Yvette was Head of Voice Training. A title she had given herself, considering there was absolutely no one else teaching voice training. Brian (Head of Drama) was Head of Drama.

Over the next few weeks we were subjected to an assortment of strange tutors, with equally strange teaching methods. In the mornings we had 'Spanish Dance' for an hour. This consisted of us all standing in a circle whilst raising our arms up and down in unison. Hardly the foot-stomping, hand-clapping flamenco that I was looking forward to. Also, we had movement classes with a bizarre Scottish woman who had her own dance troupe called Cunning Stunts. (Geddit?) I will say this though; she was 'Moonwalking' long before Michael Jackson had supposedly invented it. Another tutor, whose name escapes me, taught comedy timing. This was a ridiculously unfunny class, except for one exception.

We had all been asked to bring an inanimate object to class and perform a three minute sketch using said object for comedic affect. It was painful to watch, as we all tried to be 'funny.' I can't remember what I brought, but I do remember it being pitiful and embarrassing. One of the girls though had brought a banana, which looked promising. She then peeled it, discarding the skin onto the floor (You know where this is going, right?). She then tried to fake slipping on the skin, but actually really did slip, and shot head first into the wall, cutting her head open in the process. I actually fell off my chair laughing. The tutor had a real go at me for being cruel, but as I pointed out, was it not Mark Twain who said all comedy stems from cruelty? Didn't go down well!

Not all the classes were a waste of time though, and once a week we had to go back to Golden Lane for Fencing. Phil Palmer was a bonafide Fencing Master, who really should've lived in the 13th century. He was a bearded giant of a man who wore a huge weighted leather band on his left wrist to counter the weight of the swords he wielded. He used to carry an assortment of evil-looking instruments of death in a huge bag which, if ever searched by the authorities, would've resulted in a lengthy spell in the cells, I'm sure. Phil carried it around like a satchel. From the moment I held a Rapier in my hand, I knew that I was going to be good at this.

I started staying late after fencing class for extra lessons. I had found that the basic classes with my fellow students were not enough for me. The others, I felt, wanted to learn just enough to pass their bronze fencing award, but I definitely wanted to learn more than that. I started learning complex routines, using an array of ancient weapons that Phil had in his enormous sack. My Martial Arts training and dance lessons had given me poise and balance, essential when waving a 16th century broadsword about.

Due to a childhood injury, where my right arm had been immobilized for quite a while, I found that I was ambidextrous to a certain degree, which was definitely an advantage. Of course, cuts and grazes were inevitable, and I still carry some scars to this day, but you know what they say!

Phil used to do exhibitions at medieval re-enactment functions, and asked if I'd like to partner him, re-enacting famous duels and battles from the past. The money was good, and it meant that I got to dress up. What wasn't there to like? We did everything from fairs to medieval banquets in that first year, and Phil and I became quite good friends.

Phil never talked about his private life to me at all, but he most certainly over-compensated in the testosterone department. He didn't like women very much, and would berate any he came into contact with, with a 'not knowing a 'real man' if they saw one; kind of thing. He was so far in the closet that any skeletons that had previously lived there had long moved out.

The other thing I liked about returning to Golden Lane was that I could catch up with old friends from when I was at the school. A lot of them had stayed on to do the Musical Theatre Course, which is self-explanatory, and I often wished that I'd followed this route.

I already knew I could act. I even had, thanks to my dad's perseverance, an Equity Card, which at the time was essential if you wanted to work professionally. You couldn't work unless you had one, but you had to work for 40 weeks to get one. Theatre companies usually had one or two cards to give to new actors, but the competition was fierce, and a lot of people I know had to travel abroad to dance in some dodgy nightclub to build the weeks up to get the all-important union card. How times have changed. Now even my window cleaner has his own T.V show. The rules were more lenient for child actors though, so I never had to worry about having to sweep a stage, or dance with Ladyboys in Bangkok.

1976 had been a turning point for me in many ways. I had never been into Glam or Prog rock, and although reggae was still my music of choice, I was never going to be black. So when Punk exploded onto the scene, I felt that this was something I could relate to. I started going to a pub in Islington called The Hope & Anchor to watch bands like 999, Xray Specs and The Clash, amongst others. The actual performance space at the Hope and Anchor was at the time a Spartan and rather grubby basement space, always dank and overheated, and very smoky. But this in many ways suited the anarchic ideals of late-1970's live music scene. It was here that The Stranglers recorded their album *Live*. I also started shopping for clothes.

London's Kings Road was the place to see and be seen if you were a punk in 76, and there was a shop near Worlds End called Sex that I started buying from. Run by a young fashion designer called Vivienne Westwood and her boyfriend Malcolm McLaren, it became the Mecca for all that was Punk. All four of The Sex Pistols used to shop there, and I think Glen Matlock, the original bass player, actually had a Saturday job. The shop changed its name to Seditionaries shortly after, selling their trademark trousers and T-Shirts to kids who could afford them. I actually bought a shirt there that nearly got me arrested.

The logo said...

BEATMEBITEME
WHIPMEFUCK
MECUMALLOVER
MYTITSLIKETHE
DIRTYSLAGIAM
TELLMEYOULOVE
MEANDFUCKOFF

The copper who stopped me said, in no uncertain terms, that if I didn't take off the shirt, he would arrest me for indecency. It was okay to wear a shirt with a Swastika on though!

My mum was brilliant at making clothes as well. She once stayed up 'till the wee small hours, putting long zips on either side of my Levis, fastened to the waist with padlocks. I used to wear the keys on a dog chain around my neck.

I had also acquired a girlfriend. Tammy was in the Musical Theatre Course, and was a fabulous singer. We met in the local pub (The Shakespeare) and from the moment I saw her, I knew that there would be no other. We became 'joined at the hip' as they say, and shared a love of music. Tammy was a massive Barbara Streisand fan, and played the soundtrack album of "A Star Is Born" continuously. I thought Tammy was better than Streisand. She managed to get an evening job, singing in a new restaurant situated in the posh part of London called Encore, a supper-club that catered for the après theatre-going clientele.

The unique selling point of this restaurant, though, was that all the waiting staff were also the entertainment. Basically singing waiters, who would serve you with a prawn cocktail before bursting into an Irving Berlin song as the main course was served. It had been the brain child of a certain Terry Hammond, who'd had success with a similar restaurant in New York. It was very American, and very, very, camp.

I'd originally started hanging out there just to be with Tammy, but had quickly become involved. Some evenings I'd help out in the kitchen preparing starters and salads, and on others play the piano for any drunk customers who wanted to murder a pop song or two. Terry Hammond was great at playing 'show tunes,' but in any other genre, he was rubbish. There were about eight waiter/performers who could all sing and dance wonderfully, but as waiters, they were shit. But that wasn't the point of this restaurant. Most people came because of the entertainment and novelty value, not the food and the service. It was so much fun to watch and be a part of that if you were worried about that, you'd be missing the point. Plus, pissing off the waiters in this establishment could have repercussions.

One evening a man and his wife came in for dinner. They hadn't booked, which seemed strange for that time of the evening, but they sat down anyway and were given the menu. That's when they started moaning.

The wine was corked, the wine not chilled, the starters too small, and so on and on and on he went. He kept snapping his fingers at anyone and everyone in the vicinity, and was completely unaware of anybody else in the room who might be having a good time.

For their main course, they'd chosen the Dover Sole, with seasonal veg and stuff. But no sooner had it been placed in front of them, snap, snap, snap: IT'S NOT COOKED!!! The waiter apologised profusely, and brought the two perfectly cooked soles back to the kitchen where all the staff spat on them. They were then placed under a grill until the spit bubbled, and then the waiter returned them to the table, with the chef's compliments. So remember, Never Piss Off Your Waiter!

Tammy's parents rented her a little studio flat in Muswell Hill, and some nights we wouldn't get back there until three or four in the morning. Then we'd have to be up for college, and start the whole routine over again. It was an exhausting time, but great fun. My days and nights were filled with music and laughter.

I became lifelong friends with two of the waiters, who were obviously only doing this job until stardom beckoned. One was an American actor called Jay Benedict, who less than a year later would be featured in a movie called Star Wars, and the other was a flamboyant black singer called Leee. No that's not a typo, Leee, "Tripple E" as he liked to be called, really did spell it that way. Leee was going to be a recording artist and star, no doubts about it. We shared the same passion for music, and would spend hours at his mum's house in Hackney listening to Motown and Stax. Leee's favourite artist, though, was Diana Ross; he even sounded like her, and knew every word to every song.

One time we even recorded a song that we'd written in a little back street 8 track studio in Hornsey. I played bass, drums and piano, and Leee did all the vocal parts and harmonies. We thought it sounded brilliant.

When I left college Leee and I lost contact for a while, but then, yet again I was watching Top of the Pops (sometime around 1981) and there was Leee performing his top ten hit, "Body Talk" with his new band *Imagination,* wearing what looked like a tin-foil thong.

Leee is 'showbiz' through and through, and continues to tour the world singing wherever they will have him. He is also an Ambassador for SOS Children's Villages, an international orphan charity providing homes and mothers for orphaned and abandoned children. He currently supports the charity's annual World Orphan Week campaign which takes place every February.

No one who lived through 1976 would forget it in a hurry. It was the year that saw the shock resignation of Harold Wilson as prime minister and Britain's humiliating rescue by the International Monetary Fund. It was also the year of an unprecedented heat wave, which led to the drying up and cracking of reservoirs, record bankruptcies and the end of Sunday postal collections. There were riots at the Notting Hill carnival, and bombs seemed to be exploding everywhere. The most publicised art events were the unveiling of Carl Andre's 'pile of bricks' at the Tate Gallery, and the Sex Pistols foul-mouthed tirade on ITV's The Today Show. Keith Moon was rushed to hospital for the 2nd time in five months, after collapsing in his trashed hotel room, and the first ever punk festival was held at the 100 Club in London, where Siouxsie and the Banshees played their first ever concert. Alice Cooper was rushed to hospital after collapsing on stage, cancelling his world tour, and Elton John came out as being bi-sexual, (Hard to believe, I know.) Former Beatles road manager Mal Evans was shot dead by Los Angeles Police after refusing to drop what turned out to be an air rifle, and Eric Clapton caused outrage with his inflammatory comments at a Birmingham concert with his views on immigration. The Eagles released their album "Hotel California" and Bob Marley was shot in his Kingston home by anti-government thugs. Southampton beat Manchester United in the Cup Final 1-0, and the 1976 Olympics introduced us to the greatest American boxing team ever assembled. Suger Ray Leonard, Leon Spinks, Michael Spinks, Leo Randolph and Howard Davis Jr all won gold medals, and all but Davis would go on to become world champions. Phew...What a year!

It was now 1977 and I was in my final year of college. All of the theory learnt in the previous year would now be put into practice, as we would now be putting on productions for an audience. Back then we still had in this country (to a certain degree) repertory theatre; and even small provincial towns would support this system, where the resident company would present a different play every week, either a revival from the full range of classics, or if given the chance, a new play. It had been the tried and tested route for a young actor entering the profession for years, but even then, the days of joining a company as an assistant stage manager and working your way up to leading man were a thing of the past. Even so, we were encouraged to write letters to all the theatre companies, with the hope of getting an audition on graduation.

As I already held an Equity Card I didn't see the point; and felt that I could be a bit 'more choosy'. Never the less, I wrote to three companies, and was rejected by all of them. I didn't bother writing any more letters after that.

Appearing in films or on TV was never discussed or encouraged by any of our tutors, as 'Real Acting' was 'Stage Acting,' and anything to do with popular culture or advertising was deemed a bit low-brow. Theatrical agents were also a necessary evil.

Having a legitimate theatrical agent was essential to an actor back then, as they could bypass the letter writing process, and get you in to see a director or producer. I didn't write to any of them either.

To be honest, I thought I had wasted my time being at college, and thought that my future life would be more to do with music. Acting was fraught, it seemed, with uncertainty and I didn't take it seriously at all. Even during the productions I would get bored, and devise elaborate jokes to corpse my fellow actors. Sometimes though, my jokes backfired. In a particularly boring production of Drydons 1667 'All for Love,' which was basically just an imitation of Shakespeare's Antony and Cleopatra; I was cast in the small role of a messenger. All I had to do was deliver a scroll to Mark Antony for him to read aloud. The actor playing Antony had written the message out in long hand on to the scroll so that he didn't have to learn it. One night I replaced the scroll with one that I'd prepared earlier. Instead of the script, I had drawn a massive, spunking penis, complete with hairy balls instead. As I came on to the stage, scroll in hand, I was already shaking with suppressed laughter and it got worse. As I handed Mark Antony the scroll I was almost sick with anticipation. I couldn't look at him at all. He took the scroll, unfurled it, took one look at it, and burst out laughing, but what he did next was genius. He made his laughter look like anguish, and through his tears, whilst handing the scroll back to me said,

"This news grieves me too much. You read it."

Our final production before graduation was Anton Chekhov's 1900 play *Three Sisters*. I had been cast as Staff Captain Vassily Vasilevich Solyony, an extremely unpleasant character who would sprinkle perfume, almost pathologically, onto his hands and body to mask the smell of dead corpses. This part should've been great fun to play, but I hated it and found Chekhov as boring as fuck. People staring out of windows at ducks flying to Moscow might've been entertaining to an audience in the 1900's, but to an audience of 17 year old Musical Theatre students in their final week of college, it was theatrical Valium.

I had already started getting bored by the 2nd performance, and had started with the on-stage jokes. Gluing tea cups to the saucers was a good one, and writing saucy messages onto my eyelids in black pencil so that only my fellow actors could read them was another. But for the final night when all the parents, and hopefully any agents who had been written to, were in, something special was required.

For the part of Solyony I had been dyeing my hair black. But for my final ever performance at The Arts I spiked it and spray-dyed it alpine green. As soon as I walked out onto the stage I got a huge laugh and a cheer, which I duly acknowledged. This was a complete no-no in the theatre, and I knew that I would be pilloried for it, but it was too late now. I had already received my 'diploma' so fuck it! Now it was 'The Gary Shail Show.'

At the final curtain call, as I took my final bow, I received a standing ovation from all the students in the audience. I think some of the parents weren't too happy with my antics though, including my own, but I would soon find out when I met them in the bar. As for my fellow students, well I knew that some of them would be pissed off with me, but I really couldn't give a toss! I didn't think for one minute that I would be seeing most of them again, and I was pretty sure that none of them apart from Jon Caplan and Dave Williams would ever want to stay in touch with me anyway.

Unlike my fellow graduates, I had no ambitions to act on stage or join a company (although I would eventually do both), and although I faced an uncertain future, I felt that fate would lend a hand somehow and I would be discovered by someone—just like I had been by Marcus Kimber all those years ago in the drill hall at Hendon High. It would only be a matter of time. Actually it only took the time it took to get showered, changed, and the short journey down to the bar.

Sitting with my parents was an incredibly attractive woman with huge breasts. She was in her early 20's, and her name was Sharon Hamper. She had recently been the publicity manager for the Glasgow Citizens Theatre, but had now formed a London based theatrical agency with a friend, called Hamper-Neafsey Associates.

Sharon wanted to know if I had contacted any other agents, as she was very interested in representing me. She thought that my un-orthodox approach to Chekhov had been hysterical and that my disrespectful attitude to 'the classics' was a breath of fresh air.

I told her that none of my performance had been planned, and I was just having a laugh. This explanation certainly didn't dissuade her at all though. Sharon wrote down our phone number (no mobiles back then kids) and told me that she'd be calling me over the next couple of days. I often wonder if any of what was to happen next, would've happened had I not dyed my hair green. I doubt it.

Arts Ed production of Love on the Dole

4

"There's nowhere you can be that isn't where you're meant to be..."
John Lennon

I was now an officially out of work actor, and as I now had a diploma it meant I could sign on at the Labour Exchange as unemployed without the fear of being sent down the coal mines to work. All actors, except the fortunate few, will have had to 'sign on' at some point in their careers, and this was regarded back then as a part of the job. As it turned out though, this wouldn't happen to me for quite a while.

Sharon Hamper was as good as her word, and telephoned a few days later asking me if I'd like to visit her at her office just off London's Regent Street for a chat. As it happened, Sharon shared the top floor office space with a bloke who ran a modelling agency called Star Girlz or something equally as tasteful. There were pictures of bare breasted nubile young girls pinned to the grubby walls, whilst the equally grubby proprietor sat stuffed behind his desk smoking cigars whilst on the phone, promising instant stardom to impressionable youngsters in exchange for sexual favours. Believe me, Max Clifford wasn't the only sleazebag on the block back in the 70's.

Sharon explained that the office arrangements were just temporary, and that she was actively seeking new premises in the same area. To be honest though, I quite liked the sleaziness of that old office, and thought the new one (about a year later) was far less personal. I certainly don't remember having to sign any formal contract with Sharon, it was just understood that she would now be my agent, and I would be giving Hamper-Neafsey associates 15% of any monies earned whilst on their books.

Sharon wanted to know if I knew anything about the rock group The Who. I said that they were a little before my time, but I was well aware of their mad drummer Keith Moon. In the early 70's 'Moon The Loon', as he was fondly named by the tabloid press, was rarely out of the news. Everyone knew a story about Keith, and although most of them were usually grossly exaggerated, he was regarded as an absolute legend to anyone who'd ever wanted to throw a TV set out of a hotel window.

Sharon explained that a new film was being planned based on one of the Who's albums called *Quadrophenia*, and would I like to audition for it? What was I going to say...No?

My first audition was with the casting directors Patsy Pollock and Esta Charkham in a little office just off Carnaby Street. I was very much regarded as Sharon's new boy, but I certainly didn't know that at the time. If Patsy and Esta thought I was what the director (Franc Roddam) was looking for, then I would be re-called for a 2nd audition where I would be expected to improvise some scenes from the script. I don't remember what I said or did at that first meeting, but by the time I got home, there was already a message from Sharon to call her. Franc Roddam wanted to see me.

For my re-call audition, I took Tammy with me for moral support. We were spending almost all our time together anyway, so this didn't seem such a strange thing to do at the time. When we arrived back at the office, we were asked by the receptionist to wait whilst she let Patsy, Esta, and Franc know that I'd arrived. There were only two other people waiting in reception, one was Toyah Willcox and the other was Johnny Rotten. Obviously for a young wannabe punk this was amazing. Toyah had already appeared in Derek Jarman's cult punk film *Jubilee*, and as for Mr Rotten...well he was the most famous punk on the fucking planet. If these two were going to be involved in this movie, then I wanted in. As soon as I was called I went on the offensive.

"Shail came into the room," recalled Roddam in an interview in 1999. "He was really coming full on saying 'I want to be in your film'. I said 'Look you're great but I just don't think you have got the strength, you're a bit young looking'. 'Stand there, Stand there!' he howled. 'Go on, Attack me! Attack me! Kick me!' 'For fuck sake,' I muttered and took a big fucking kick at him. He did a backward somersault and landed ten feet away."

I don't remember it being quite like that. For instance, it was a backflip, not a somersault. But whatever, I certainly had made an impression, and as I was leaving I introduced Tammy to Franc. By the time Tammy and I had travelled home to Hendon, there was already a message from Sharon to call her. I had got the part, and what's more, so had Tammy.

When making a film, you sometimes only get to meet your fellow actors on the actual day of filming. The only rehearsals you normally get is for the benefit of the camera people and sound department, and then it's 'Action,' and off you go. *Quadrophenia* was nothing like that.

Franc wanted his leading cast to act and behave like a gang of kids who'd grown up together, so for that to happen, we had to get to know each other.

Quadrophenia was Franc Roddam's first feature film, and he'd previously only done documentaries. He'd made an extremely harrowing film called *Dummy* about a deaf and dumb prostitute, and was also responsible for the first ever reality 'fly on the wall' documentary *The Family*. So it was plain to everyone involved that Quad wasn't going to be a 'sugar-coated' foray into London's swinging 60's scene.

Once the cast had been finalized, certain activities were arranged for us, such as dance classes to learn all of the 60's moves. These lessons were held in a little studio above a strip joint in Soho, and I remember them as being great fun. Gillian Gregory, a renowned choreographer who had previously worked on *Bugsy Malone* and *Tommy* was drafted in to teach us, but we also got a few tips from an old iconic face from the 60's called Jeff Dexter who spent ages with Sting, who's part as 'The Ace Face' had to be a dancing marvel.

One day during a break in dance rehearsals, I got chatting to Sting. He was wearing his classic green flying suit. On his lapel was a badge that just said 'Police' and I said, "What's that?" and he said "That's the name of my band," and I said, "What a fucking stupid name for a band!"

We also had to learn to ride scooters. Back then you could ride any bike up to 125cc on a provisional licence, so the production team hired us all little Honda 125s which we were allowed to ride around on all over London. Before we were let loose though, we all had to go to the Hendon police training school to learn some basics. It was brilliant fun, except for poor Leslie Ash who received some very unwelcome attention from an extremely fat sweaty copper who insisted on instructing her personally.

Trevor Laird, who was to play Ferdy the drug dealer, just couldn't get the hang of it at all and to this day I don't think he has ever ridden a bike. Trevor justified this by saying that his character Ferdy would be far too cool to ride a scooter anyway, and certainly wouldn't risk getting 2 stroke oil on his handmade mohair suit.

One night, as part of our preparations, we were all summoned to an 'arranged' party. Held at an old mods house in the East End of London, our host, Tommy Shelly, had actually been one of the original mods who'd fought the 'rockers' on the beaches back in 1964.

One of the production team (and I'm not saying who) thought it would be a fab idea to give us all some blues to see how we'd interact under the influence of drugs. What had started out as a rather polite get-together to discuss Tommy's recollections soon turned into a full on 'knees-up', and we were all asked to leave.

Driving my little 125 home whilst pilled-up at 2 in the morning through the streets of London was a tad precarious, but certainly a useful experience for when we actually started filming.

On another day, we all went down to Bill Curbishley's office in Wardour Street to get the official Quadrophenia Cast T-shirt. Powder blue, with a little Target Motif and the word Quadrophenia stitched beneath, they were really quite cool.

Bill told us that we could only have one each, and told his secretary to keep an eye on us before leaving to go to a meeting. The office (on the 1st floor) had two main rooms, and all the boxes containing the shirts were in the back one. Whilst me and Mark Wingett kept the secretary occupied, Phil Daniels and Trevor Laird started throwing T-shirts out of the back office window to Phil Davis, who was on the street below. I think we all got two or three each. We were definitely starting to act as a team.

We could now ride a bike and dance The Twist, The Pony and The Locomotion, but for me, the moment I became a mod, was when we got the clobber!

A company run by two former mods called 'Contemporary Wardrobes' were hired to make, or source, the costumes for the film, and you could tell that the tailors, Jack English and Roger Burton, loved doing it. They told us great stories about Brighton in 64, and how they'd spend an hour getting the knot just right in a tie, and wouldn't sit down on buses in case they creased their suits. We were definitely in the right hands, and this was the attitude that I would need to accurately portray the role of Spider. That's all bollox… I just liked dressing up!

Franc wanted us to live in these costumes for at least two months, so we had lots of choice in what we thought our characters would actually like to wear. As it was going to be late September, (when we were scheduled to start filming in Brighton), everyone was issued with a parker. For some reason I reckoned that 'Young Spider' hadn't got one yet, so I chose a military style green rain coat, and imagined that he'd got it from his dad.

Mark Wingett, who was playing Jimmy's best mate Dave, was only 16years old at the time. Esta Charkham and Patsy Pollock had seen Mark in a National Youth Theatre production, and had suggested him to Franc. They met at Franc's house, and after a few improvisation sessions, Franc had offered him the part. Mark was the perfect punk! He was in every way the spirit of 1977, infused with the punk spirit that had enlivened every boring corner of teenage Britain.

Mark had only recently been working for 40p an hour at a petrol station in Portsmouth, so this whole experience must've been extraordinary for him. We were being picked up in chauffeur driven cars and taken to places like The Nashville Rooms (a famous West London punk venue) to watch bands, and also the Southgate Royalty I seem to vaguely remember. Mark and I became great mates.

Mark didn't have a permanent address in London, and had been 'dossing it' with mates. I think he even stayed with Phil Daniels and his family for a while. So when I told this to my mum and dad, they immediately offered him the bottom bunk in my tiny bedroom. Mark Wingett was now family.

One day Mark and I were walking up the road heading for the tube station. Following a few yards behind was my mother, who was off to the shops. Mark and I were dressed in exactly the same leopard skin tight trousers with matching shirt and black leather biker jacket and boots. (How fucking camp is that!) We walked past a woman standing at her gate and said 'Good Morning'…as my mother reached the woman at the gate she said, "I pity their poor mother." And my mum said, "I am their poor mother!'

I believe it was Phil Davis who gave Mark Wingett his nickname after a witnessing yet another example of his infectious exuberance. A name that is still whispered with fear in certain circles: Brain Damage!

Even though Tammy was going to be in the film as my on-screen girlfriend, we actually started seeing less of each other in real life. We knew that we were going to be booked into separate hotels in Brighton, which was fine by me, and apart from some in the main cast I don't think anybody else actually knew that she was actually my real girlfriend.

Franc put Tammy in with all the other modettes, where they were busy forming their own special relationships.

Mark and I already knew that we'd be sharing a hotel room. We were only a week or two away from going to Brighton, when something terrible happened.

"Someone suggested putting 'This film is dedicated to the memory of Keith Moon' on *Quadrophenia*.
And I said, "You don't need to say it. *Quadrophenia* is Keith Moon." Pete Townshend 1979

Keith Moon **23/8/1946 – 7/9/1978**

The death of Keith Moon, ironically from an overdose of Clomethiazol; a sedative aimed to combat the symptoms of severe alcohol withdrawal, threw the whole Quadrophenia project into jeopardy.

Roy Baird (the producer) recalled in 2007 that he was in Los Angeles discussing the film's U.S. release when he got the call from London.

"Suddenly an operator came through and said, 'Sorry, but we've got a very important call coming through from London.' It was Bill Curbishley, and he said, 'I've got some very bad news, Keith's dead.' It was a huge shock. So I got on a plane and came back, and we thought that was the end of the film. As it was being financed by the record company, they probably thought, 'no Keith Moon, No Who.' So that was a big problem. It could've been the end of the film before it started."

Even so, assurances came from the rest of the Who (and Bill Curbishley) that even though this was a monumental loss to both group and fans, the band would continue on, and into the future. So even with such a huge blow to overcome and the tangible sadness in the air, work would continue, and we started packing for Brighton.

"Roy Baird said to me, 'you're not going to have a director's chair. I said, 'I always wanted a director's chair.' And he said to me, 'You won't have time to sit down'." - Franc Roddam, 2007

Filming started, as scheduled, on Tuesday, 26th September, 1978. Whilst Phil Daniels was busy filming his iconic final ride along Beachy Head, we were left to check into our various hotels and guest houses along Brighton's seafront. Franc Roddam and most of the crew were booked into The Grand (of course,) but for the rest of us, the surroundings were far less salubrious. Mark and I were booked into a hotel at the 'unfashionable' end of Brighton called The Salisbury. The room was about as basic as you could get, with only two single beds and a walk-in shower in the corner of the room, but we didn't care, we were making a fucking movie.

After everyone had acclimatized themselves, a roll call was convened in the lobby of the Grand Hotel, allowing everyone to check their call times for make-up, hair and wardrobe for the following morning. It looked like it was going to be a long day.

Light was always going to be a big issue for the Brighton shoot, as we were filming in September when it was supposed to be May. So for most days we would have to be ready and on-set before sun up. This is not a good time at all for teenage boys, and Mark and I were no different, except that now we didn't have my mum shouting at us to get up. I think we managed the first morning call by not sleeping at all.

As I've already said, Phil Daniels had been filming the end scenes for the film first, and these would include the scooter flying off the cliff top onto the rocks below. We saw Franc and the cameraman (Brian Tufano) after they had finished shooting this scene, and they didn't look very well at all. Franc Roddam would recall this moment in 2011.

"The guys had scientifically worked out the physics of it. I decided I'd be in the helicopter. I thought it would be fun to see this thing coming towards you while you were in the chopper.

They worked it all out with block and tackle to catapult it into the air, but the calculations were wrong, and it literally almost hit the helicopter. Afterwards I thought it was pretty hilarious."

YEAH RIGHT!!

We had now been given our own scooters, and we were actively encouraged to ride them around, even when we were not being filmed. I am reliably informed (Thanks to Graham 'Mod' Webb) that mine was a Spanish made LI 150 Eibar, series 3 Lambretta, and it moved like a boat!

Unlike a conventional bike, you couldn't really lean into the bends, and if the wind caught you on the side panels, it would blow you all over the road like a crisp packet. What's more, we would be riding these things with girls on the back, and no crash helmets. Never the less, I loved my scooter, and named her 'Winnie', after my mum.

Brain Damage (sorry) Mark Wingett was always in trouble! He'd just fuck off without letting anyone know where he was, which can be quite annoying when you are playing one of the leading roles in a film. One night, he just disappeared completely, but turned up for breakfast the next morning with something that looked like it had just crawled from the sea.

I'm not saying that I am the bastion of good taste, but this girl had definitely fallen from the ugly tree and had hit all the branches all the way down. What's more, she had left Mark with a couple of mementos from their night together on his neck. Two of the nastiest looking love bites I have ever seen were clearly visible to everyone, including the make-up department whose job it was to try and cover them up. They went ballistic!

John Peverall (assistant director) gave Mark a real bollocking, not only for the love bites, but for his general time keeping and attitude in general. Mark told John to 'Fuck Off' and said he had had enough of being told off and was leaving. I don't know where he thought he was going, but he was definitely off. News of this quickly reached Franc Roddam, who recalled the incident in 2005.

"What I did was, I had a shirt that Johnny Rotten had given to me. He'd got it from Sid Vicious. Johnny had attacked Sid with an axe and Sid had puked up all over the shirt, and it had safety pins and drawings on it and puke. Anyway, this shirt had been given to me as a grand prize. I gave it to Wingett so that he would stay on the film. Being a punk, that was enough — it was a great bribe and he now has this famous shirt." - Franc Roddam

Even though we had mobile caterers supplying the cast and crew with food and drink, we took to eating and hanging out in the beach I between takes.

The woman who ran it (Maureen Wells) wouldn't take any shit from anybody, so we started calling her Mum. Franc Roddam thought she was brilliant and cajoled her into playing the waitress on screen.

In one scene, Dave (Mark Wingett) parked himself on one of the tables and Maureen instinctively objected. Dave...or was it 'Brain damage' told her to piss off! This time he got another bollocking from Maureen. This scene was totally ad-libbed, but was captured on film and made the final cut. Unfortunately for Mark, the scene where he eats an egg sandwich wasn't improvised and he had to do it 12 times. I don't think he has eaten one since. Once all of the café scenes were completed and in the can, it was time to start filming the lead-up scenes to the riot.

A lot of rumours about who first came up with the unscripted and impromptu idea for the "We are the mods! We are the mods!" chant, have surfaced over the years, but I can categorically say that it was me.

Franc Roddam wanted some sort of vocal reaction to the photographer taking pictures and it was the only thing I could think of at the time. To be honest I thought it was a shit idea and half expected Franc to yell 'CUT' and ask for something else. But the chant gained momentum, and before anyone could say "Hang on a minute, are we sure this is authentic 60's banter?" everyone had joined in and it ended up as the mods battle cry.*

The next scene, where we attack the rockers, was 'hairy' to say the least. I remember thinking that if I didn't get in there quick I would get crushed to death by the onslaught. So as soon as Franc shouted 'Action,' I did my best Linford Christie impersonation and didn't look back. It was just as well, as a few moments after I had slammed through the café doors, one of the camera men lost a tooth! Linda Regan who was playing the head rocker's girlfriend recalled in 2012.

*'We are the Mods' is now the name of a radio show in Dallas, Texas, a clothing range in Great Britain, the name of its own movie and a countless number of web-sites on Facebook and Twitter. Not such a shit idea after all then.

"I remember the pin-ball machine flying right in front of my nose. I stood there at the end of the take and I remember Franc yelling "CUT!" and I thought 'Thank God for that,' because my hair was covered in shattered glass." - Linda Regan

The rest of the day was just as hectic, and as we rioted (on cue) through the streets of Brighton, injuries were inevitably sustained by cast and crew. Leslie Ash got knocked to the floor, Toyah hurt her arm quite badly, and one of the extras got knocked over by an ambulance. Franc Roddam also suffered when he got hit on the head by a camera. An extremely 'spooked' police dog bit one of the camera guys on the leg, who then turning sharply away, struck Franc full on with his heavy equipment.

After filming all the street riot stuff, the action was moved to the beach where little vignettes of violence would be filmed. The one where Toyah's character Monkey puts the boot in to some poor prostrate rocker is a favourite of mine, as is Mark Wingett's out-of- character judo throw. But the one where my character gets attacked by two rockers came completely out of the blue, as Franc obviously forgot to tell me it was going to happen. That look of surprise on my face was definitely not rehearsed.

With all the riot stuff safely in the can, we still had a few scenes left to film before heading back to London. One of these is the moment where we stop and look down on a beautiful panoramic view of Brighton. In reality, no such view exists. In fact, it's actually Eastbourne that we are all looking at. Over the years, many *Quadrophenia* 'anoraks' have pestered me with their observations of what is 'historically wrong' with the film, but not once has anyone ever pointed this one out.

Another last minute scene required only lasts for a split second, but is still one of my faves. As Jimmy sits on the beach looking mournfully out to sea, a lone swimmer is seen in a bathing cap. Remember that this was filmed at the end of September, and the water was fucking freezing. The guy swimming was actually the stunt co-ordinator Peter Braham who had to be treated for mild hypothermia shortly afterwards. This guy was one of the all-time greats. Peter had choreographed fight scenes for Lee Marvin and John Wayne, so a little bit of Hypo didn't worry him too much. Peter Braham and I became good friends.

With my first pay-cheque, (about £700) I bought a little yellow Yamaha 125 which allowed me some freedom from London Transport, but would also give my mum sleepless nights. I was always trying out new things on it such as wheelies and jumps. Peter asked me one day if I'd ever thought of doing stunt work. Of course I hadn't. Being a stunt man was the ultimate in cool as far as I was concerned, and it seemed like a secret society, almost impossible to join.

Peter had his own stunt team called 'Special Action Services, (SAS) and wanted to know if I'd be interested in joining. I jumped at the chance, not really knowing what was involved, but eager to learn. I would be a probationary member for at least a year whilst I honed some new skills, such as horse riding and high-diving. I was definitely fearless, but not complacent. Everything was always worked out meticulously to give the stunt performer his best chance of survival, but sometimes things could go horribly wrong, as we would all find out.

One scene, not shot in London, was when all the mods are scootering down to Brighton and collide with a group of rockers, filmed on a secluded road near Denham. We were denied permission from the police to film without crash helmets...But we did it anyway.

There is a story that the reason for the crash was because the film crew refused to hand over some cash to a group of local travellers, upset at us for filming on their stretch of road. So, unbeknownst to us, they pushed an old car into the road—on the bend!

As Phil Davis 'Chalky' (closely followed by 20 rockers riding high performance large British motorbikes,) came around the bend, he had no choice but to swerve drastically to avoid the car. This caused a huge pile-up, and people were flying everywhere. By the time me and the rest of the mods had caught up, there was devastation.

Linda Regan: "It was terrifying. We came around this bend and there was this car in the middle of the road. John Blundell (Head Rocker) somehow managed to steer the bike off the road and in to some hedges. He effectively saved my life. I remember looking back at the road and there was carnage everywhere, with people moaning in agony. Moments later, I heard sirens from emergency services approaching."

Whilst most of the injuries were mainly superficial, stunt man Gareth Milne had taken the full brunt of the collision and received a wound to his leg that was so severe, he had to be air-lifted by helicopter to hospital.

Before the police arrived, helmets were hurriedly handed out and strategically placed around the crash site. Such was the indestructible nature of stunt men; Gareth Milne was back on set only two days later to re-shoot the same scene. Ironically, the derelict car that had caused such mayhem was still at the roadside, and can be clearly seen in the final shot. We re-named Gareth, 'Legend.'

Franc Roddam orchestrating the Rockers

Spider continuity photo

Mark Wingett

We are the Mods!!

Spider, Ferdy and Jimmy

Spider takes a kicking

Who the fuck do you think you are?

There's a party 'dahn' Kitchner Road

Looking back at *Quadrophenia*, it is difficult to realize sometimes just how much talent flourished from this film. Timmy Spall, Danny Peacock, Julien Firth, Kathy Rogers, John Blundell, John Altman, Jessie Birdsal, Gary Holton and Nicholas Lyndhurst all gave fantastic but brief appearances, but it is Holton that I have some stories about.*

A couple of years after *Quadrophenia* I had been offered a fantastic role in a new play for the Half Moon theatre, called *H.M.V.* The play explored the evil side of the music industry, and I had been given the leading role of Wally Burk. Wally had a band, and when he signs a record contract...that's when his troubles begin. Gary Holton was playing my dad!

All the music for the show was played live, so every actor in it had to be able to play something and sing. We had to rehearse as a band, as well as tell the story as actors, so it was great fun to rehearse and eventually perform the show.

By this time I was renting a little one bedroomed flat in West Hampstead, whilst Gary Holton only lived half a mile away in Maida Vale. Gary started giving me a lift to rehearsals every day. He'd split from his wife Donna and was now living in a smart regency block with his new lady Sue, and he was very happy.

Gary was now something of a TV star in his own right since appearing in the hit show '*Auf Weidersehen, Pet*' as 'Cockney-Charmer' Wayne, so things were going great.

I don't think we did one show or rehearsal sober. Some nights I was amazed that we actually got to the theatre, let alone the stage. As always though, as soon as we heard the audience coming in to the theatre we somehow sobered up enough to do the show. The reviews were brilliant, as was the music.

People started asking where they could get a cassette of the music from. Gary and I booked the Tin Pan Alley Recording studios in Denmark Street, and we recorded all the songs, and sold the cassettes in the foyer. They always sold out.

The whole cast was remarkably talented. A very young Michelle Collins played my girlfriend, and a brilliant drummer and actor called Dorian Healey played my cousin. We also had Sid James's daughter, Raynor, playing my mum and the keyboards.

After the show there would invariably be drinks in the pub next door,* and then Gary and I would drive in to London's West End to a club—or three. We'd get in at about 4am, and then meet at the pub the next day and prepare for another show. One night Gary scared the fuck out of me though. I always knew that Gary liked heroin, but I was more into cocaine and alcohol so he didn't do it around me at all, except for one night in 1982.

---

*In 2013, I was kindly asked if I'd like to contribute to a book being written about Gary Holton Called 'Fast Living', written by Teddie Dahlin and published by New Haven. The piece 'Wot I Wrote' is directly responsible for me writing this book.

*The Blind Beggar pub is notorious for its connection to East End gangsters, the Kray twins. On 9 March 1966, Ronnie Kray shot and murdered George Cornell, an associate of a rival gang The Richardson's as he was sitting at the bar.

One night we were in a little pub in Chelsea's Kings Road when we were joined by a strange looking woman, whom Gary Holton knew quite well. After a few drinks we went back to her extremely smart flat where we had more drinks and some lines of cocaine. She then disappeared briefly and then re-appeared carrying a small leather pouch. Inside was a small dirty silver spoon, a length of rubber tubing and a hypodermic needle. All the paraphernalia for main-lining smack. I must admit, I was intrigued and more than a little curious as she produced a fresh lemon and proceeded to squeeze a small amount of the juice on to the silver spoon. She then produced a small bag of brown powder and poured a little of it into the juice. Using an onyx table lighter, she heated up the mixture before sucking it up into the syringe and flicking the tip of the needle with her perfectly manicured fingernail.

I'm not sure if Gary had told her that I'd not done this before, but before I had the time to really think about it, I was stripped to my vest, with the rubber tubing wrapped round my bicep. I looked at Gary, who just gave me a devilish grin as the strange woman tightened the tourniquet and began slapping my arm to raise a vein.

As soon as the heroin had entered my blood stream, I could taste it. Then suddenly it felt like someone had poured a bucket of hot water over my head. Within seconds I was not of this world! I felt so content and worry free, you could've told me you were going to cut my leg off with a rusty bread knife and I would not have cared. Now I knew why Gary Holton loved this drug so much. And why I never did it again.

Since doing *H.M.V*, Gary and I had often talked about doing something together music wise. And in 1983 an opportunity presented itself completely out of the blue. The band 'The Actors', was formed out of necessity rather than design. Due to the popularity of *Auf Wiedersehen Pet*, Gary was asked to appear on a television show called *The Tube*. Transmitted live from a studio in Newcastle, the show, which was presented by Jools Holland and Paula Yates, had proved popular with music fans in England. It often featured un-signed bands playing live, unlike its BBC predecessor Top of the Pops, where chart success was a requisite, and 'miming' was the order of the day.

The new band (The Actors) would consist of me on bass guitar, Dave Williams (my old school friend) on drums. Dennis Stratton, who'd only recently left Iron Maiden, on guitar, a keyboard player whose name escapes me and Gary Holton on Vocals.

Gary had already written the song ('Long-legged Blue-eyed Blonde') which in retrospect is very un-pc, but even now still makes me giggle. Joe McGann, who was also the lead singer in my band, was drafted in to manage rehearsals and organise train tickets, expenses etc. Out of all of us, Joe was probably the most sensible.

I can only remember us having one rehearsal before we all went to the pub. After all, this wasn't rocket science, just good old fashioned 4/4 rock and roll. How we'd managed to get Dennis Stratton still eludes me to this day, but even after a skin-full he was a fucking genius! Putting him and Gary in the same country, let alone on the same stage, was going to be risky, but Joe McGann made us promise to behave ourselves until we'd finished the show. And we did.

We all turned up at the TV station, on time. We didn't forget anything, or abuse our fellow travellers in any way. We arrived at the TV studios on time, were polite to the security men on the gate, did a run-through for the cameras and sound guys, and then waited patiently in our designated dressing room for the show to start.

Paula Yates was on a break from the show at the time, and had been temporarily replaced by Leslie Ash who had also starred in *Quadrophenia*, so we all felt comfortable with Gary's impending interview.

First off, they showed a clip from *Auf Wiedersehen Pet* featuring Gary and Timothy Spall, and then the red light went on for the interview. All was going well until Leslie mentioned Gary's time in Germany, upon which Gary launched into a graphic story about being seduced by a Ladyboy...feeling his/hers bits and bobs etc. I was pissing myself laughing. This was being broadcast live for fuck sake, at 6 in the evening. Poor Leslie was bright red and at a loss for words. God knows what the producers thought he was going to say next. Leslie quickly rounded up the interview, and suddenly we were on, and then we were off and it was all over.

We were invited to stay on for after-show drinks, but Joe, in his wisdom, declined the offer thinking it safer to get us all on the first available train heading south. So within the hour we were back at Newcastle train station.

Unfortunately the train was packed, with not enough seats for us all to sit together. So Joe suggested we move to First Class and pay the extra ticket price to the conductor if and when he came to check. So that's what we did. The first class carriage was empty, so we made ourselves comfortable before heading off to find the bar.

Back then trains had proper bars and not those ridiculous trolley things that get in your way when you are trying to get off the frikkin' train!

Once we had located the bar, we bought it! All of the beer we could carry, and as many miniatures of spirits that we could stuff into our pockets were purchased with the rest of the expenses, and we 'clanked' our way back to first class. After about an hour of serious drinking, Gary fell asleep curled up on his seat, whilst the rest of us stared drunkenly out of the windows at the English countryside flashing by.

Suddenly, the carriage door was flung open, and a weedy voice demanded: 'TICKETS PLEASE'. Gary didn't move.

Joe tried to explain the situation and offered to pay the excess fares, but Weedy was having none of it, and insisted we move back to second class, and stand for the rest of the journey. Gary still hadn't moved.

Joe protested politely, but I could already see that Dennis Stratton was getting wound up, and this was going to get messy. Weedy then turned his attention to Gary, who was still sleeping soundly. 'TAKE YOUR FEET OFF THE SEATS SON.' Dear old Weedy grabbed Gary's legs and Gary came to with a start, quite accidentally kicking poor old Weedy in his nether regions. It must've been terrifying for Gary. One minute he was in dreamland, and the next confronted by a screaming man in uniform clutching his bollox! I couldn't stop laughing, which made wincing Weedy even angrier. He backed out of the carriage stating 'YOU LOT HAVN'T HEARD THE LAST OF THIS,' and we hadn't.

After about 20 minutes the train started to slow down. I was sure that the next station was not a scheduled stop, and I was right. As we pulled into Grantham station (Birthplace of Maggie Thatcher,) we could already see the police lining the platform, and some of them had dogs!

Everyone sobered up immediately, or at least tried to, and Gary, who was now wide awake, suggested going on the offensive. As soon as the train had stopped, we hopped off the train looking as calm and as cheerful as possible.

Gary took complete control of the situation and explained who we were, and what had happened. He was so charming and reasonable, that even the dogs were mesmerized. The fucker even signed autographs for the police, who then arranged for another train to make an unscheduled stop to pick us up. In fact, the train we got on actually arrived in London before the one we got chucked off of. Genius!'

Due to filming commitments on both sides, Gary and I didn't see much of each other over the next few months. But then, in early 1985, we met for a drink in Maida Vale.

He was still filming *Auf Wiedersehen Pet*, but told me he wasn't enjoying it anymore. The Tabloid press had been writing stories about his personal life, and he had money troubles. I could tell from our conversation that he was using heroin again. He looked terrible. He kept telling me that we should get The Actors back in the studio, and arrange a tour. I think we both knew that it was never going to happen though. That was the very last time I would see Gary Holton alive.

The *Quadrophenia* scene where Gary Holton and the other rockers attack Spider and his girlfriend was filmed outside a pub somewhere in West London. I know that I could've probably given you the exact name of the pub, as there are now web-sites dedicated just for Quadrophenia locations. But I really couldn't be arsed!

The scene took most of the night to shoot. Peter Braham had assured Franc Roddam that I was more than capable of doing the fight, but to tell you the truth, I was more worried about my scooter which had to crash to the ground when the rockers threw me into it. For this reason Franc wanted to shoot the whole fight in one take, film it from three different angles, and edit it later. So we filmed it three times (I think.) It was a brilliant night for the actors as they had kept the pub open all night for us. Every time the crew had to set up for another angle, we had another beer. Or in Gary Holton's case, a large brandy and a beer.

Gary had brought his wife Donna with him for the night, so whilst we were filming she was getting the drinks in. Gary and Donna Holton looked and behaved like rock stars. That's cos Gary Holton was a rock star! Gary was the lead singer of a band called The Heavy Metal Kids who'd had a hit record in 1977 with a song called 'She's no Angel.' Gary looked like Ronnie Wood, and probably took more drugs. But Gary was also a fab actor and entertainer in his own right. He behaved like a star.

Another actor playing 'a rocker' was Jessie Birdsall. Jessie was already a rocker before he put the costume on. He was a real 50's retro head, with a quiff and brothel creepers, who also bought and sold rockabilly records when he wasn't acting. I really liked him. And so did my girlfriend Tammy. About a month later she chucked me and moved in with Jessie. I remember being really upset about this at the time. Tammy was dating a faaaking rocker!! And this wouldn't be the last time I would lose a girlfriend to a Quadrophenia cast member.

Sting had been doing rather well. His band 'Police' (not 'The' Police) had a record being played on radio 1, called "I Can't Stand Losing You", which had excited everybody. I had already heard Sting play "Walking on the Moon" and "Roxanne" on his acoustic guitar in our hotel room in Brighton, so I knew that their debut album was going to be great.

One afternoon Sting was given the afternoon off and helicoptered to Manchester to perform on the BBC's flagship contemporary music show 'The Old Grey Whistle Test'. It was brilliant for us to watch Sting doing what he did best, even if he did look like a twat in those sunglasses he wore. He told us later it was because the make-up girl had squirted hair lacquer in his eyes just before he went on. I reckoned Stuart Copeland had poked him in the eye with a drum stick.

Tammy and me

One night we all went to see them play at Dingwalls in Camden Town, and there was hardly anybody there except us. I think me and Phil Daniels sat on the edge of the stage for most of the gig. They were polished though, and as tight as Pete Townsend's wallet. You just knew they were heading for the big time. Within two years they had embarked on their first World Tour, often playing places which had seldom hosted foreign performers, including Mexico, India, Taiwan, Hong Kong, Greece, and Egypt. Gordon done good.

Once the film had been roughly edited together, we had some Post Synching to do. A lot of dialogue had to be re-dubbed due to poor sound quality. I didn't have that much to do, but I know Daniels was in the dubbing suite for quite a while. It's horrible for the actor. You think you have already given the performance, but now you'd have to re-create it again in a studio environment at the drop of a hat. It takes real skill.

Years later, (if you continue to read), you will learn that I ended up working in this environment for a living in the late 80's and 90's, but in 1979 this was a new experience for me, and I loved it. Just going in to London's Soho district to work was exciting.

Soho was still pretty seedy in the late 70's, with the sex shops and the like, but it was also home to Denmark Street. Famous for its music shops and recording studios, anyone who was anyone had recorded here at some point in their career. The Sex Pistols lived in the basement of number 6, and had recorded their first demos there. Elton John wrote his famous 'Your Song' in this street, and Hendrix, The Stones, The Beatles, and The Clash had all spent time in Denmark Street at some point.

I would spend hours looking in the guitar shop windows, vowing that one day I'd have enough cash to actually go in the shop. But for now, just being there was great.

Once everything had been edited and dubbed together, we were invited to see a rough-cut press screening of Quadrophenia at The Plaza One in Lower Regents Street. I went with Toyah and Sting.

Toyah was really disappointed, thinking that most of her part was now on the cutting room floor, so she left. Toyah says in Simon Wells' book 'Inside the Making of Britain's Greatest Youth Film', that we all left together, but I don't remember doing that. Yes...a lot of what everyone did was cut in the final edit, but the film is about Jimmy, not Monkey or Spider. To be honest, I was just happy that I was in it at all. I don't blame Toyah though—she was a lot more 'Full-On' in 1979.

The Premier for *Quadrophenia* was on 16th August 1979 at The Plaza One Cinema on Lower Regents Street. My seat numbers were L26/27. My date for the evening was a beautiful girl called Shelley Haynes (obviously not Tammy) and I wore a sky blue suit from Johnsons.

The party afterwards was a lavish affair, with lashings of champers and nosh, and that's about all I can remember really. Oh yes—the critics hated it!

WORLD GALA PREMIERE

ⓆUADROPHENIA

Plaza 1, Lower Regent Street,
Thursday, 16th August 1979
7.15 pm for 8.00 pm

Black Tie

L 27

Well, they didn't actually hate it as such, but the initial reviews were not great. I think the language in the film shocked many, and was regarded by some as unnecessarily violent. *Quadrophenia* was even initially played as a double bill with an American Gang movie called *The Warriors*, which in my view was much more violent.

The best thing for me, though, was seeing the poster on my local tube station wall. Almost everyone I knew would see that!

Everyone involved in the making of *Quadrophenia* has a story to tell. I hear new ones all the time. In 2014 I was at an event, and met up (after 35 years) with cameraman Brian Tufano. Brian was talking about his long and illustrious career, working on films such as *Trainspotting, East Is East, The Wall, Kidulthood*, etc. and I asked him what his first feature film was. It was *Quadrophenia*.

5

1978 had been an incredible year for me, and 1979 was proving to be just as eventful. Once I was free from my *Quadrophenia* commitments, I signed on to make another British film called '*The Music Machine*'. *Saturday Night Fever*, starring John Travolta, had been a huge worldwide success, so it was only a matter of time before the British would try to cash in on the Disco Craze that seemed to be sweeping the world. *Music Machine* would be it.

Directed by Ian Sharp and starring Gerry Sundquist and a cabaret singer called Patti Boulaye, it told the story of a young lad learning to disco dance to win a competition. Despite various attempts to thwart him in this venture, (normally from my character) he wins the competition, gets the girl, and triumphs over the bad guys.

Music Machine had a fantastic cast, which included Clarke Peters, Brenda Fricker, Mickey Feast, David Easter, Ferdy Mayne, Ray Burdis and even Mark Wingett, who'd managed to get cast as one of my henchmen.

The whole film was shot in Camden Town and at the actual Music Machine nightclub over a period of about three weeks, and was brilliant fun to make. Unfortunately the fun didn't transfer to the finished film, and it was atrocious! I do believe it is actually on the 100 worst films of all-time list, and if it isn't—it bloody well should be. The music for the film was terrible, and poor Gerry Sundquist just couldn't dance. The poor man had two left feet, and just looked totally embarrassed by the whole affair.

Another reason why the film was such a shambles could've been because almost everyone involved was snorting cocaine–me included!

Gerry Sundquist was a lovely bloke, but obviously had deep personal problems. On the 1st August 1993, after a long battle with depression, he committed suicide by jumping in front of a train at Norbiton Train Station.

I was in Manchester during the General Election of 1979 when Margaret Thatcher became the first ever woman Prime Minister. The biggest news for me, though, was the death by heroin overdose of Sid Vicious.

I'd been cast in a new play written by Peter Flannery, called *Jungle Music,* for a Manchester based theatre company called Contact. They had been looking for an actor who could also play guitar and sing, and after meeting with the director at my agent Sharon's office, I was given the part without having to audition. Obviously this job would mean having to move up north for the duration, but I no longer had a girlfriend, or any other reason to keep me in London. Plus, I thought it would be good fun to work with an established company of new actors. I hadn't previously arranged for anywhere to live, so when I arrived at the theatre I had to sort out digs.

A lovely actress called Caroline Pickles*, told me that she had a spare room to let in the house that she was renting in one of the suburbs. It would cost me £6 per week, so I was pretty sure that it wasn't going to be in the Cheshire countryside, and I was right.

The house was in the middle of what looked like something out of the Blitz. They were actually demolishing the area whilst people were still living there. Some nights we couldn't even be sure that our house would still be there when we got home. All my room had in it was a double mattress on the floor, and I didn't dare venture into the kitchen.

After the first couple of rehearsals, they still hadn't cast an actor who could play the drums. So I suggested they use my old school mate David Williams. I explained that he was still in his final year at The Arts Educational, but if given an Equity card could be persuaded to leave early. They agreed, and so did Dave, although he would have to change his surname because there was another David Williams already registered with Equity. He called himself David John.

It was brilliant having Dave in the show, not only because of his brilliant musicianship, but also because of his infantile sense of humour, which I shared completely. We had discovered the 'Derek and Clive' album, which we played continuously until we had learnt every disgusting word. Unfortunately, our fellow cast members didn't share in our mirth and seemed to be taking this acting lark very seriously indeed. We rarely socialized, and I felt a certain amount of resentment coming from them, probably because they'd all worked together as a company for ages, and also that they'd had to get outside help for this production. There were some good moments though.

In one scene in the play, I had to procure the services of a prostitute. The role required the actress playing the part to kiss me, and then lead me off stage. It was such a small role that it was given to a young student who was studying drama at Manchester University. After a few rehearsals one thing led to another, and I ended up back at her flat for a night of 'How's Your Father'.

*Carolyn Pickles is an English actress who has appeared in West End theatre and on British television. She played Shelly Williams in the ITV series *Emmerdale*. She is the daughter of the late Judge James Pickles, a niece of actress Christina Pickles, and great-niece of Wilfred Pickles. She has recently appeared in the hit ITV drama *Broadchurch*.

Many years later, when I was working in advertising, an actress who was quite a well-known TV personality at the time came in to do a voice-over for a commercial that I was producing. Afterwards I thanked her for her work and was escorting her to the door, when she suddenly stopped and said, "You really don't remember me do you?" (Yes you've guessed it.) She saw the funny side (or so she said) but I felt like a total heel!

Mark (Brain Damage) Wingett, who was still living at my mum and dad's in Hendon, had decided to come to Manchester for the press night. I was extremely nervous.

Mark decided to calm my nerves with a huge spliff of Moroccan black which completely knocked me bandy, and as I went on stage that night, I was getting some pretty strange looks from the stage management and my fellow actors. What happened next is still an utter mystery. I remember going on, and I remember coming off...but what happened in between is anybody's guess.

The next day I was dreading going in to the theatre, sure that I was going to get fired, but instead everyone was congratulating me. On the notice board was a review from The Manchester Evening News. It said: "Blah...Blah...Blah...Gary Shail is an extraordinary actor who somehow manages to spit in the eye of the audience and still gain their applause at the end. On this showing Gary could soon have another career as a pop star, given his musical abilities." PHEW!! I'd gotten away with it.

I loved smoking dope! And it's true when us 'Old Gits' say that drugs were better in the good old days. I feel sorry for today's youngsters as they have no choice. Skunk Weed is all that seems to be on the menu these days, but back then there was a complete smorgasbord to choose from: Lebanese, Moroccan, Temple Balls, Oil, Thai Sticks, and good old faithful Jamaican Herb, all were available for a price. And music always sounded better after a spliff!

On the 18th August 1979, I got to hear The Who play live for the first time. Kenny Jones from The Faces was brought in as a replacement drummer for Keith Moon for the Wembley show, which I thought must've been the hardest gig of his life. In fact he was totally laid back about it, which disappointed me somewhat. All the Quadrophenia cast had been given 'access all-area passes,' which was amazing!

Also on the bill were The Stranglers, ACDC, and Nils Lofgren. Only a couple of years previously I'd watched The Stranglers at The Hope & Anchor Pub, and now I was drinking with them backstage at Wembley Stadium. And fuck did they drink. The Who didn't just have a backstage bar, they had Transit Vans. Each truck served a different drink with mixers. Vodka and guava juice with a constant supply of Jack Daniels chasers is what I vaguely remember drinking.

I do remember watching The Stranglers from the side of the stage, but then having a little lie down whilst ACDC and Nils Lofgren played their sets. I then woke up just in time to have a quick chat with John Entwhistle in the Gents Toilet, just before he was about to play in front of 80,000 people.

I asked John, as casually as I could, if he was nervous about playing to such a huge crowd, and he said, "You know the Album…why don't you do it?" Funny Fucker!

Around the end of August, 79, I decided it was time to move out. Mum was always having sleepless nights, and she said she couldn't rest until she heard me coming home on the bike. My uncle Andy had had a serious accident on one a few years earlier, and had been left severely injured, so I thought that by getting my own place, Mum might now get a decent night's sleep. Also, bringing girls back to the house had proved difficult. Mum and Dad were by no means Victorian in their attitudes, but I had two younger sisters and a baby brother to think about. So I started looking for somewhere to rent.

I'd found a little two bedroomed maisonette advertised in the local paper, which was above a little chemist shop in Colindale. Only a couple of miles from my mum and dad's, it was just what I was looking for. The landlord was a young (ish) bloke called John, who told me that he worked with children with special needs, and ran the local boys' football team. He also said that every now and then he would be staying at the flat for the odd night, but I would rarely see him otherwise. I remember thinking that it all sounded a bit strange, but I was so enthusiastic about having my own place, I brushed my concerns under the carpet and agreed a one year lease.

I had a friend from college days called Pete Lee Wilson who'd agreed to share the rent and deposit with me, and Mark Wingett, although not officially a key holder, would be moving in too. It was going to be fantastic!

Mark and I had been out on the tiles one night, and when we got back to the flat the following morning we found Pete in a complete state of panic and packing his bags. Apparently, Pete had been asleep in bed the previous night when he was awakened by John standing at his bedroom door stroking his erect penis in complete make-up: lipstick, eye-shadow, blusher–the lot. Needless to say, we didn't hang about. So now Mark and I were back at my mum and dad's, and back on the bunk beds. We wouldn't be there for long though.

I had seen a play in 1978 called *Class Enemy*. Performed at the Royal Court in London's Sloan Square, it had completely changed my attitude to theatre.

Written by Nigel Williams* and set in a vandalised South London schoolroom, it told the harrowing story of six school children so terrible that no one is prepared to teach them. Left without a teacher, they form their own hierarchy, and out of sheer boredom, decide to teach themselves with stories of their bleak lives.

This was the kind of theatre that I wanted to do, so when my agent informed me that a tour of the play was being planned by The Oxford Playhouse, I was definitely going to be in it. Mark Wingett now had an agent called Jonathan Alteraz, who happened to be good mates with mine, so an audition was arranged for both of us at the same time.

---

*Nigel Williams most successful work has been the 2005 TV drama *Elizabeth 1*, being himself nominated for an Emmy Award for his script and winning multiple awards for the film and its star, Helen Mirren.

The director (Nick Kent) never stood a chance! I think Mark actually threatened to kill him if we didn't get the parts. Mark got the role of Iron, a dangerously violent minor with homicidal tendencies, and I got the role of Nipper, a 16 year old punk rocker whose racist outlook on life had been influenced by his alcoholic father.

The play, although controversial, had received glowing reviews in London, but now we would be performing it at regional theatres all over the country. First stop though, would be Oxford.

We had rehearsed the play above a pub in Putney, so getting to work on our bikes hadn't been a problem, except for one time when it had snowed heavily and my dad nearly wrote off his car sliding us to work. But now we had to relocate to Oxford for the final rehearsals, so we would need to find digs.

Mark and I rented a houseboat, on the river, in the middle of winter. The boat was fucking freezing, so we had to keep the cooker on constantly to keep hypothermia at bay, and most nights we'd have to sleep fully clothed. But it was a brilliant laugh. One morning, Mark slipped on some extremely smelly swan shit and nearly fell into the icy river. He spent the rest of the day planning revenge on the culprit, and looking at recipes for swan stew.

The rest of the cast were good fun too. An actor called Keith Jayne, who was playing a character called Racks, did all the driving. Keith had been a children's TV favourite in a show called 'Stig of the Dump' in the early 1970's, playing Stig. He was a brilliant laugh and a top bloke. He was also a crazy driver. He used to play a game in the car (when we were hurtling through poorly-lit country roads) called Chicken. He would turn off the headlights, and the first person to scream would be 'clucked' at for the rest of the journey.

Another great guy was an actor called Peter Lovstrom, whose grandfather had fought for the Norwegian resistance in the 2nd World War. He was also an incredible gymnast and dancer, but was also a terrible giggler. I could barely look at him sometimes whilst on stage, and if he'd decided to get me, which was most nights, I would be reduced to tears trying to hold it together.

The violence in the play was extreme to say the least, so had to be choreographed meticulously. School furniture had to be broken every night, and that brought problems of its own.

One night Mark Wingett was trying, without much success, to break a chair onto the stage. It just wouldn't break no matter how hard he slammed it down. Eventually with one last effort it broke, and a piece of it disappeared into the darkened auditorium followed by a muffled yelp. Some poor woman sitting five rows back had been hit full in the face by a piece of the shattered chair. She received some 'on the spot' first aid, but refused to leave the theatre until Mark had signed the bit of chair that had hit her.

In some towns on the tour the reputation of the play had preceded us, and we were warned by some theatre managers to behave ourselves or else. We, or should I say Mark, would normally tell them to 'Fuck Off!' These kinds of confrontations only added to the adrenaline as far as we were concerned, but sometimes could backfire when trying to book into a quiet little guest house. Especially when Mark insisted on signing the register as Adolph Hitler!

The *Class Enemy* tour was a lot of fun, and by all accounts quite successful, but there is nothing like playing in your home town. So when we learnt that the show was being transferred to London's Young Vic Theatre, we were all over the moon. The memories from the Royal Court production were still fresh, so anyone disappointed at missing it the first time around would now get the chance to see our production. We were almost guaranteed a good audience.

As soon as the tickets went on sale, it sold out! Even today, 35years later, I still get people telling me that they'd seen that play. Only very recently a new production of *Class Enemy* was staged in Sarajevo, set against the backdrop of the civil war. And it has also been adapted for audiences in Singapore, Shanghai and Romania, as well as Slovenia and Serbia.

I often wonder, given that Nigel Williams became so successful with his TV writing, that he never adapted *Class Enemy* for television. Maybe he did, and I just missed it.

One night, during the show, I became aware of someone sitting in the front row who seemed to be writing something on a pad of paper every time I moved. It was quite off-putting to tell the truth. Afterwards there was a knock at my dressing room door, and a very attractive lady introduced herself as Theresa Topolski. She said that her dad Felix would very much like to meet me for a drink in the bar.

Her dad, Felix Topolski, was a contemporary artist who'd come to Britain from Warsaw in 1935 after being commissioned to paint King George V's Silver Jubilee. He had been working on his 'Memoirs of the Century' project in his London studio under Hungerford Bridge for years, documenting key moments from history on canvas, as well as on the actual walls of his studio. He had painted everyone from Ghandi to Jagger and now he wanted to paint me.

Actually, it wasn't really me that he wanted to paint, but my character (Nipper) from the play, as he thought that would sum up 1970's youth. I arranged to go to his studio, in costume, for the sitting. My agent, Sharon, thought that this was a fabulous publicity opportunity, so she contacted the Evening Standard newspaper who jumped at the chance to document the event.

Felix Topolski's studio was amazing. There were paintings and drawings everywhere, piled high to the ceilings in some places, with just a double bed in the middle of the wonderful mess to sit on.

The painting, which was about the size of a door, only took less than an hour to paint. Felix had that enviable talent of being able to create with one stroke of his brush what others would take all day to create. The picture was stunning and the Evening Standard called me "The Immortal Punk".

When Felix died in 1989 at the age of 82, his 'Memoirs of the Century' was opened as an exhibit to the general public, and this included my picture. In the brochure list of the pictures mine was number 79 and titled…Gary.

Felix's studio is still there under Hungerford Bridge, but is now a I/Bar serving drinks and light lunches. His work is obviously still all over the walls, but I do wonder if the punters really look at it, whilst munching on their steak sandwiches, and checking their mobile phones. Or am I just being cynical.

Felix Topolski

The Immortal Punk

6

"The music business is a cruel and shallow money trench, a long plastic hallway where thieves and pimps run free, and good men die like dogs. There's also a negative side." — Hunter S Thompson.

Even though I was busy as fuck, I would always find time to make music. I must've driven my friends crazy, playing cassette tapes of my latest tunes at them over and over again. But if I did, they never told me, and anyway, the tunes were brilliant.

Phil Davis, who'd played Chalky in *Quadrophenia*, had written some lyrics for a song called 'Blown It'. It was a simple and poetic story about a young lad at a party who drinks vast amounts of alcohol to acquire enough Dutch courage to chat up his dream girl. He drinks far too much though, and is eventually too drunk to dance with her.

One day Phil and I sat at the family piano and worked out some music. I loved it, and played it to my agent Sharon. Sharon had a mate who was the Music Publisher for Rocket Records, a guy called Eric Hall.

Eric Hall was a complete force of nature! He had an office with a big desk, had gold records all over the walls, smoked a big cigar and thought that everyone and everything was MONSTER! This was the time of the Record Companies*.

Eric wanted me to demo the song the way I heard it in my head. Even though I could play and sing the song at the piano ballad-style, I felt that I could do more with the arrangement and give it a more up-tempo reggae feel.

I was given two full days at E.M.I's studio in Manchester Square, and told I could use my own musicians. I would play piano and bass, I got a mate from Brighton called Bernie Richards on drums, and Mark Wingett got me his mate from Portsmouth on guitar. His name was Lawrence Dexter.

Lawrence was one of the nicest, most decent 'sober' people you could ever hope to meet. He was a talented guitarist and great to work with. When we finished the demo for Eric Hall, I didn't see Lawrence again. Then, about 30yrs later, whilst living in Portsmouth, I got a message on MySpace from a Lawrence Dexter saying 'hi', and that we should meet up for a drink. I had absolutely no idea who Lawrence Dexter was! After some skilful questioning on my part, it turned out that he'd played guitar on a demo I did back in 1980 for Rocket Records. We met for a drink...And I still didn't remember who he was.

*The Rocket Record Company was a record label founded by Elton John, along with Bernie Taupin, Gus Dudgeon, Steve Brown and others, in 1973. The company was named after the hit song "Rocket Man". The label was originally distributed in the UK by Island and in the US by MCA Records, both of which Elton John was also signed to.

Eric seemed to like the demo but you could never really tell if Eric liked anything or not, as everything was always just 'MONSTER, MONSTER!' He did feel though that it would need a good producer at the helm, and he knew just the man. I said that Phil and I should have some say in who produced the record, but when Eric told me that Steve Harley the singer from Cockney Rebel* had already heard the demo and wanted to produce it…I shut the fuck up!

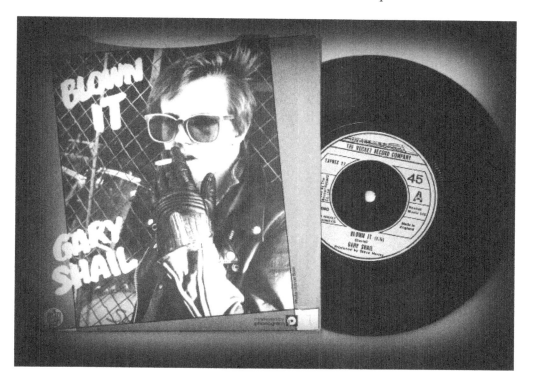

It was totally brilliant. Elton John's record company was going to sign me and Phil for a single deal, Steve Harley was going to produce it, and it would be released with 'monster monster' backing from all the departments concerned.

One night Phil and I were taken to a flash Chinese Restaurant in the West End part of London. Eric and Steve Harley were there, as was a strange and very camp bloke called Tony Toon. Tony was Rod Stewart's Publicist and he was fucking outrageous!

The restaurant had one of those tables that could spin, so you can easily share the dishes. Tony Toon was chopping out lines of cocaine, and then spinning the table round to each person in turn for a toot. I think we ordered 20 or more dishes, and never ate one!

*Steve Harley & Cockney Rebel are an English rock band from the early 1970's. Their music covers a range of styles from pop to progressive rock. Over the years they have had five albums in the UK Albums Chart and twelve singles in the UK Singles Chart.

59

We recorded the record at Morgan Recording Studios in February, 1980. For the up- tempo reggae version, Phil sang the song with a full backing band, and for the ballad I sang and played the piano accompanied with a solo violin.

Rocket wanted to release it as a double A-sided record, and obviously use the Quadrophenia connection to publicise it. It was decided to emit a lyric ('pissed') from Phil's version, but would still be included in mine as we thought it far too tame to cause any offence. We were wrong, and the BBC flatly refused to play it. It got a couple of so-so reviews, but with no radio play… it was dead in the water as far as Rocket was concerned.

Eric Hall was still interested in listening to any other songs that I had though, as he thought I would be a good writer for other artists on the books. He arranged a meeting for me to meet the head of EMI's MOR division, to play him some of my songs and ideas. His name was Vic Lanza, and he'd been responsible for financing massive hit records for the likes of Cliff Richard and Kiki Dee, amongst others.

At EMI, I was greeted by a cute little receptionist who informed me that Mr Lanza was expecting me, and I should go right in. Vic was (I suspected) in his 50's, overweight and gay (although he probably had a wife and two kids seconded in a semi somewhere in Edgware). He shook my hand delicately and said he was very much looking forward to getting his hands on my cassettes. (Okay, I made that up).

Vic played my demos at a volume that actually shook the windows in his office, but he just stood clicking his chubby fingers (out of time) to the beat, whilst I sat squirming in my chair.

After the meeting, I asked the cute receptionist if Mr Lanza always listened to music at that level of volume, and she said, "He has to—he's deaf!"

Angst

Obviously, I wasn't going to be the pop star that I thought I'd be. So I thought I'd just hang out with some instead.

It was now the 1980's, and the London club scene was exclusive enough for me to want to join it. I'd been knocking around with a dancer called Libby who formed her own dance troupe called Angst, and they had a residency in a nightclub called Munk-berrys.

It was a tiny place, with a small restaurant area, DJ booth, dance floor, and a small stage with dressing rooms either side. I loved going to their shows. Dance was the new rock n roll, and other acts were starting to get noticed too. Hot Gossip were ruffling a few feathers with an act that bordered on pornography, and a band called Shock, featuring two robotic dancers called Tik & Tok, were playing to full houses around the country. Suddenly every pop star wanted to be supported, or surrounded, by dancers. Shock supported Gary Numan on his British tour, and Angst supported David Essex for his London shows. As for Hot Gossip, they got massive exposure on TV thanks to The Kenny Everet Show, where complaints from self-appointed moral guardians like Mary Whitehouse only made people want to watch them even more. I loved going to Munkberrys. It was my first club.

One night, we were at our usual table in Munkberrys, when there was a commotion at the door. It was a very small place, so even with the loud music; you could still hear everything that was going on. Suddenly the manager came rushing over to me, saying that there was a pissed-up bloke at the door saying he knew me, and could I vouch for him. I looked over to the door… and it was Pete Townshend!

Work-wise, things were just ticking along nicely. In March, 1980, I did a play at The Bush Theatre, where I worked with a company of real northern professionals. The play (Viaduct), written by actor Paul Copely, was set in West Yorkshire where the characters led the story: a young textile worker, a newly married couple, a mysterious old man, and a Puck-like boy proficient in the acrobatic art of balance. Guess what role I played?

I loved doing theatre, as it didn't interfere too much with my very important social life.

Once rehearsals were finished, you'd have the days free. Lots of time to recover for the next show. Plus, I really loved meeting and working with new actors. It had been a bit strange for me in Manchester, but in London, I guess I felt more secure. Also, dressing room politics can be brilliant. I learnt more about Margaret Thatcher's proposed plans for the mining industry from the other actors in this show way before it actually happened. And the way that they described and pontificated their socialist ideals was like watching stand-up comedy. Believe me; back-stage was rarely boring.

I was having so much fun it was un-fucking true! I was working steadily, and I was in London. I certainly wasn't making a fortune, but more than enough to keep me in the company of beautiful woman at a nightclub of my choice. And at the age of 20, that's all you need. So what did I do? I got myself a new girlfriend.

Tracy was a dancer who'd also trained at The Arts Educational School, but she'd been on the ballet course. I hadn't been aware of her whilst I was there, but she had once dated my ex flatmate Pete Lee Wilson, and I remembered thinking 'Cor'!!!

Tracy and I were brilliant together for a while, and even got engaged at Albert Wong's Chinese Restaurant with all my family and friends in attendance. My mum and I chose the ring from Argos at Brent Cross Shopping Centre, and we did the whole 'shubudle' (Is that a real word? It should be) and just assumed that we would be a normal couple.

Drugs were available everywhere in my world in the 80's. But I rarely saw them out of that world. None of my Hendon friends snorted cocaine for instance. Cocaine was expensive and not that easy to find, unless you knew someone, or knew someone who knew someone. And I most definitely knew someone. I knew where to get my Charlie from before it got messed with, as buying from a stranger in a club toilet could prove hazardous and costly. I know 'cos I once paid £60 for a gram of baking soda from a geezer in Chelsea who swore it was pure. Yes it was...pure fucking baking soda! I hated being ripped off, so I made friends with the dealers.

"At the top of the chain, drug dealers are really quite normally balanced human beings. It's the customers who cause all the drama."   - Anon

My dealer was called Janine. A mother of two and strikingly beautiful. Janine was the main man when it came to supplying cocaine to the movers and shakers of the 1980's entertainment world. She was also an incredible song writer and singer, but still had to pay for her own demos like the rest of us, hence the cocaine selling.

I loved working on Janine's songs, as it meant I would get free Charlie all night, and the songs I liked anyway. One night, she let me have sex with her and drive her classic Carmen Gia sports car (Not at the same time, I hasten to add). But I crashed it, and Janine had to phone a friend to get rid of the car. Then she reported it stolen and got the insurance on it.

If I'd had the photo technology that we have today back then, I could've made a million in blackmail, or as the Tabloids liked to say...investigative journalism. Some of Janine's clients were really big household names, in all areas of show business. But everyone knew the rules back then, and no one was crying on about their terrible sex and drug shame just to get on the Telly. No, the drug trading, dealing, buying and taking was really quite well-organised, it seemed to me.

Once you had your little envelope of white powder, the next problem (if in a public place) is where to take it. Now traditionally this would have to be in a toilet cubical of some description. Unisex facilities were not readily available back in the 80's, so trying to share a line of coke with a young lady brought problems of its own.

The traditional way, and for my money the most stupid way to take cocaine, is to lock yourself and a friend in a toilet cubical saying 'Shhhhhhhh', whilst trying to find a relatively clean flat surface (normally the toilet seat) to line out your cocaine. You then tentatively unwrap your little envelope, careful not to drop any, and then scoop some coke with your gold Amex card onto the toilet seat to chop. Then whilst saying 'Shhhhhhh..' start banging the credit card down on to the tiny white chunks, sounding like a Morse Code operator with Tourette's, before shooting it into your brain with the help of a rolled-up £50 note.

The other way, (if you had bothered to embrace the whole drug paraphernalia scene) was to buy a solid gold, diamond-encrusted, little spoon that was worn around the neck. You would have just enough slack in the chain to be able to scoop a spoonful of powder from a little brown bottle up to your nostril, without making too much of a public statement.

I remember having a solid silver straw with a diamante encrusted dragon riveted to one side. Not pretentious at all then.

One night, Libby gave me a tab of Acid. Even though I was now engaged to the doll-like Tracy, I was still seeing Libby. She was older than me by only a couple of years, but to me, at 20 years old, it was like having a sugar mamma. Libby loved reggae music, and always had the latest Bob Marley album before I did. She also liked crazy shit like the B52s, and once choreographed a piece of contemporary dance to Rock Lobster, I seem to remember. She had a little studio flat in West London, and liked to stay up late, smoke dope, and listen to music-three of my favourite things to do in my early 20's. If the evening ended up with some hot sweaty sex, then that would make it four.

I truly never went over to Libby's just for sex though. She was an incredibly intelligent and totally focused young woman when working on a project. And very, very, sexy! I just adored being in her company.

One night, Libby handed me a tiny little red pill, telling me not to make any plans for the next 18 hours. She then handed me a glossy magazine, telling me to concentrate on the front cover for about 20 mins, or until my brain exploded. All of a sudden I was tasting colour and touching sound. The magazine melted into the carpet, and I loved it...and the sex was incredible!!

Some weeks, especially in the winter months, I would rarely see daylight. I'd get home just as it was getting light, and wake up as the sun was going down. Tracy would usually come over late afternoon, have a cup of tea with my mum, and then wake me up with a blow-job. I loved Tracy. She was in every sense the perfect girlfriend. I loved going out with her, and she always looked great whenever we did. She was a good laugh, a great dancer, and even though I took advantage of her loyalty time and time again, I knew that Tracy would always be there.

To compensate for my atrocious behaviour, I would buy her expensive gifts whenever I had the cash. Once for her birthday, I had a made-to-measure white leather suit designed for her, and I was forever in ladies' shoe shops. I didn't care about the money though; I just wanted my Tracy to be happy with me.

Sharon (Agent) had been busy getting me auditions for anything and everything. Auditions can be a strange experience at the best of times, and some of the jobs I went for I knew I would never get, so I would go just for the laugh.

Sharon sent me to some swanky London hotel for a movie audition. The film was called *Cop Killer*, and would star an American actor called Harvey Keitel. During the improvised workshop audition Harvey almost strangled me to death. I had bruises behind my ears for a fucking week! The role eventually went to Johnny Rotten.

Then one day I got a call saying that I had to be in London for two auditions. One was for a new family friendly TV Sit-Com, for London Weekend Television, called *Metal Mickey*. And the other was for a part in the follow up to the *Rocky Horror Picture Show*.

The Rocky Horror Show had been around since its London debut back in 1973, and had toured consistently ever since. It was a theatrical success story that had become legendary. I knew loads of actors and dancers that had been in it at some point, but it had never been on my radar. It just wasn't the kind of show that I was into, or right for. So when the film came out in 1975, I didn't really notice.

The Rocky Horror Picture Show was even more of a phenomenon than the stage show. So in 1980, writer Richard O'Brien and director Jim Sharman came up with an idea for a sequel. It was going to be called *Shock Treatment*, and I was auditioning for the part of Oscar Drill.

The only person at my audition was the musical director Richard Hartley, and it was held at his very smart flat, in the trendy part of Fulham whilst sat around his grand piano. He basically sang me the song (Breaking Out) whilst banging the piano, and then asked me what key I'd like to sing it in.

The build-up to filming *Shock Treatment* was crap though. It was winter 1980 and freezing cold. I was happy though, because *Shock Treatment* was being filmed entirely on location in Texas. That is, until an American Union strike fucked it all up, and we ended up filming it in a studio in Wembley, only a five mile drive from my mum and dad's house.

To say that I was disappointed is an understatement. It was only a tiny part in film that I'd agreed to do, so I'd agreed to do it because it was going to be made in America. Not bloody Wembley!

The final scenes of *Quadrophenia* had been filmed here, so I knew the studios well. I could get a number 83 bus from West Hendon Broadway that would take me the entire way in less than an hour for 50p. How fucking glamorous, I thought. Some days I would see old school friends on the bus on their way to work, and I'd tell them I was visiting a sick relative.

There is a story that when Richard O'Brien and Jim Sharman were reviewing their options one of the suggestions submitted was to film *Shock Treatment* as a live show in a theatre. This apparently gave Richard the idea of setting the entire movie in a television studio.

If this story is true then Richard O'Brien really is clairvoyant, as the Kings Head Theatre in London have just announced that *Shock Treatment* (The Stage Show) will debut there in 2015. So you may well have already seen it. (I hope it was good.)

Shock Treatment (The Movie) takes a remarkable glimpse into a future that we are now living in. O'Brien predicted a world of Reality TV and Popularity Contests, presided over by an evil Overlord Television Producer who bears more than a passing resemblance to Simon Cowell. He was spot on! In 1980 though, this was all just in Richard O'Brien's head.

Sometime around 2006 (-ish,) I received an email from a young guy living in San Francisco called Jared Wilkes, who wanted to know if I was 'The Real Gary Shail'

who'd appeared as Oscar Drill in a little-known movie called *Shock Treatment*. Apparently he was dressing up as Oscar regularly, and performing with a thing called a 'Shadow Cast' at a theatre in the Bay Area. When I told him that I was indeed the actor who'd played the part 30yrs' earlier, he bombarded me with questions about everything concerned with the film.

One detail that he needed was what was written on a certain T-shirt that I was wearing in the film. These shadow casts are meticulous when it comes to detail, so I looked at an old photo, but could only see certain obscured letters. The only ones I could make out were...CK & KE.

I thought about it for a while, and came up with COCKSNAKE!

Jared seemed happy with this explanation, and then invited me on an all-expense trip to San Francisco to appear at a Shock Treatment themed Party. When I got to the theatre, everyone was wearing Cocksnake T-shirts!

Once I'd got off the number 83 bus, and walked through the doors of Lee International Film Studios Wembley...I entered the world of Denton U.S.A. The Home of Happiness. The cast list was impressive, and some of the original actors from the Rocky Horror Picture Show were also involved.

Patricia Quinn who'd played Magenta, and was responsible for the iconic 'Rocky Lips,' was cast as Dr Nation McKinley, the incestuous sister to Richard O'Brien's character Dr Cosmo McKinley. And Little Nell Campbell, who'd originally played Columbia in the *Rocky* Film played Nurse Ansalong. The rest of the ensemble included Charles Gray, Ruby Wax, Barry Humphries, Barry Dennen, Betsy Brantley, Chris Malcolm, Ugene Lipinski and a very youthful Rik Mayall playing a character called Rest Home Ricky.

Rik Mayall was only a couple of years away from changing the face of British comedy forever with his TV show *The Young Ones*. But at the moment was just biding his time and writing poetry about Cliff Richard.

Claire Toeman and Sinitta

Richard O'Brian and Patrica Quinn

My character (Oscar Drill) had a band called The Bits (Geddit) and all the Bit actors were younger than me. Not by very much, but younger none the less. My great friend David John who'd I'd been to school with, and more recently in Manchester, played the drummer in the band, and a strapping young bodybuilder called Gary Martin played the bass. We nick-named him 'Hunky'.

Rik Mayall, Patrica Quinn, Richard O'Brian and Little Nell

Oscar Drill

The guitarist was played by a super talented young actor called Donald Waugh, who'd first appeared in a film called *Bugsy Malone*, and was now ambitious beyond belief. Whenever Michael White (Producer) came on set, Donald would go into a complete song and dance routine. He was brilliant! There were girls in the band too. My sister Brenda Drill was played by Claire Toeman and Frankie was played by a very young lady called Sinitta, who ironically would end up dating Simon Cowell.

I was in the recording studio on the 10th November 1980, recording Oscar's song 'Breakin Out' for the *Shock Treatment* Album. It's hard to forget, as it was also my 21st Birthday.

It was a real show-bizzy birthday. Once we'd finished recording, Richard O'Brien and Richard Hartley presented me with champagne and a cake, or should I say a very attractive woman in a fur coat presented me with the cake, before dropping the fur to reveal stockings, suspenders and a garter. It was the perfect 21st birthday present!

Even though my career as a recording artist had been less than successful, I still had ambitions to create music. David John and I had been working together on bass and drum stuff for some time now, and had some limited studio experience whilst recording the songs from the play we'd done in Manchester. Inspired by bands like the Jam and Police, I thought a three piece outfit would be the way to go. All we needed was the third piece.

My old school friend, Jon Caplan, had been working part-time in a trendy shoe shop in the Kings Road called R.Soles (geddit?) and had become friendly with a co-worker called Joe McGann who'd recently travelled south from Liverpool to make his mark on the world.

Joe was, and hopefully still is, a strapping good-looking six footer, with all the witty banter that us soft southerners had come to expect from anyone from north of the border. Joe played guitar and sang–or so he said.

An informal get together was arranged with Dave, John and I at Joe's flat in Maida Vale to discuss musical strategy, and to get pissed! So armed with a bass guitar, a bottle of scotch and Dave's portable bongos, we started on that wonderfully ignorant journey that all young men should experience before they become cynical and bald.

Joe's flat in Maida Vale wasn't actually Joe's flat in Maida Vale. It was actually his girlfriend's flat in Maida Vale, but Joe acted like it was his flat in Maida vale.

His girlfriend was an extremely smart and attractive lady called Sarah Inigo Jones who worked in theatrical design, and it was her flat in Maida Vale. Why she ever thought Joe would be good boyfriend material was beyond me, but posh birds seemed to like all that working class bollox back then, and Joe had it in spades. His musical repertoire was incredible though, and he could've made a small fortune standing on the corner of Oxford Street with nothing more than an acoustic guitar and a hat if he'd wanted too. I had bigger plans though.

We started writing songs almost immediately. Lots of them! One of the first songs was called 'Backchat', and we loved the title so much that we named the band after it. We also started rehearsing at a local studio to get the arrangements right.

I always knew that when we eventually recorded, I wanted it to be as tight as possible and not rely too much on overdubs. For me, this was a magical time. I loved being in this band so much that it completely consumed me. Dave, Joe, and I became closer than brothers. We shared the same taste in almost everything, from humour to politics, and even to the steak and kidney pies we ate every lunchtime. We worked and played almost every day, and often Tracy and I would stay over for the night. Sarah and Tracy got on really well too, which helped enormously as they also shared our enthusiasm for the music we were creating.

Often we would get visitors. Gary Holton and his new girlfriend Sue lived locally and often popped into the studio for a drink and a smoke. Alcohol was forever present. Usually just beers, as whenever we drank anything stronger we would row about something stupid. Dave rarely drank as he was always driving, but Joe and I could easily polish off a bottle of Scotch or Tequila in one session. And if Gary Holton was there, then all bets were off, and if Mark Wingett turned up as Brain Damage then all the local hospitals were notified.

It soon became clear to me that we should be recording something, but studios were not cheap. Lucky for us then that I was about to start earning again.

7

My lovely agent Sharon had secured me an audition for a new London Weekend Television situation comedy called *Metal Mickey*. I was told that I was too old for the part, but it would be worth going to, if only to meet the casting director who was a lovely old queen called Richard Price. I would also get to meet the director, a completely mad Monkee called Micky Dolenz.

L.W.T. was situated on London's South Bank. Just a stone's throw from The National Theatre and a short walk over Waterloo Bridge into the West End. I travelled to my audition on my little yellow 125 Yamaha, dressed in my bright red motorbike leathers, and was now sweating in reception awaiting the call.

All over the walls were pictures of LWT's biggest stars. Bruce Forsyth, Little and Large, Russ Abbot and even Orville the Duck had all been allocated space for their publicity pictures which had been blown up to a ridiculous size and now gazed down at you like mad clowns. I actually found the experience unsettling. Suddenly my name was called, and I was in the elevator hurtling towards the 12th floor. The elevator at LWT was brilliant. It actually took your breath away it was so fast. I remember getting in one morning with a young lady who'd never been it before, and she actually screamed the whole way up to the top floor.

I had been a huge fan of The Monkees whilst growing up, and Micky Dolenz certainly didn't disappoint. He was like a loose electric cable with the power still running through it, and he never sat down. Even though I'd been told that I was too old for the part, Micky insisted that we read some scenes from the script together and not worry too much about the age thing. It was brilliant fun. Micky has this wonderful enthusiasm that is so infectious you just go along with whatever he suggests.

I must've been in Richard's office for about an hour, which seemed like an awfully long time for a TV audition, but Micky just kept going on about some amazing Robot that talked and danced the boogie. It all sounded a tad mad to me though.

After the audition, I decided to drive into the West End and do a bit of window shopping in Oxford Street. I was standing outside some trinket shop that sold 'I LOVE LONDON' T-shirts, when I felt a tap on my shoulder. I turned, and there was Micky Dolenz who was taking a lunch break. What were the chances of that?

I was contracted to make a Pilot Episode of *Metal Mickey* that, if successful, would then be turned into a six part series to be shown on Saturdays (at tea time) after the football results. It was proper prime time television, and I would have to make a commitment to make further episodes if the show was popular. After reading the first script, I thought that was extremely unlikely.

Once my fee and contract had been brilliantly negotiated by Sharon, I was invited to a meet-and-greet in the foyer of LWT to meet my fellow cast members, including Metal Micky. It was the strangest morning of my life to date. The rest of the cast seemed as bemused as me, and we all just stood around smiling inanely at each other whilst LWT's publicity department did their thing. Humphrey Barclay, who was the Head of Light Entertainment, had first seen Metal Mickey on *Jim'll Fix It* a couple of years earlier, and had thought that kids would love him.

I should imagine that footage of that first appearance of Jimmy Saville with Metal Mickey is now locked in a vault somewhere off the coast of Borneo, never to be seen again until Saville's vile crimes become common history and studied in the classrooms of the 23rd Century. I'm sure that Vlad the Impaler was probably worse, and Genghis Khan, with his systematic rape and torture of most of the women and children of Northern Europe would probably come as a close second. But we have Jimmy Saville for now. How will future generations rate our villains I wonder? Or will we just air-brush them from history like we do with everything else these days?

I would be playing Steve, the youngest member of the Wilberforce family, and from what I could gather from the script, the most normal.

Colin Bostock-Smith, the writer, had re-written the part of Steve as a 15year old teenager, which meant I would be playing six years younger than my actual age. In fact, I was older than the actors who were playing my elder brother and sister in the show. Lucinda Bateson was playing my sister Hayley, and Ashley Knight was playing my big brother Ken. A very attractive and, I thought, extremely sexy actress called Georgina Melville played the mother, and a lovely old actor called Michael Stainton was the dad. There was also a next-door neighbour called Janey, who we were led to believe was Ken's girlfriend. The part of Janey went to a very tall and striking black actress called Lola Young*.

For me though, and the most exciting thing about working on this show was that I would be acting alongside a bonafide comedy legend. The part of my Granny was to be played by Irene Handl.

Irene had had roles in such landmark films as *Night Train to Munich, Spellbound* and *Brief Encounter*. Her most notable appearances included *I'm All Right Jack* as the wife of Peter Sellers' union leader Fred Kite and Tony Hancock's landlady in *The Rebel*, which in my view is one of her funniest performances. She'd also played Sherlock Holmes' housekeeper Mrs Hudson in '*The Private Life of Sherlock Ho*lmes', and had small roles in two of the *Carry On* films.

---

*Lola Young unsurprisingly gave up acting after *Metal Mickey*. From 1990 to 1992, Lola was a lecturer in Media Studies at the Polytechnic of West London. In the following year she was lecturer, senior lecturer, principal lecturer, Professor of Cultural Studies and in the end Emeritus Professor at the Middlesex University. In 1995 she published Fear of the Dark: Race, Gender and Sexuality in Cinema. Young became Project Director of the Archives and Museum of Black Heritage in 1997, she was Commissioner in the Royal Commission on Historical Manuscripts in the years 2000 and 2001, and Chair at Nitro Theatre Company in 2004.Lola was appointed an Officer of the Order of the British Empire (OBE) in the 2001 New Year Honours. From 2001 to 2004 she was Head of Culture at the Greater London Authority, following which she was created a life peer on 22 June 2004 taking the title Baroness Young of Hornsey, in the London Borough of Haringey.

On television she appeared as a guest in a number of comedy series, notably as a regular in the 1958 series *Educating Archie*, and as Cockney widow Ada Cresswell in *For the Love of Ada*, which would later be adapted for the cinema. She would also appear in *Maggie* opposite Julia McKenzie. She appeared in a rare aristocratic role in *Mapp and Lucia* and as another aristocratic character in Eric Sykes' 1982 television film *It's Your Move*, where her chauffeur was played by Brian Murphy from *George & Mildred* fame. She also appeared as Madame de Bonneuil in the BBC's film of Hotel du Lac in 1986.

Metal Mickey was basically a giant toy robot remotely controlled from a man-sized black box that contained a bloke called Johnny Edwards, who was Mickey's operator and voice. He was also its creator.

The robotic voice was created using a device called a vocoda*, the same one that Jeff Lynn from E.L.O uses on "Mr Blue Sky". Mickey could perform a multitude of tasks. His head alone had about 10 functions, all controlled by Johnny Edward and a joystick.

Johnny Edward had been many things. In the 1960's he'd been a pirate radio DJ, in the 1970's he'd run a successful entertainment agency, set up his own independent record label, and would eventually write and produce the song "Save Your Love" for Renee and Renato in 1982. The song entered the charts at number 57 but would eventually go on to become the Christmas number 1.

Johnny Edward owned a complex of recording and rehearsal rooms in South London that were available to hire. And this was music to my ears! I was tired of rehearsing Backchat in rooms with water dripping down the walls. Johnny's studios were twice the hire price, but the facilities were luxury compared to what we'd been used to.

Each room had its own PA system and a backline designed for that specific space, and all had lovely carpet which all musicians will tell you is essential, not only for comfort, but for sound as well.

Rehearsals for Metal Mickey were held in an old church opposite Waterloo Station which was fantastic as it was only a stone's throw from LWT, and only a short walk to the Young Vic Theatre which I knew well. The producers weren't too happy about me riding a motor bike though, and although they never banned me (I would've told them to fuck off probably) it was suggested that it wasn't me that they were worried about, but all the other maniacs on the road that might crash into me. I started using the London Underground shortly afterwards, which was horrible, but at least it gave me time in the mornings to learn my lines, plus it meant I could have a little 'drinky' at lunchtime.

---

*A vocoder (short for voice encoder) is an analysis and synthesis system, used to reproduce human speech. The vocoder was originally developed as a speech coder for telecommunications applications in the 1930's, the idea being to code speech for transmission.

There is a little bar almost at the bottom of the steps at Waterloo Station called 'The Hole in The Wall' that I started frequenting. Sometimes Colin Bostock-Smith (writer) would join me for a few ales at lunchtime when he came to rehearsals, but normally it was just me knocking back a pint and a whisky chaser before running to LWT to take advantage of their subsidised lunches. You could get a T-Bone steak with all the trimmings for about 2 quid, and a jam roly-poly with custard for about 20 pence.

We would have the read-through on the Saturday morning, and then rehearse from Monday to Thursday. Then on Friday we'd be in the studio all day rehearsing for lighting and sound, and then at 7p.m. sharp we would record the show in front of a live studio audience.

We had precisely three hours to get it right, otherwise the lights and cameras were switched off by some un-seen union official with a love of stop watches. It never happened.

I was now theoretically getting paid a considerable amount of money to behave like a naughty teenager, so I did. Micky Dolenz was just as bad. He never stopped laughing and joking throughout the day and it was definitely infectious. I remember rehearsals as being one big laugh from start to finish. Irene Handl was a fucking OAP hooligan though. She was 79 going on 18, and totally evil. I fell in love with Irene Handl the day she told me this.

One day about four days into rehearsal, I politely asked Irene (who took her two rat-like dogs with her everywhere) why they had no teeth. Now, you have to remember that Irene actually ferried these ugly little fuckers around in her bra. And she said to me, "I had the vet remove their teeth 'cos they was biting my nipples!" I very nearly wet myself.

Irene was as sharp as a switch blade though, and didn't suffer fools at all. She hated it if anyone treated her like a senile old lady. I once saw a make-up girl talk loudly to Irene, thinking she may be a little hard of hearing. Irene pretended that she was deaf, and made the poor make-up girl shout at the top of her voice for the rest of the day.

She was also a terrible giggler. She would think nothing of changing a line mid-scene if she thought it was funnier than the script, trouble was...she never told anyone when she was going to do it. Watching her forget a line and then getting out of it was always a comedy treat too.

I think it can be safely said that I was totally enamoured by Irene Handl. Over the next three years she would continue to inspire, amuse, and terrify me in equal measure. I have so many lovely memories and stories about her, and will venture to slip one in every now and then, especially when I have a sense of humour breakdown.

The pilot show for Metal Mickey was aired on LWT on Saturday the 6th September, 1980 at 5.30pm, just after the national football results. It was, to my complete and utter surprise, an instant hit.

The show would eventually pull in audiences of over 12 million people a week, which by today's standards is astounding when you consider that even top shows today only get 4 to 5 million viewers. Of course, back in 1980, there were only three TV channels to choose from, and I'm sure that the show's given timeslot helped enormously. For me though, everything changed.

Once the show came out, the phone never stopped ringing, both at home and at my agents. I was asked for interviews for all the girls' mags my sisters read. My Guy, Jackie, I was in all of them. I don't think my sisters were too happy about that. Once there was a competition in Jackie Magazine, and the prize was spending a whole day with me.

It had been arranged that the winner of the competition would spend an entire Saturday with me, including watching a rehearsal and meeting Metal Mickey in person, and then she would come back to mine for tea. As I was still living at home this would mean meeting the whole family and the people from Jackie magazine thought this was great. When we arrived back at the house, I had no need to introduce the young lady to my sisters as they were all at the same school anyway. My sisters thought it was hysterical. We all shared the Shail name after all. Surely the clues were there that we might be related? This very embarrassed girl could've come over at any time to meet me if she'd wanted to.

Socially, things were definitely looking up. Although I'd tentatively knocked on the door of London's club scene, now I was being handed the keys. I was offered membership to all the top clubs including Stringfellows, The Embassy Club, Bootleggers, and if I included Munkberrys in that list as well, I could get to all four clubs in one night, on foot if necessary. My great friend and fellow actor Jonathan Caplan came along for the ride.

Jon Caplan was the perfect friend to have at this time of my life. We had known each other from Hendon High, and had suffered two years of drama training together. So there was no way Jon was going to let a little bit of fame go to my head. We shared the same taste in almost everything, and that included drugs.

One night Jon and I were on our way somewhere after just purchasing a gram of coke. We were driving through Maida Vale when the police stopped us for a routine check. I'd no time to chuck the offending evidence out of the window, so I kept it in my hand. As soon as the police had checked Jon's licence, and could see we weren't pissed, they let us go. Once we were back on the road, I opened my hand, to reveal a small pile of sweaty mushy paper. We ate it anyway.

Jon's acting career hadn't been quite as meteoric as mine, but all that was about to change once he'd been offered a leading role in Britain's best loved soap opera, *Coronation Street.*

Jon would be playing a character called Martin Cheveski, who, if you know your *Coronation Street*, was Elsie Tanner's grandson. He was supposed to be from Birmingham, so why the fuck they cast Jon in the role was a mystery to me. His accent was abysmal, but he looked great and got loads of fan mail, so no one said anything.

Jon spent the week up in Manchester filming, and then hired a top of the range Granada Saloon on the Friday to drive down to meet me from LWT, and then we would go clubbing.

Once I'd finished the first six episodes of *Metal Mickey* though, I could now visit Jon in Manchester. One of Jonathan's co-stars on *Coronation Street* was an actor called Chris Quinten who played the part of Brian Tilsley. Jon and Chris had become good pals, and were regulars on the Manchester night club scene where they abused their celebrity statuses mercilessly.

Chris managed to persuade some star-struck club owner to let him have his own night, promising a steady influx of fellow celebrities and footballers to boost trade and profile. The gullible club owner agreed, and Chris set about arranging a star studded opening night party for all of his mates. I went back with Jon to Manchester after one weekend, and stayed for the entire week.

It was amazing to meet all the Coronation Street stars that I had grown up watching throughout the years. Jon shared a dressing room with Geoffrey Hughes, who played the loveable bin man Eddie Yeats, and Peter Adamson who had played builder Len Fairclough* since 1961. They were both very friendly to me.

The biggest star of Coronation Street, though, was Pat Phoenix. Pat had played the fiery devil-may-care Elsie Tanner in the show, firstly from the very 1st episode in 1960 until 1973, and then again in 1976 until 1984, and been divorced twice. Both her ex-husbands had been actors, and now she was going out with another one called Tony Booth.

Tony was a legendary hell-raiser who'd often appeared in the tabloids due to his drunken escapades and womanising. He was a fine actor though, and had achieved stardom playing the Scouse Git Mike Rawlins in the hit show *Till Death Us Do Part*, which ran from 1965 until 1975. Six years later ITV continued the sitcom, calling it '*Till Death*, and from 1985 to 1992 the BBC produced a sequel called *In Sickness and in Health*.

Pat and Tony had first met on *Coronation Street* in 1960 and remained good friends ever since. In 1979 Tony nearly burnt himself to death when, during a drunken attempt to get into his locked flat, fell into a drum of paraffin whilst smoking a cigarette. He spent six months in hospital and needed 26 skin graft operations. Shortly after his discharge from hospital he went to visit Pat. She took him in and nursed him back to health, and they lived together ever since.

Pat Phoenix was going to be the guest of honour at Chris Quinten's party. He'd even persuaded her to dress up as Boudicca and pull up to the club on a horse-drawn chariot. Jon Caplan and Pat had become very good pals indeed; so on the night of the party, Pat offered to pick us up from Jon's flat in her chauffeur-driven Bentley.

I couldn't fucking believe it! I was sitting in the back of a Bentley with two of the nation's biggest TV stars. Tony Booth, who still had to wear surgical gloves and a neck scarf to hide the burns he'd suffered, was absolutely brilliant. He and Pat were obviously devoted to each other and acted like teenagers. I obviously didn't know it at the time, but here I was sharing a ride with the future mother in law and father in law of our future Prime Minister Tony Blair.

Pat married Tony Booth in September 1986. Suffering from lung cancer, she died eight days later aged 62. Tony Blair and his wife Cherie were among the mourners at her funeral.

---

*In February 1983, Adamson was suspended from *Coronation Street* after selling stories about the show and cast to a tabloid newspaper. Following his arrest for alleged indecent assault in April 1983, Granada Television decided not to support him financially through his legal problems. Although he was cleared of the charge in July, he was sacked from Coronation Street by producer Bill Podmore on 26 August, 1983 for breach of contract when it was discovered Adamson had sold his memoirs for £70,000 after the previous warning in order to pay the £120,000 legal debts from his trial.

Adamson died from stomach cancer in Lincoln County Hospital in January 2002.

"The trouble with fame is, if you get caught breaking the law, every fucker knows about it!"   - Russell Crowe.

A few months into Jon's Coronation Street run, we were out and about in London's Soho. We had been to see the world's finest drummer Buddy Rich at the legendary Ronnie Scott's jazz club when we got stopped by the police walking back to the car. This time we were not so lucky.

Jon had in his possession a small bag of weed which the coppers found, and he was arrested on the spot. The Sun newspaper ran the front page headline 'ELSIE TANNER'S GRANDSON IN SOHO DRUGS SWOOP'. What a load of old bollox. But the damage was done, and even though the bosses at Granada TV seemed sympathetic, Jon's contract was not renewed.

Me and Jon Caplan

Now that I was free from Metal Mickey for a short while it was time to get back to what I thought was far more important: music. Joe McGann, Dave, John and I had been rehearsing at Johnny Edward's place for some time now, and thought we had at least four songs worth recording. I also now had enough money to pay for a decent recording studio to do them in. So, thanks to a connection that Joe had, we booked ourselves into The Portland Recording Studios.

The studio, owned by Chas Chandler of *The Animals* fame, had had a long and illustrious list of past clients that included Jimi Hendrix, Deep Purple, The Rolling Stones, The Small Faces, and Slade, who had recorded all six of their number 1 singles in this studio. It was the real deal. We had decided to record at night, which for me has always been the proper time to be creative, as there aren't the distractions that the daytime can bring.

I have over the years had to record during the day, but there is always something like lunch breaks and phone calls to contend with, and it really pisses me off.

We would have none of that here though, and the people who visited us were by invitation only. Our engineer for the sessions was another Scouser called Andy Miller who was a great bloke and would later become a good friend for many years to come. He and Joe knew each other from Liverpool days when they worked on some project or other involving music. Whatever, Andy 'Killer' Miller, as we christened him, was just the man I was looking for.

Thanks to the constant and regular rehearsals, the songs were now as tight as Roger Daltrey's wallet, and now I had the chance to record them as I heard them in my head.

All my reggae influences and ideas could now be realised in the music, and Andy knew just how to achieve them all. Delay, echo and distortion were all added where I thought necessary, and it sounded fucking wicked! It may well have been the drugs, which were in constant supply thanks to my wealthy friend Stephen Hyer, but when the sessions were finished I really thought that we would have record companies queuing to sign us. It didn't happen!

It seemed to me to be the same old story of 'it's not what you know...but who you know'. We had a band meeting at Stephen's flat in Hyde Park to discuss strategy, and it was decided that we would need the services of a named producer with hit records under his belt.

Stephen Hyer, although knowing nothing about the music industry, decided that he would manage us in this venture. His logic being you only need two things to succeed: money and experience, and if you don't have both, then one or the other usually worked. Money would now no longer be a problem. One night I was 'round at Stephen's flat, and after smoking a lot of dope, we all got the munchies. There was a fab but very expensive Chinese restaurant about a five minute walk away and I was designated to get a takeaway. Stephen told me to get some cash from a bottom drawer in his bedroom. When I opened it...it was entirely filled with £50 notes.

The meeting with Nick Tauber was held at Stephen's on a Friday night, I seem to remember. Nick definitely had great production credentials under his belt. He had produced three of Thin Lizzy's early albums, and had given them their first hit record "Whisky in the Jar". He'd also produced Marillion, Spear of Destiny and Def Leppard, whom he'd discovered for the Bronze Record Company. Apparently, Bronze had refused to sign Def Leppard on Nick's say-so, so he left the company so he could produce the band on his own terms.

Nick was currently working on my old mate Toyah's debut album at the Marquee Studios in Soho. We played Nick the Portland tapes and he seemed to like them, although you can never be totally sure when you are dealing with hard cash. I have produced lots of people who think they can sing that obviously can't, but it's amazing how one lies through their teeth when money is being offered.

Nick also assured us that he had excellent record company connections, and that getting a deal with one of the major labels wouldn't be a problem. This was just what we all wanted to hear. I didn't really want to know how much all this was going to cost, but Stephen assured us that money was not an issue, and we could pay him back once we had sold a million records. So that was it. Even though no contracts of any description were ever signed, we now had a top record producer and would be recording in the famous Marquee Studios.

What could possibly go wrong? Well actually, quite a lot. I was astounded at just how little Nick Tauber's input as producer was. He was a great bloke, but it seemed to me that the engineer was doing all the work whilst Nick regaled us with stories about Thin Lizzy's drink and drugs consumption. I would suggest doing an overdub or something and Nick would just say, "Yeah...Whatever."

I was never happy with the sound we got at The Marquee, and thought it all sounded tinny and over-compressed. To be honest, I thought the original recordings from Portland were far more organic and spontaneous. But what did I know?

Needless to say, once we'd finished recording and the bill was paid, we never heard anything from Nick Tauber or any of his record company contacts again. How naive was I?

To be honest, it wasn't entirely Nick's fault. Having cocaine on a recording session back then was common place, and we should've spent more time in the studio listening, instead of sitting in the lounge outside talking bollox and pretending to be Rock Stars.

In early 2015 whilst researching for this book, I came across Nick Tauber's Facebook page. We got in touch via telephone, and he told me how much he had enjoyed working with us back in 1980. I was pleasantly surprised, as I didn't think he would've remembered me at all. So, with my 2nd attempt at a career in music back in the toilet I concentrated on my social life once again. At least I had my loyal and faithful girlfriend Tracy right? WRONG!

Tracy, Jonathan and I started spending a lot of time at the Embassy club in London's West End. It was as exclusive as you could get back in the early 80's, and catered for anyone who the management thought worthy and rich enough to be admitted. One day you could be standing outside queuing in the rain, but after one hit record or a successful TV show, you would be ushered past the hoi polloi and treated like a long lost cousin. I loved it.

The bar staff were all male, probably due to the club manager's penchant for pretty boys, and there always seemed to be plenty of fresh-faced youths liberally scattered throughout the club who nobody knew. Most of them seemed to be northern lads down on a day trip. Every now and then you would see one of them disappear, only to reappear an hour or so later with more cash than he'd left with. Everyone knew what they were up to, and we all joked that if all else failed then becoming a Rent Boy was a viable employment option. These boys knew exactly what they were doing though, and I certainly don't remember anyone ever forcing any of them into the back of a car at gunpoint.

All of the Bar Staff wore singlet vests and tiny gold shorts, and all were waiting for their 'big break' in show business. One of the boys was a budding singer with big hair called Chris Hamill, who would eventually change his name to Limahl once he became the front man for a new band called Kajagoogoo. Another was someone I knew from working on *Quadrophenia*, John Altman. It was great to see John again, and I introduced him to Tracy who must have been dazzled by the Golden Shorts, as within a couple of months she had left me and moved in with him. I couldn't fucking believe it! I remember being quite upset about this at the time, as I now had lost two girlfriends to *Quadrophenia* bit-part players. So much so, that John and I didn't speak for the next 27 years.

In 2007 we had a Quad reunion of sorts at London's Earls Court, where we were asked to sign photos and do a Q&A. I had seen most of the other guys separately over the years, but not all together in one room. John Altman was there, who by now was a big TV star from appearing in 'Eastenders' as Nick Cotton, and it was actually really good to see him. We have since seen quite a lot of each other, and speak often on the phone.

Quite recently we were both at The Birmingham NEC, when he told me he had a present for me back at his flat in London. I visited John at his home, and he gave me back the green raincoat that I wore in *Quadrophenia*. Apparently I'd given it to Tracy, and she left it at his place. John kept it, awaiting the right time to reunite me with it. How lovely was that?

On Dec. 8, 1980, I was sat watching TV drinking a cup of tea with my mum when the phone rang. It was Joe McGann, who told me that John Lennon had been shot to death outside his house by some fan. He had only just turned 40.

Once all the leftover Christmas turkey had been scoffed and the New Year hangover but a distant memory, I was back at work. It was 1981, and it had got off to a good start. Roy Baird, who had been the main producer of Quadrophenia, called me to see if I was busy. I told him that I would soon be starting on the 2nd season of Metal Mickey, but at this precise moment I was doing fuck all.

Roy explained briefly that he had a contract to produce a recruitment film for the Ministry of Defence (MOD) and would I like to be in it. It would mean training with the British Army for a few days in the Brecon Beacons, and then a trip to Germany to film at the North Rhine-Westphalia army base. The money wasn't particularly brilliant, but I felt that I couldn't pass up the chance of pretending to be a soldier and maybe get to fire a machine gun. Roy Baird arranged a meeting in a pub in Soho for me to meet my fellow actors.

I would be playing Private Wentworth, Jeremy Bulloch would be playing a Sergeant Major and Gareth Hunt was the commanding officer. After a few ales in the pub, it became very clear that this job was going to be eventful for all the wrong reasons. We all looked on it as being a bit of a holiday really, and a great opportunity to sample some real German beer. And some real German women.

Jeremy Bulloch* was charming and very witty, a real 'old school' actor and raconteur. He'd appeared in loads of stuff over the years, and had some recent commercial success in a LWT show called Agony, playing the gay friend of Maureen Lipman's character Jane Lucas.

Gareth Hunt was famous for all sorts of stuff though. In 1976 he had starred with Joanna Lumley and Patrick Macnee in ITV's *The New Avengers*, playing the secret agent Mike Gambit, and was currently known nationally for his series of Nescafe coffee ads.

After spending the afternoon drinking with Gareth and Jeremy I knew that I was in for an education in bad behaviour.

My few days training in Wales had been exhausting but rewarding, and we'd even managed to shoot some interior shots in the local pub that I was billeted in. I'd also been taught to abseil out of a helicopter, fire a semi-automatic weapon, and launch a rocket out of a device called a Milan (Missile Infantry Light Anti-tank). I'd even had to sign the Official Secrets Act, as I now knew how to strip and put together this devastating piece of deadly equipment.

I would have to demonstrate how to do this on film, so I took the training seriously and stayed relatively sober. This all changed though, even before we got on the plane to Germany.

I met Gareth, at his request, at Gatwick Airport four hours before our flight, and we got hammered in the bar, and even more so on the plane. It was only a short flight to Germany and when we landed I had to carry Gareth off the plane. And it didn't get any better.

Gareth Hunt was a top bloke, and he never stopped making me laugh, so much so that I really thought that I'd broken a rib one night when he tried to teach me how to do 'The Sand Dance'. It was about 2 in the morning, when I heard muffled giggling outside my hotel room door. It was Gareth, bleary-eyed and still drunk. I opened the door to find him stripped to his pants with a towel wrapped around his head. He led me down to the foyer where he had emptied the fire buckets of sand all over the lobby floor. He then proceeded to hop back and forth like a demented Egyptian, whilst laughing like a schoolgirl.

*Jeremy Bulloch is now best known worldwide for his costumed appearances as the bounty hunter Boba Fett in the Star Wars films 'The Empire Strikes Back' and 'Return of the Jedi'.

It was okay for him though, as he didn't have to do all the fucking work. Me, on the other hand, I had to demonstrate what it would be like to be a new recruit in the British Army. The real soldiers were at first a bit sceptical about having a poofy actor in their ranks, but after the first days filming I'd hoped they could see that I was trying to take it seriously, and   was chuffed when they invited me to have a drink with them later on that evening in the Mess Bar.

They were a boisterous bunch of lads, and I was amazed and in awe to a certain degree just how young some of the commanding officers were. These very young men were being trained to take serious responsibility, with life and death decisions made whilst under fire. The least I could do was not take the piss and try and do them justice. A lot of footage would have to be shot from the air, so a helicopter pilot called Geoff was commandeered. Geoff had seen action. Either that or he'd watched *Apocalypse Now* a 100 times, but Geoff flew that thing like it was part of his body. The camera crew dreaded going up with Geoff, as often he would take them to the location at low altitude and at battle speed. I couldn't wait to go up with Geoff. One lunchtime I got my chance.

Geoff the helicopter pilot had been asked to fly back to the unit base to pick up some forgotten piece of equipment. I asked if I could go along for the ride, and Geoff said no problem. It was absolutely thrilling. Whilst flying across army land, he flew so fast and low that we could've cut hedges. Then he would pull back on the joystick, hurtling the machine into the clouds, before levelling out high above the beautiful German landscape.

One of the filming locations was at The Wewelsburg Castle. In 1941 the castle was re-named "The Centre Of The World" by Adolph Hitler's best buddy Himmler, and this is where he'd planned to run the conquered world with the help of the twelve most high ranking SS officers in the Third Reich. These would be known as Himmler's Knights. Himmler even had a round table, which they would all sit at whilst planning the final solution and other beastly things. It was an evil place.

We were always laughing and joking, but when we entered that room where all those evil decisions were made we stopped laughing. Obviously Castle Wewelsburg had had a long history before Himmler and the SS, but this has been largely forgotten, and the castle is now a museum, and the first permanent exhibition in the world to address not just the crimes of the SS, but its ideological basis and involvement with science and art, and also its political and cultural ambitions.

The final shot of the film was of Gareth, Jeremy and me in full uniform on the parade ground. We would all be saluting as tanks and armoured trucks passed by. At one point, and only for a brief second, we stopped saluting and all held hands. We thought that someone would notice and yell 'CUT', but no one did. We had to tell them to re-shoot. Can you imagine if we hadn't?

The journey home was just as eventful as the flight out. Gareth got so pissed at the airport that I had to wheel him through passport control in a baggage trolley.

The pilot even had to be called to inspect Gareth to see if he was fit enough to travel.

Private Wentworth

Making that little film had been a once in a lifetime opportunity for me though, and it had been everything I'd hoped it would be. It had been a real boys' adventure.

Back in London, Gareth and I stayed in touch. Gareth loved to party. We started hanging out at my flat, drinking claret and playing guitar. Gareth was a really good singer and songwriter. If we went out to the pub he was always recognised —mainly for the Nescafe Ads- but Gareth was always so gracious to the fans who asked him for his autograph and I learnt a lot about dealing with that side of the business from him first hand.

In 1982, I even managed to get Gareth into an episode of Metal Mickey. By now I had suggested a lot of my actor friends to Micky Dolenz and the casting department, if I thought they were right for the part. They nearly always agreed with me. So when I told them I was a good friend of Gareth Hunt, they jumped at the chance of having him in the show. Like most actor relationships, Gareth and I lost touch, and when he died in 2007 I felt obvious personal sadness, but also the sadness of losing yet another badly behaved, immature, hard drinkin', funny and brilliant actor to cancer. In1999, Gareth Hunt suffered a heart attack and had to withdraw from a Pantomime in Malvern. And in July 2002, he collapsed again whilst on stage in Bournemouth. Gareth died in 2007 of Pancreatic Cancer.

Gareth Hunt 7/2/1943 – 14/3/2007

8

Season 2 of *Metal Mickey* was far more relaxed than the first one had been. The show was still ridiculous, but now we knew that it worked, and the viewing figures were fantastic. I'd even started to receive fan mail, some of it quite saucy and explicit. The LWT publicity department had organised a photo shoot so that I could reply to the letters (once my whole family had read them) and enclose a signed photograph. I replied to everyone.

It was great to see all the cast again after the break, and especially good to see Irene. During rehearsals, she would make me sit between her legs to comb out my hair, which was normally still sticky from the previous night's lacquer. She would also comment on how she thought the rehearsals were going. These comments were usually very scathing, but extremely funny. Micky Dolenz couldn't direct traffic; Lucinda and Ashley were as funny as a runny nose and Metal Mickey was just a dustbin with a face. I often wondered what she said about me when I was not around.

One of the great things about the show was when we had guest performers for an episode. Micky Dolenz said he had worked with an amazing actor on a film project back in the USA, and had hired him to play a very camp hairdresser for episode 1. His name was Robbie Coltrane (He did well, didn't he?).

On that same episode I met a young actress called Lucy, who I thought was absolutely stunning. I asked her out on a date and we became an item for a while, but it was never going to go anywhere. We did have a lot of fun though, and would often book into a little hotel in Sloane Square where we would drink champagne and order room service. I loved being able to afford to do things like that. I still hadn't gone as far as getting a credit card yet, but I was going through cheque books like nobodies' business.

At the end of each month I would hand over the empty books to my dad, who would then write down all my outgoing expenses in an account book that would then be presented to my accountant at the end of the financial year. I used to dread giving Dad those books.

I loved shopping, and thought nothing of spending £250 on a jacket from Johnsons and another £150 on the boots to match if I saw them. Remember, this was the early 80's where fashion was really coming in to its own. The New Romantics now ruled the roost, and 'preening' was now considered cool. I never started wearing make-up, well not that much, but it did mean that I could start wearing smart suits.

Johnsons had a complete range of fantastic two-piece suits in various designs and colours, and I wanted them all. After hours of indecision, and a couple of ales in the Kings Road, I settled on the salmon pink, a powder blue, and the tartan. I was sat, resplendent in my Johnsons' tartan suit with Billy Connolly and Pamela Stephenson, at the top table at Stringfellows on New Years' Eve, 1982.

Billy loved my suit and wanted it badly. Billy, who at this point was still drinking, wouldn't take no for an answer. So after another bucket of champagne, I apparently let him have the jacket. The next day, I woke up on the bathroom floor of my flat, and then spent the whole morning drunkenly searching for my jacket. I phoned the cab company in case I'd left it in the car, I even phoned Stringfellows to see if it was still on the back of a chair. Suddenly I had a flashback to the night before. Bollox!!'

Jonathan Caplan had introduced me to a friend of his called Mike. Mike worked for his parents in the Rag-Trade. Doing what? I had no idea, but Mike was a really-really nice guy. His parents bought him a fantastic basement flat in Belsize Park, just two minutes from the underground station, and fifteen minutes from Hampstead Heath. Mike also played guitar, BADLY! But Mike loved music in a big way. He had a fab record collection, which was played on Mike's 'top of the range' Hi-Fi, and he drove a Japanese sports car like a Formula 1 racing driver. Mike spent all day in an unfashionable suit doing whatever, but come 7p.m. in the evening Mike would get changed, put on some eyeliner, and hang out with me. Mike became my un-paid driver, companion, and soon-to-be flatmate. It was only a one bedroomed basement flat in a block, but the location was brilliant. Mike would have the living room and I would have the bedroom, which was slightly smaller. We never used the kitchen-ever, and I can't remember how much rent I paid, if any. It was brilliant.

I walked down to Camden Town and bought a Futon. In fact, I went Japanese crazy. The Futon came with a bamboo base that turned the whole thing into a table and sofa. I had black carpet laid and painted the walls pure white. I put a Japanese silk screen (bought from Camden market) across the window to hide the dim basement light and whatever daylight got through made the screen shine.

I bought some original art work for the walls from an amazing shop called Parallax, which had just newly opened in the Piazza at Covent Garden. The shop was owned and run by two of the most visionary artists that I'd ever met. Hamish and Larry were so ahead of their time, they needed drugs just to slow themselves down. I started buying stuff from the shop that I knew no one else could possibly have. Hamish and Larry had been working with new photographic techniques using lasers and had come up with the hologram. In the last 35 years holograms have become part of everyday life (just look at your credit card), but in the early 80's this kind of technology was in its infancy and not cheap to buy. I can remember seeing a hologram for the first time and being blown away. It was just a piece of photographic glass, but when hit by the light would give you a clear 3D image of a dripping tap. I paid £175 for it and had no idea what I'd bought.

Hamish and I became good friends, and I started hanging out at the shop. One Saturday after rehearsals Hamish asked if I'd like to work in the shop. Of course I jumped at the chance, but someone recognised me and within the hour...the shop was full of girls. Parallax was just the tip of the iceberg for these guys though, and they would eventually sell the technology on for big bucks. Holograms can now be mass produced. Back then though, every hologram was an original piece of art. Just writing this is painful, knowing that I just let things like that disappear from my life and have no idea what happened to them. Hamish, on the other hand, was last seen hanging out with Keith Richards in Barbados.

My little Hampstead basement flat was ready to Rock and Roll. Lucinda Bateson, who was playing my sister in MM, had bought a new car with her newly acquired wealth and loved driving it. So much so, that I somehow managed to persuade her to pick me up in the morning and take me to rehearsals. This was totally brilliant as it would give me at least an extra hour in bed. I was not getting home (ever) before 4a.m., so if I came home alone, I would only get four hours at the most to get my shit together. But now, thanks to Lucinda, I would get five. More than enough to sober up and look professional.

Some mornings though, Lucinda would have to wake me up and I would spend the entire journey to work in a deep sleep- normally drug and alcohol induced. When I wasn't asleep, I got to know her, and apparently we'd met before.

"Gary and I first met at school. We were both at the Arts Educational School, but he was at the co-ed London Branch, and I was at the all-girls school in Hertfordshire. When we were about 14, we girls were deemed responsible enough to visit the London school to take part in joint productions twice a year. I remember that Gary's particular brand of roguish charm was already well developed, and we had to be fetched from the prop room under the stage on more than one occasion.

Not long after we left school, we played brother and sister in the LWT show Metal Mickey, produced and directed by Micky Dolenz of The Monkees. It was a great show to be part of and Gary and I used to travel up to rehearsals together every day. I have to say, he was often asleep in the car, recovering from the night before. But it seemed like the way things should be.

My 21st birthday fell during a filming day and Gary decided he would take me out and show me the sights. I was excited and nervous in equal measure having never "seen the sights" and imagined all sorts of things. I needn't have worried. Gary may be a rogue, but he is also considerate and understanding. I had an absolute ball and Gary made sure I didn't come unstuck. There were a lot of iconic clubs in the early 80's, and I think we sampled all of them, starting at Annabelle's. Gary seemed to know everyone and I remember at one point standing at the bar with a gang of celebs, musicians, and actors, whilst Gary taught me how to do Tequila Slammers.

We arrived back at his parents' house in the small hours of the morning slightly the worse for wear, or at least I was, and sat downstairs drinking coffee and "chatting". I think we must've been "chatting" a bit louder than we thought, because eventually Gary's mum appeared to tell us to quieten down.

There was a bit of re-shuffling, and I was put to bed in his sisters' room and Gary was sent off to his. This was all accomplished without any fuss, as if it was the sort of thing that happened every Friday night. Next morning there was a wonderful cooked breakfast and I went home with a big smile and a rather sore head

Gary and I have remained friends ever since, and even though there have been long periods when we haven't seen each other, I know I can count on him, whatever happens."   -Lucinda Bateson (now Rose Freeman) 2015

I'd had no idea that Lucinda had been one of those glorious Tring Girls from under the stage.

If I got lucky and had the pleasure of a lady's company for the evening, then I would have to make sure she was up and out of the flat before 8am. I was never really into one-nighters, but sometimes an opportunity would present itself and, as I was now single, I couldn't see the harm in the odd impromptu dalliance.

I was sat at the end of the bar by the piano in Stringfellows on my own one night, when the barman presented me with a bottle of house champagne, saying that the lady at the other end of the bar had sent it. Of course I had the good manners to invite her over to share it with me and, after another two bottles, we jumped in a cab back to my place.

Before leaving the club she had retrieved a holdall from the cloakroom, saying that it was her clothes for work the next day. I did find it a bit strange that she would be working on a Sunday.

We had a great night snorting, smoking, fucking and drinking, and eventually collapsed into bed at about 4am. At about 7am she woke me to ask where the bathroom was and could she take a shower. Whilst she was in the shower, I ventured into the kitchen to see if we had any coffee or tea, but of course there wasn't. She said it didn't matter as she had to rush to catch a train. Eventually the bathroom door opened and suddenly there was a policewoman in the house! She worked for the Thames Valley Police.

I just stood there whilst she gave me a kiss on the cheek before saying that she'd had a lovely time, and hoped to see me again sometime. And then she was gone. If I'd known that she had a police uniform in her holdall, I would have made her put it on hours before. Bollox!

As I have said, I was never really into one-night stands, preferring actually to talk to and get to know the women who I was spending time with, before trying to have sex with them. I did like the dating rituals though, and I don't think any of my exes will say that I didn't always behave like the perfect gentleman whilst out on a date. In fact, I am still very much in touch with a lot of ex-girlfriends via social network. Some of these friendships have lasted nearly 35 years now, and we have all grown up together. To still have these friends after so many years, even if only on Facebook, is a wonderful and comforting thing. What is probably more wonderful and certainly more comforting for all my exes is that I am not going to list them in this book. Not all of them anyway.

Mother: Why has Steve got a tea cosy on his head?
Father: He's turned Muslim!
Mother: Awww, and he was so looking forward to Christmas.
                    -The Demon Barber. Series 2, Ep. 1, 1981

The part of my mother in Metal Mickey was played to perfection by an actress called Georgina Melville. If I'd been born sooner, I'd have loved to have met her as a teenager, 'cos she was sexy as fuck, so god knows what she'd been like at 19. I fancied her rotten, and told her often that I did, normally as she was about to make an entrance on set as my mum.

We became really good mates and started having lunch together in different places around the South Bank. I remember once meeting up with her friend Rula Lenska for lunch at The Young Vic and being well impressed. Rula had been one of the stars of a great TV show back in 1976 called *Rock Follies* and I'd been a big fan. Georgie was also good friends with Mathew Kelly, who was one of the presenters on a new LWT game show called *Game for a Laugh*. She told me that Mathew was actually a brilliant actor who'd got the presenting job by accident. Obviously Mathew had been good at it, because he went on to present lightweight Saturday evening entertainment shows for the next 20 years. It wasn't until 2005 when I saw him play the part of a serial killer in ITV's *Cold Blood* that I realised Georgina had been right. Mathew was a brilliant actor.

Georgina lived at number 8, Friendly Street, Deptford, SE8 with her husband Rory and their baby daughters Jessica* and Cordelia. I loved going to Georgie and Rory's house for supper. They were joyous events fuelled with humour, witty banter, and copious amounts of wine and marijuana. Rory was (and is) a Renaissance man* and a top bloke to boot. He is an artist, musician, author, film director, special effects co-ordinator and all round flash git who is also the younger brother of Lord Julian Fellowes who wrote *Downton Abbey*. He was (and is) an interesting guy.

Georgina and Rory had successfully grown a shit load of Ganga Weed in their back garden one year. It was so successful that the neighbours commented on it, and wanted to know what the plants were. Georgina told them she was growing tomatoes, but then got so paranoid she spent an entire night stringing baby tomatoes to the marijuana plants. She then offered some of them to the neighbours a couple of days later.

---

*Jessica Fellowes has been the deputy editor for Country Life, a columnist for the London Paper and writes for The Daily Telegraph. She has published five books to date: Mad & The City, The Devil You Know, The World Of Downton Abbey, The Chronicles Of Downton Abbey and A Year In The Life Of Downton Abbey.

*A person whose expertise spans a significant number of different subject areas, referring to the renaissance time period.

Georgina smoked for other reasons though. I didn't know it at the time, but Georgina had Multiple Sclerosis and marijuana—as a lot of people now know—is a fantastic pain reliever for people suffering with that terrible illness.

But if you ever met Georgie, you would never have known that anything was wrong at all. Which is why I was almost shocked beyond belief a few years later when I realised to what extent Georgie was suffering. But in 1982 things were still good. Rory and I started 'hanging out'. I remember going to a late showing of *Hitcher* starring Rutger Hauer at the Leicester Square Odeon and then on for a Chinese in town.

"I met Gary in 1982, when he was starring alongside my then-wife Georgina Melville in Metal Mickey. She played his mother, though if that had been the reality it would mean she had given birth to him when she was about ten years old. Well, they were actors, they made it seem plausible. It's very funny, completely surreal and bonkers.

We became friends and have remained so ever since. Sadly, Georgina died in 2004, but Gary and I have stayed in touch, and when I have had sufficient training and rest I like to get together with him. I can usually take a night or two before falling exhausted by the wayside while he steams ahead, unstoppable bundle of energy that he is.

I have one particular memory of Gary. It was my 40th birthday, October 1986. We gave a party at our house in Deptford, in the memorably named 'Friendly Street' (they called it that, so I'm told, because when it was called George Street it was notorious for crime and prostitution, and they hoped the change of name would improve its character. I don't know how quickly that worked, but when we lived there, it was indeed a friendly street).

Gary showed up with a pal, Jon, a fellow actor. He was his usual rambunctious self, strolling in early on in the evening, yelling greetings to us all, Georgina, me and our five year old daughter Jessica. Jess was still upstairs in her bedroom changing for the party. You'll see why I mention this in a moment.

Gary had decided in his inimitable way that it would be amusing to bring along an emergency flare, meant for use at sea. He stood in the middle of our sitting room on the ground floor and set the damn thing off and then ran through the ground floor with it. In minutes the house was filled with a thick cloud of red smoke. It was like standing in a Victorian London smog, but red and glowing and stinging the eyes.

"What The Fuck" I yelled at him, but he ran on, laughing like a hyena. He went through the ground floor then upstairs, making sure he had got his fiendish smoking joke to all corners of the house. I ran after him, throwing open windows as I went, to try and clear the smoke.

Jess started screaming. She thought the house was on fire! I ran upstairs, opening more windows on the way, and got her. I calmed her down and brought her downstairs. We went outside. Our neighbours were coming out of their houses. Red smoke was pouring out of all the open windows. People were panicking; all of them assuming the house was in danger, and with it, their houses. Someone phoned 999. A police car came roaring up the hill and stopped outside the house. I put on my best Queen's English accent, "yes officer, no officer, sorry to bother you officer, just a prank, officer", etcetera.

Gary came out, still carrying the smoking flare. He probably would have told the police to piss off if I hadn't stopped him. He was still laughing his mad head off. Eventually, the coppers took it all in good humour and drove away, telling me not to do it again. ("Of course not officer, thank you officer" I drivelled as they started up their car.) I persuaded the neighbours that nothing serious was happening and they drifted away, back to their homes, shaking their heads at the behaviour of those folk at number 8. Slowly the smoke cleared, drifting away into the autumn night. I went back through the house and closed all the windows. By now the house was freezing, but after I pumped up the heating the warmth returned and we got down to celebrating my birthday. I was turning 40, except I had just aged an extra five years. The party got underway. It was a great night, and like all disasters avoided, it became an amusing story. But boy! Be warned: if you invite Gary to a party, search him at the door."

-Rory Fellowes, 2015

At least you will never forget your 40th birthday Rory.

The great thing about working at LWT was that I was on their casting radar. Even though I was playing a 16 year old in a sitcom, it didn't mean I was overlooked for meatier roles. Esta Charkham (who had cast me in Quadrophenia) was the casting director for a show called *The Professionals*. Every actor wanted to be in it, and I really-really wanted to be in it!

A part came up in season four for a young homeless heroin addict called Jimmy who'd been living in a squat whilst trying to find out what had happened to his girlfriend. She had been killed by a bad batch of heroin supplied by a dealer with links to the Triad. Bodie (an undercover CI5 operative) persuades Jimmy to talk to the police, but before Bodie and his boss Cowley (played by Gordon Jackson) get to him, he is found hanged from the ceiling.

The director was a lovely man called Douglas Camfield, and the actor playing Bodie, who I would be playing opposite, was a TV heart-throb called Lewis Collins. Filming *The Professionals* with Lewis and Douglas was a joy, and I also got to spend an afternoon chatting to Gordon Jackson in the back of his car about working with Steve McQueen, plus anything else I could think of to ask such an iconic British actor. Lewis and I swapped phone numbers.

The Professionals ran for five series and made Collins a star and a national sex symbol. As one wag said: 'Men want to be him, women want to be patted down by him'. His character was foul-mouthed and sexist, with an explosive temper. Though only 5ft 11in, he could lift bigger men by the lapels and throw them across the room. When one girlfriend tried to slap him, he dumped her in a horse trough.

In 1982, as *The Professionals* was ending, Lewis auditioned to become the new James Bond. I think he would have been perfect for the modern Bond movies, as a tough but damaged 007 (sounds familiar). Producer Cubby Broccoli took only seconds to consider Collins, all short fuse and suppressed violence, and decide that he didn't want him. Instead, Lewis played an SAS captain in a film based on the Iranian embassy siege, *Who Dares Wins*, which was to be directed by Ian Sharp, with whom I'd worked with on the ill- fated *Music Machine*.

After *The Professionals* ended, Lewis actually applied to join the Special Air Service, and passed the initial selection stages for the territorial unit 23 SAS, before senior officers ruled that his celebrity status made him a security risk. Lewis Collins lived opposite The Old Bull and Bush Pub in Hampstead, and it soon became a regular Sunday lunchtime hangout. Lewis's interests outside of acting were basically just an extension of his role as Bodie in the professionals, and quite often I would be introduced to obviously military-trained men who looked like they could kill you with a single blade of grass.

Lewis loved skydiving more than anything though, and even managed to get me drunk enough one Sunday to agree to jump from 16,000ft out of a perfectly good aeroplane, strapped to his chest without any real training at all. He told me that it was the best buzz in the world. He wasn't wrong!

Sometimes Lewis's persona would get him into trouble though. One ex-girlfriend sold a ridiculous story to the tabloids, which stated that he liked to dress up as a commando before having sex, and regularly fired a shotgun into the ceiling of his flat when he couldn't get his own way. This last part meant that he was interviewed by the police for several hours before common sense prevailed. After all, surely the people upstairs might've noticed something fishy with all those pellets flying through their floor, doncha think? As usual, I lost contact with Lew for a couple of years, but in 1987 we were reunited in a pub, on a film set in Victorian London, for a TV production of *Jack the Ripper*.

1982 ended on a very bad note for me and my family. My granddad, Benjamin Hudson Shail, died suddenly from heart failure on Boxing Day, and my father was made redundant at the age of 46 from his job at Smiths Industries.

I think losing his job actually galvanised my dad into action. He never spoke with any great joy about his job at Smiths Industries, but it had provided us with a lovely home and enabled me to be privately educated. So even though it was obviously a worrying time for my parents, we all knew that Dad wouldn't be sitting around the house all day moping and twiddling his thumbs.

No, what Dad did was start his own landscape gardening business. He bought a van and all the gardening equipment that would fit in it, and swapped his suit and tie for a flat cap and a pair of wellies. The business flourished and he became a completely new man, working to his own time scale until his retirement at the age of 70. He is now 78, and still shows no sign of slowing down. He still does gardening work for past clients who can't imagine employing anyone else to prune their roses and hydrangeas, and will never really retire whilst he can still start a petrol driven strimmer and still be able to see well enough to clean it afterwards.

Season 4 of *Metal Mickey* would be the longest one yet, with 17 episodes to record. With each new season my contract had been re-negotiated by Sharon, and as my character Steve had proved so popular with the viewers, this was made evident in my pay packet. It also changed the way I looked in the show.

In the early shows Steve was just an annoying little twat, but in the final episodes he was a very expensively-dressed annoying little twat. LWT had given this series its biggest budget yet, and most of it I spent on Steve's wardrobe. I was given my own costume lady who, after the Saturday morning read through, would take me (and the company credit card) shopping in the Kings Road for the next show's costumes. There was no way that a 16 year old suburban schoolboy could've ever afforded this clobber, but by now reality in the *Metal Mickey* show had gone completely out of the window.

For one episode I wore a shocking pink Johnson's suit, which cost a frikkin' fortune. I planned to steal it afterwards, but made the mistake of telling the writer Colin Bostock-Smith. He re-wrote the script, so that me and the suit ended up being dunked into a huge vat of custard. The suit was ruined, and very nearly my face as well.

For the last shot of that show, I was supposed to get lowered from the roof upside down into a large pot of custard. It was huge and the catering department spent all afternoon ferrying buckets of hot custard from the kitchens to pour into it. By the time we were ready for me to be dunked, a thick skin had formed, and it took three or four attempts before the skin broke, and I was dipped head first into what felt like molten lava.

Most of the costumes I got to keep though, and because I was such a good customer, I usually got a good discount from all the shops I bought Steve's clothes from. Even when the show ended I continued getting discounts for a good couple of years, until the shop owners realised that *Metal Mickey* was no longer being aired on TV.

I was also now the unofficial casting director for *Metal Mickey*. I think that I was definitely one of the most generous actors in the world during Metal Mickey. Whenever I got a new script, I would always try and suggest parts for my friends.

In one episode I got two old college fiends (Nigel Miles Thomas and Ashley Gunstock.*) parts as foot-ballers, and in another Jon Caplan played my screen sister's love interest. Pete Lee Wilson also got an episode playing a school friend, and for one segment I got my entire band involved, including my flat mate Mike. I even got a part for my little brother Keith, who was only about 6 years old at the time, playing me as my younger self.

The one person I never suggested, though, was Mark Wingett. Mark hated me doing this show and told me that I had sold out to commercialism. This coming from a man who would spend the next 25 years acting in *The Bill*.

Joe McGann and I were inseparable for a while, but I think he wanted much more than just being my wing-man, and the cracks in the band were beginning to show. I loved it when we drove up to Liverpool in Dave's little yellow Mini to see Joe's mum and dad and four siblings. Joe had three younger brothers, Paul, Mark and Stephen and they also had a younger sister Claire.

All three of the brothers would enter the business, and all would have varying degrees of success. Paul would go on to star in the 1986 cult film, *Withnail And I*, as well as becoming a Dr Who, Mark would play John Lennon in various films and productions, and Stephen is currently playing the village doctor in the BBCs *Call the Midwife*. And they could all sing.

---

*Ashley Gunstock was a candidate in the Green Party of England and Wales leadership election, 2008. He lost to Caroline Lucas by 2,559 votes. He is a Theatrical Producer, Artistic Director, English Teacher and qualified Football Association Coach.

With Paul McGann

At the end of 1982 the McGann brothers were all cast to appear in a show called *Yakkety Yak*, based on the songs of Leiber & Stoller. Also in the show was the Be-Bop group Darts, who'd had a few hit records in the 70's, most notably their re-working of the 1957 classic "Daddy Cool". The show was first produced at the Half Moon Theatre and then got a London transfer. On the 18th January, 1983, it opened at the Astoria to some great reviews, but closed only a few months later due to dwindling ticket sales.

The opening night party was brilliant though, and I remember someone telling me that the two very pretty young lads posing at the bar were going to be the next big thing.

They had called themselves WHAM!

9

Even though I was living in North London, I spent very little time there and very rarely socialised with anyone in that area. I preferred the West End and the company of like-minded people, not estate agents and money brokers. In the early 80's Maggie Thatcher had single-handedly created a society of money-grabbing twats who all seemed to congregate in the wine bars and pubs of Hampstead, bragging loudly about how much dosh they'd made that morning on the stock exchange. Greed was good, and Michael Douglas was their pin-up boy.

This mentality had absolutely zero effect on me or anybody I knew. All the actors and dancers I hung out with, if not working, would either be auditioning for something or taking a class. Libby (my sugar mamma) taught contemporary dance at a place called Pineapple* in Covent Garden, which was a great place to network and meet up with friends.

Often after class, everyone would congregate in a little pub on Long Acre called The Kings Arms. This would become my home from home, and a little sanctuary from the crap and bullshit thrown at me in the supposedly real world. The Landlady of the Kings Arms was a lady called Lillian Florence O'Brien (Lil) who sat at the end of the bar barking orders at her son, Terry, who took absolutely no notice of her whatsoever. He, in turn, would then bark the orders to his wife Jayne, who took no notice either. They were a great family who lived, including their two daughters, above the pub and ran their place the way they wanted to.

None of them gave a flying fuck about celebrity, who you were, or what you'd done. In fact, it was positively frowned upon to talk about your latest show or production as you ran a very high risk of being cut to pieces by Jayne O'Brien's very sharp tongue. I actually saw Jayne threaten to throw Wayne Sleep and Lorna Luft (Liza Minnelli's sister) out one afternoon for being too loud. It was probably the only time I ever saw Wayne Sleep speechless. I loved the O'Briens.

Of course, I was not the only regular customer at the Kings Arms. This was also the home of Charles Augins. Charles was big, black and bald. He'd been born and raised in Virginia, USA, but had lived in London for years where he worked as a dancer and choreographer.

---

*Pineapple Studios was founded by former model, Debbie Moore, who had started dance lessons to alleviate weight gain caused by hypothyroidism. Following the closure of her local dance studio in Covent Garden, she failed to find a suitable alternative, so decided to open her own studio in the area. Pineapple Dance Studios opened in 1979, based in a former pineapple warehouse, from which the company gets its name. The site continues to house the dance studios, as well as being the headquarters of the Pineapple Performing Arts School and the studios' associated dancewear and clothing brand.

Charles also taught dance classes at Pineapple which were renowned for being the hardest and most painfully strenuous classes in London. Think ballet, gymnastics, and osteopathy and you get some idea of what Charles Augins put his poor students through. After class though, Charles would most probably be found at The Kings Arms drinking a very large gin & tonic whilst planning the next day's torture.

Charles Augins lived in a large house near Swiss Cottage with three women, one of which I knew. Sinitta and I had worked together on Shock Treatment (Chapter six) and stayed in touch. We weren't exactly dating per-se, but we were definitely seeing enough of each other to warrant me being introduced to her mother and aunt, with whom she lived. Sinitta's mum and aunty were both singers. Miquel Brown (Mum) had had a couple of Hi-NRG hit records in the late 70's, and her aunt Amii Stewart had scored a massive hit with a re-working of Eddie Floyd's 1966 hit 'Knock on Wood'. Miquel and Amii were both Divas.

I was standing in this very large living room looking at a wall covered in gold and platinum records and feeling very impressed. When I looked more closely though, I soon discovered that they were all for the same record: "Knock on Wood". It had been a hit all over the world and had given Amii a Grammy nomination.

I think Charles was a bit surprised at seeing me drinking tea and passing pleasantries in his living room, but he already knew from the pub that I wasn't one of the bad guys, and whatever he said to Sinitta's mum about my character must've been favourable, as Miquel Brown and I would spend almost the next decade working together on various musical projects. Some of which I will describe in more detail later in this book.

The upstairs bar of The Kings Arms Pub had almost become a private members club. We even had our own 'Dodgy Geezers' who would ply us with their wares. One such character was called Rolex Reg (for obvious reasons), who looked like a middle aged businessman, carrying his brief case and having a quick drink before heading off home after a hard day at the office. In the first year that I knew Reg, I bought a Cartier, a Tag Heuer, three Rolex's and a Casio. All fake as fuck of course, but no one at Stringfellows would ever know that.

The great thing about the early 1980's was that faking luxury watches was still a relatively new thing, and as modern Dubai was still just a glint in a young sheik's eye, still quite hard to get. If someone I didn't know well ever asked me if my watch was fake (and it didn't happen that often), I would always answer with the same line.

"Do I look like the kind of man that would wear a fake?"

10

The date is 12th February, 2015 and I have just found out that Steve Strange has died. I had already planned to tell a story about Steve and Rusty Egan but didn't expect to be writing it tonight. I'm not sure if anyone has ever written their memoirs in Real-Time, but it just seems strangely appropriate somehow.

As I walked into the bar at The Embassy Club I saw Rusty Egan, and it was daggers on sight. We had both been invited to a party one evening, and we already knew each other well.

I had been to the Blitz club a few times, but found it too cliquey and pretentious for me, as I liked to be able to talk to someone in a club without the risk of getting a Hat-Pin stuck in my face. I much preferred The Camden Palace, which I knew well. It was a huge place with lots of nooks and crannies to get up to no good in.

Steve Strange and Rusty Egan were making a small fortune, as the club quickly became one of the most famous clubs of the era. My lovely friend Sally Anne Cooper* was head of PR, and Steve worked the door, vetting, then sorting the princes from the peasants and loving it. I actually saw grown men cry if they were turned away for obviously not 'Getting it Right,' but vowing to try again next week. It was brilliant.

Steve Strange was nothing but politeness and nice to me and any guests I may have had, and was nothing like the flash Rusty Egan who had a degree in flash-gitness and a diploma from the University of Twat. For some reason, Rusty Egan had taken an instant dislike to me and the feeling was entirely mutual. Rusty was a great musician, but so was I. Rusty had a lot of fans, but so did I. Rusty had a massive....You get the picture I'm sure.

Well, one night Rusty was working the door instead of Steve, and as I tried to just bypass the throng and just walk in (as usual), Rusty had the doorman stop me (and my guests) and I was told (loudly) to go to the back of the queue. I was fuming!

This party at The Embassy Club would be the first time I had seen Rusty since that event. Sparks were going to fly!

The party was the usual mix of Pop Stars, Wannabe Pop Stars, Models, Wannabe Models, Drug Dealers, Actors, Hookers and Rent Boys. I was there with my best friend Jon Caplan, who for some bizarre reason had a spear gun in the boot of his car. I have racked my brains to remember why. I know it was 30 years ago, but I'm sure that if Jon Caplan was into spearing big fucking fish in 1983, I would have definitely clocked it. So unless Jon Caplan reads this book and can tell us why, then I guess we will never know. Why is this important? I will tell you.

*Sally Anne Cooper has worked as a PR consultant for Jasper Conran, Trevor Sorbie, Arlene Phillips, and Hazel O'Connor. She was the PR behind The Camden Palace for three years before joining Decon Blue's management team 86/90. Sally was Mica Paris's Manager for her 1st Platinum selling album 'So Good' and followed it up with the 2nd album 'Contribution'. Sally Anne lives in Brighton, which is where I first met her when we were 16yrs old at a Brass Construction concert.

Rusty Egan and I avoided each other for the rest of the evening, which was hard for me because Rusty had good friends that I liked. I'd never really been a big Visage fan, but there was no doubting the talent and commitment that had gone into the project.

Rusty Egan was actually everything I wanted to be, I suppose, and I would've loved to have sat and chatted with him about his musical journey. He played various instruments to a high standard, and had success with many acts that I liked. I just think he just saw me as just being a Kid's TV Star who was far too mouthy for his own good. He was definitely right about me being mouthy, but no one was ever going to tell me what was good for me.

As the evening wore on, the word went out to inform a portion of the gathered revellers that someone was having a private house party after The Embassy emptied. Jon and I had been given the wink, so armed with an envelope of pharmaceuticals and the promise of scantily-clad woman, we set off in Jon's little white Mini to a promised night of debauchery.

On our arrival we were lucky enough to be able to park the car right outside the house, but as we got to the front door, which was already open, I saw Rusty Egan and an extremely large black dude welcoming guests. As soon as Rusty saw me, it was very clear he had no intention of letting us in, so it kicked off, and then it started to get messy.

Rusty and Steve

Rusty and his personal fucking bodyguard gave me the distinct impression that they were quite prepared to get 'Ugly On My Ass', or in words not connected to Quentin Tarantino, give me a right good kicking. I told Jon to open the boot of his car.

Rusty Egan and Mandingo (if that really was his name) looked on almost quizzically as I retrieved the spear gun and started to pull back the rubber firing device that would enable the gun to shoot the barbed spear into a speeding shark at about 100 miles an hour. With no shark on the horizon I aimed at the next best thing: Rusty Egan's head.

Needless to say, no one wants a row with a heavily drug stimulated mouthy Kid's TV Star armed with a spear gun, so they backed off slowly back into the house and then very gently closed the door.

11

My next job was about as far removed from *Metal Mickey* as you could get. BBC2 were running a series of one-off television plays called *Playhouse*. They were highly regarded within the industry and always received a lot of attention from audiences and critics alike.

I was to audition for a piece called *Easy Money,* which was about a young unemployed youth called Terry who is put on a government 'back to work scheme' where he is befriended by two West Indians. Trouble is, Terry has a girlfriend who is a leading member of the National Front.

The play had been written by Michael Abbensetts, who'd had considerable success in the late 1970's with a series called *Empire Road*, and it would be directed by Gillian Lynne, who was much better known for her choreography for shows like *Cats* than she was for TV direction.

I knew it was going to be tough for me to secure this part, as by now I was totally typecast as the extravert Steve from *Metal Mickey*, whereas the part of Terry was as introverted as a dormouse.

At my meeting with Gillian, I thought it best to try and steer the conversation away from any fears she might have and talked about her work in the theatre instead, of which I knew plenty. I could even tell her most of the names of the cast of Cats, which was hardly surprising as I was hanging out with most of them upstairs at The Kings Arms Pub. We also discovered that we had trained at the same school, obviously not at the same time, but at least it gave her the impression that I was not a one-trick pony and I could be moulded into the character of Terry with the right direction. Whatever, my bullshit worked a treat and I got the part. The rest of the cast was impressive, and I knew almost all of them by reputation alone.

Derek Smith, whom I'd watched for years in everything from *Black Beauty* to *Are You Being Served* was playing a nasty character called Mr Kemp, and Stanley Lebor, who played the Russian gay lover to John Hurts' Quentin Crisp in the much feted *Naked Civil Servant*, was playing a down and out called Stewart. My girlfriend Marcia was played by a beautiful first timer called Kim Thomson who I think was even more nervous than I was. But for me, the real treat was the casting of my two West Indian friends, Trevor Laird and Norman Beaton.

Obviously, I had known Trev since *Quadrophenia* and we had stayed very much in touch ever since. Trevor had done some great stuff since those pill popping days in Brighton, including a lovely cameo in the classic *Long Good Friday* and a barnstorming performance as Beefy in the movie *Babylon*.

Norman Beaton was a living legend to me though, as he'd played the dad in the first accredited Black family TV Sit-Com in the country *The Fosters*, which had also starred the very young up and coming comic Lenny Henry. He also had the reputation of being a hard drinker.

The rehearsals for *Easy Money* came as a bit of a shock, as Gillian Lynne had obviously not heard that actors such as Norman Beaton like to stay up late in the hotel bar regaling less experienced actors like myself with stories of daring doo, whilst quaffing vast amounts of vintage whisky. No, Gillian had other plans for us that did not include eating sausage sandwiches and drinking coffee in the morning. We had a fucking dance class.

Gillian's philosophy was simple: healthy body, healthy mind, and it did work. Whatever alcohol was still lurking in our veins was completely gone within the hour, and I think even Norman was pleasantly surprised that rehearsing without a hangover had its benefits. We were a happy team.

I loved the work and was involved in every scene. This would be the first time that my name would be the first on the credits, so to fuck it up would've been a real shame—so I didn't.

Yes I did have a couple of ales in the bar at the end of the day, but the thought of the next day's work kept me relatively sober throughout. Plus I had shit loads to learn. Gillian directed like we were going to perform *Easy Money* live, so she wanted us all to be word perfect before we even got a glimpse of a camera. Again, Gillian was right. We started looking for the sub plots in the script, and why our characters did and said the things they did. Working with Kim Thomson was a bit of a problem for me though, as I fancied her rotten.

A lot has been said by actors about doing love scenes, and I have never met one yet who will say that they are enjoyable experiences. Something that normally happens naturally has to be rehearsed meticulously for lighting and sound, and unless you are a porn star this is certainly not a natural experience.

During rehearsals, once we got to these specific scenes, Gillian would say not to worry and all would be fine on the day. I said that I wouldn't mind rehearsing the scenes in the comfort of my hotel room if Kim was agreeable, but it was laughed off as a typical Gary joke. I wasn't joking, Kim was (and is) stunning.

When the day finally arrived, Gillian insisted on a closed set. This means that only the essential people involved in the shooting of the scene will be there. So all we had was the camera man, his assistant, the lighting man, the makeup department, the director and wardrobe. Kim and I felt a lot easier now.

One nice touch though, the wardrobe people had given Kim and I pink and blue matching dressing gowns to wear, I wore the pink one.

Gillian wanted no visible signs of elastic marks, so Kim would be completely topless, but as I was choreographed to be on top of her, her breasts, Kim was assured, wouldn't be an issue. Well it certainly was for me! I really wasn't sure how my body would react given this situation, but I guess I was about to find out whether or not I had the makings of a porn star after all.

Before we got into the bed the makeup girl sprayed us with glitter, which under the lights, we were told, would simulate sweat. It was not remotely horny in the slightest, and being stuck to a topless nubile young actress for the entire morning was not as I had imagined it would be.

In between takes Kim and I tried to keep some semblance of normality by discussing the hotel's evening menu, but every time we moved the glitter stuck and made little farting sounds, which I kept profusely apologising for. Certainly broke the ice though. One interesting footnote to this story is that Gillian Lynne told me she had hired an exceptional actress who was destined for great things. It was her first professional job and she only had one line. Her name was Imelda Staunton.

The reviews for *Easy Money* were better than I could've hoped for. The Guardian said that my performance had been understated and gentle; the Daily Mail said that I'd given a true and sensitive performance and the Sun said, 'GARY SHAIL GAY OR WOT?'

I enjoyed living with Mike in Belsize Park, but by now I think I'd outstayed my welcome somewhat, so I moved to a little top floor, one bedroomed flat in West Hampstead. This would be the first time I'd ever lived on my own. Not that I was ever really alone though, as I often woke up to unexpected, impromptu house guests, who would often stay for days on end. I didn't mind though, I have never liked being on my own for too long, but my craving for human company would often nearly get me into trouble.

One night I let a couple of guy's crash at my flat for a couple of days. They said they were professional musicians, but from the amount of cocaine they had on them, I was pretty sure that they were professional drug dealers. They'd been very generous with their coke though, so I was rather disappointed when they said they had to leave.

As I was not particularly busy at the time, they asked if I'd like to go to Manchester with them for a couple of days, just for the ride. I was seriously considering it when the phone rang. It was my agent Sharon telling me I had an audition for the BBC the following day, so I declined the offer.

About two weeks later I was chatting to a mutual friend who informed me that the guys who I'd let stay had been busted by an undercover cop in a bar in Manchester, trying to sell a kilo of cocaine. They got 7 years in jail apiece.

Even though my band (Backchat) was now defunct, Joe McGann and I continued to write and record music. We needed to find somewhere that was cheap and cheerful though, and somehow found ourselves walking down the stairs of 22 Denmark Street to the world famous Tin Pan Alley recording studios.

Run at that time by a great guy called Crispin Buxton, whose family had once owned most of Scotland until King Edward 1st had them all evicted or hanged, it was a studio steeped in musical history.

Crispin had a very relaxed approach to business, and more often than not, what started off as a 10hr session would last all night long until the pubs opened the next day. It had no natural light source, so once you were in it never mattered what time of day it was anyway. It was perfect! Crispin had lots of different people casually working for him at this time, and one of them was a young lady called Kate Latto. She completely made me fall in love with her, and I have never got over it, even to this day. She was funny and smart, beautiful and sexy, and going out with Julian

Lennon. Bollox! Even I couldn't compete with that, but my day would come I thought, and it did, but not for a few years. It was a strange relationship really. Kate knew how I felt, and I was a typical Scorpio male, prone to jealousy. But for some unfathomable reason, I only ever wanted the best for her, but I vowed that one day we would be married. Still time eh?

I made Tin Pan Alley my headquarters for the foreseeable future and tried not to look at Kate.

Some of the best times of my early life were spent in that place, and I learnt the art of 'old skool' production and editing at a time when music production computers were still being devised and built. There is nothing more satisfying than cutting up a master tape, putting it back together, and getting it right.

It's about time I explained who Stephen Hyer was. I have mentioned him a few times so far with no real explanation as to who he was. I say was…because he is sadly no longer alive. I know he would've loved to have known just how well his kids are doing and that he now has grandchildren. He would've been so proud.

Jon Caplan and I first met Stephen Hyer at a strange party somewhere in London. The actor Peter Wyngarde* was there, and that was strange enough for me. My mum had been a huge fan of his and had never missed an episode of *Jason King* back in the early 70's, but in 1975 Peter had been arrested, convicted and fined £75 for an act of "gross indecency" in the toilets of Gloucester Bus Station.

Back then people were even less forgiving about this kinda thing than they are now. When George Michael got nicked for doing exactly the same thing in 1998, he got a small fine, a number one album, a concert tour and a completely new audience, whereas poor Peter Wyngarde's career had come to a complete end.

He had been a real housewives' favourite, but the scandal was huge enough to never fully recover from. He was in the 1980 film *Flash Gordon*, playing General Klytus, but wore a mask throughout.

Peter Wyngarde was certainly not the only high profile practising homosexual in London during the 70's and early 80's, but if you were famous, you still had to keep your sexual habits to yourself. If, on the other hand, you weren't famous at all, but had all the other assets that success required, you could do what the fuck you liked. Stephen Hyer was a man like that and Jon Caplan and I had found him.

After about an hour at the party we all left, and we were driven by Stephen in his pure white convertible Corniche Rolls Royce registration SH17, back to his exclusive flat in Hyde Park Street, which had once been the home of W.H.Smith.

---

*Wyngarde was interviewed for the News of the World and the Birmingham-based Sunday Mercury, and asserted that the arrest was due to a misunderstanding; in his defence after a second incident, he claimed he had suffered a "mental aberration". Although it affected his image, particularly with his audience who largely identified him as the ladies' man Jason King, Wyngarde's homosexuality was actually well known in acting circles, where he was known by the nickname of "Petunia Winegum".

Stephen lived on the top two floors of this incredible detached classic Georgian house, bang in the middle of London's Lancaster Gate region. Stephen's I had been extravagant but tasteful (if there is such a thing). For instance, the wallpaper in the main living room had been specially designed and woven with threaded silk green plants, on closer inspection the plants were all Marijuana leaves. Stephen had a fish tank the length of the entire room and a top-of- the- range Bang and Olufsen stereo system. Stephen also had a fully stocked bar with at least three of everything in case you got bored with drinking vintage brandy one evening and decided to mix it up a bit with some extremely rare Russian vodka.

Stephen used a machine to roll his marijuana spliffs, which he then kept in a beautiful hand carved wooden box, and Stephen also ran a successful clothing manufacturing business making women's' dresses for Marks & Spencer, called Paisley Hyer.

Stephen had always known that he was gay, but due to a fairly traditional Jewish upbringing which had included a marriage and two children, he left it relatively late in life to "come out" to his family and friends. When he did, he discovered two things. 1, his parents were fine about it, and 2, his wife was also a closet gay, and was going through exactly the same thing.

So now Stephen and his ex-wife were the best of friends, which meant the kids, who were about nine or ten at the time, were often at the flat for weekends and holidays. Stephen also had a live-in boyfriend called Greg, who was a fucking maniac.

Greg was training to kill people in his spare time and collected replica guns and knives. Some evenings he would leave a replica shooter outside the elevator, and I would have to try and negotiate getting up to the next floor without getting ambushed or stabbed.

He was also a very good Martial Artist and trained hard. Sometimes we would spar together in the living room downstairs, but once, when we were both completely hammered, we went out onto the outside ledge that skirted the building and practised there. It was a fall of about 80ft onto iron railings if we lost our balance.

Yes, it can safely be said that Greg in his younger days was a bit of a handful. But he was also as loyal a friend as you could ever have wished for, and just the kind of friend you'd need in a scrape, of which there were quite a few, normally caused by Greg himself.

Once, it was Jon Caplan's birthday, and Greg decided to put the cake into his face. He enjoyed doing it so much; he decided to make it a yearly event, and find out where Jon was each year on his special day, just to cake him. After about three years we had to keep Jon's birthday location a secret. He'd even do it again now, if he knew where Jon was.

Stephen Hyer* and I became great friends. He let me have keys to the flat, and introduced me to the housekeeper so that she wouldn't freak if she saw me emerging from the shower room in the morning. He didn't mind me taking women back there at all, and if I needed to go by car to anywhere special he would drive me in the Roller to my destination. He became a great friend to my family too, often turning up on a Sunday with a massive box of cream cakes from Patisserie Valerie for my mum and a bottle of scotch for my dad.

On one such Sunday my dad remarked that he'd always wanted to drive a Rolls Royce. Stephen just threw him the keys and told him to get on with it. Yes, Stephen, Greg, and the kids became family.

I became quite close to the children and took them on a tour of LWT when I was doing Metal Mickey to meet all the stars from the show, which I am assured they have never forgotten. In fact, we all became so close, that even though I was not Jewish, Stephen asked me to be the kids' godfather and guardian if anything were to happen to him. It was a sweet thing to do, and if not entirely practical, a great honour too. I took it seriously.

When Stephen's lad reached 13 years of age, it was time for his Bar Mitzvah and he had to learn a reading from The Torah in Yiddish. Stephen told me that as I was his godfather, I too would have to learn it and say it with him out loud on the day. I had lots of sleepless nights over this, until Stephen told me that it was just a wind up. Fuck me, I was relieved!

If you are the star of a successful children's TV show, then you will always, at some point, have to interact with some of the children that watch you. I had not even thought about the really young fans of *Metal Mickey*, of which there were millions. I had given even less thought to the very young disabled fans of *Metal Mickey*, of which there were thousands.

The only fans that I ever got to meet were normally about 5ft8, slim, blonde, and hopefully carrying a birth certificate. All that changed when I met a very glamorous Jewish lady called Shirley Greene who worked for the Royal Variety Club of Great Britain. Sounds very grand doesn't it? Well it was back then.

The Variety Club was a nationwide fund raising charity organisation that raised money for disabled and disadvantaged kids. Ran by some of Britain's best known entertainers and sports personalities it was regarded as a bit of an honour to be asked to do anything for them. It would usually mean just turning up and signing a few autographs, but it meant that you were now considered within the industry to be well known enough to sign autographs. Plus I have never met anyone who could say no to Shirley Greene.

* Stephen died from a heart attack on the 30th December 2002. Stephen Hyer's old flat in Hyde Park Street recently came on the market for £4,850,000

The first charity event that I did for Shirley, I don't remember meeting one disabled child. That's because I spent most of the day with a true musical legend that no one knew.

I'd been asked to turn up and sign some autographs at a charity event called "The Henry Cooper Walk-About" at a sports stadium somewhere in North London. When I got there I was basically told to just hang out and mingle with the crowd, having photos and signing autographs if asked.

There was a roped-off section just for us "celebrities" where there was a bar serving libations to anyone who'd found the day too stressful and needed a double gin & tonic before meeting with their adoring public for a selfie. Seemed reasonable enough to me.

Whilst talking bollox to Bonnie Langford, who I'd known from school, Esta Charkham ,who had cast me in *Quadrophenia* and *The Professionals* and had now become a good friend, asked me if I would look after a singer who didn't really know anyone. She then introduced me to fucking Jimmy Cliff*. If you were a soul man, it was like meeting James Brown, if you were a rock man it was like meeting Joe Cocker and if you are a One Direction fan, you can fuck off now! You know what I mean though. Jimmy Cliff was, and is, reggae royalty, and I owned all of his albums. It was brilliant walking around the stadium getting mobbed by Metal Mickey fans, whilst Jimmy looked on bemused. He was brilliant though, and even took some pictures of me with the fans. I kept wanting to say...DOESN'T ANYONE REALIZE WHO THIS GEEZER IS? But no one did.

When I met disabled kids for the first time, it broke my heart.

Today we are bombarded with images of disabled children, and there are so many more charities around today, raising far more money than we could've ever hoped to raise. Today, charities are run like multi-nationals, with publicity overheads and expenses, but back then it felt more grass-roots.

I would go and meet kids at their homes, if their parents thought it might give their child a boost. I once Gaffa-taped a young lad with a muscle wasting disease to the back of my bike, and took him for a spin at 80miles per hour. He talked about it for months, and then I kept in touch with him for years, whilst he suffered numerous painful operations. I also visited a children's burns unit in Sheffield which I found stressful, as I was warned beforehand by a nurse that some of these poor kids would be in continuous pain for many more years to come.

*Jimmy Cliff, OM (born James Chambers, 1 April 1948) is a Jamaican reggae musician, multi-instrumentalist, singer and actor. He is the only living musician to hold the Order of Merit, the highest honour that can be granted by the Jamaican government for achievements in the arts and sciences. In 2010 he was inducted into the Rock And Roll Hall Of Fame.

I visited children's hospitals like Great Ormond St, which I was familiar with, as my little sister had been treated there for severe eczema when she was younger, and I remembered just how frightened and vulnerable she'd felt whilst in there. The hardest thing though, especially with burn victims, was trying to look and act like nothing was wrong and that everything was going to be alright. During my visits I would be 'punky irresponsible Steve' from Metal Mickey, but once I'd waved goodbye the tears would flow at my sheer inadequacy.

I tried to do as much as I could with local charities too. I opened church fetes and jumble sales, and always turned up with a joke, a smile and a half bottle of scotch in my back pocket for medicinal purposes, in case I should die of boredom.

My face would ache at the end of the day from all the smiling and my brain would hurt from all the names that I was expected to remember. But I always threw myself into whatever fund-raising activity I was involved with, and tried to follow the cash raised to its intended use. Sometimes this has proved difficult.

I was once involved in a small fundraising venture with a *Quadrophenia* fan called Vinnie. His hobby was restoring old scooters back to their former glory in his garage in Portsmouth, which he then sold privately to enthusiasts all over the country. Our plan was to take a completely knackered Vesper scooter, rebuild it from scratch whilst filming every step of the re-build for social media, and then get the complete cast of *Quadrophenia* to sign the finished product, and then auction it for no less than £10,000. Sounds simple.

As soon as I announced my intentions in the local press I was contacted by a representative of the British Heart Foundation, who turned up to our first meeting in a Porsche and a pencil skirt. She explained that with the BHF's help and support, we could also help raise awareness, as well as boost much needed research funds. I explained that some of the local charities only needed the £10,000 I was planning on raising, and I would rather it went to one of them. My reason being that some people didn't have the money or luxury of time to wait for a cure, so the money was needed now!

This very expensively dressed young woman was talking about pink T-shirts and badges, and I think she actually suggested at one point painting our scooter pink. I said that I was happy with our plan, but if they had any other suggestions, I'd be happy to hear them. A few days later I had a local scooter shop manager on the phone telling me they were going to donate one of their new range of scooters in my name for the British Heart Foundation. He then explained that I wouldn't have to worry about any health and safety issues (I wasn't aware that I had any) and they would be dealing with all the publicity. I told them as politely as I could to fuck off.

In the next issue of the local paper, it was subtly suggested that I was raising money without any proper sponsorship, and not telling anyone what the money was for. That kind of thinking ruined it for me, and I cancelled the entire project.

Woman were, and are, very important in my life, and I have always remembered all of them—except the ones I can't remember.

I had been in love more times than I cared to remember, but still believed that it was always worth all the crap that went with it. The trouble with me though, was whenever I found the perfect girlfriend I would almost certainly do something to fuck it up, therefore creating the crap that I was always trying to avoid.

I met a lovely young lady called Karen Embry outside the studios of LWT one day whilst shooting some photos for some girls' magazine. Karen and her friends knew someone who worked in reception, and they were there to pick up some tickets for some show or other, but just happened to be there as I was being snapped. The photographer thought it would be a good idea to use Karen and her friends in one of the shots, looking like they were asking for my autograph. In fact, I don't think any of them actually had a clue who I was at that point, but Karen certainly made an impression.

Karen was only 15 and still at school when I first met her, and I was just 21. She started coming to LWT on Friday nights to see the live recordings of Metal Mickey, and afterwards I would have her escorted to the bar where I would be meeting with family and friends. There was no doubting the attraction that I had for Karen, but she was still far too young to really consider her a possible girlfriend. She had even invited me to her 16th birthday party, which I attended with my flat mate Mike Needleman, who couldn't believe I was taking him to a party filled with 16 year old girls. This all changed though, once Karen had reached 17 and had passed her driving test.

Karen would drive all the way from the Kent borders to pick me up from wherever I was, sometimes having to use a road map and a torch to find me, and then we would go clubbing.

I took Karen to all the hot clubs in London just to show her off. She turned into a superstar right in front of my eyes, and always looked a million dollars. I introduced her to all my show-bizzy friends including Micky Dolenz, John Entwhistle, and Peter Stringfellow, who always kissed her on both cheeks when we went to his club, and she didn't drink. This should've been perfect. Karen was so innocent it was fantastic!

She loved meeting my mum, who showered her with fake jewellery and tea, and never, ever argued with me. I never had to worry about other men chatting her up, as she stuck to my side like a limpet, which I adored. So why didn't we live happily ever after?

I always knew that Karen was far too nice a person to have to deal with the real Gary Shail. No, what Karen got was the "wild & crazy guy" Gary Shail who drank just to be sociable and took recreational drugs 'cos it was cool.

My reality was too far removed from what Karen considered to be the norm, so I would only see her when I was not working or if I didn't have someone else on the go. We could go months and months without seeing each other, but when we did, we always had fun catching up.

Karen was eventually spotted by a top modelling agency and started seeing the world. She was no longer my little Karen Embry from the sticks, but now Karen Krystel, a fully paid up member of the bullshit society, of which I was President.

I remember her once surprising me one evening by turning up un-announced to a pub in the East End of London that I was drinking in after a show. She was wearing the tightest blood red dress ever, which left little to the imagination, and matching red stilettos. She moved through the crowded pub like a gazelle. The people at my table were actually open-mouthed when she came straight over to me and kissed me full on the lips. I was so fucking proud of her!

Karen had so many other talents though. After modelling, she learnt to play the guitar and started to sing and write songs. As most of her songs were country influenced, she started visiting America. In particular Nashville, Tennessee, where she made some fantastic new friends and contacts. She would eventually move there in 2002, and now owns a home in the town where country music was invented. She has also become something of a celebrity whilst out there. Karen has her own radio show, writes, and produces her own TV and stage productions, including all the original music and songs, hosts events and considers Dolly Parton and Keith Urban amongst her good friends. Not bad for a bird from Farnborough.

I have always thought that reason that Karen and I are still such good friends, almost 35 years later, is because she never experienced what a monster I could be. I never let that "bad boy" out of his box whilst I was in her company.

Karen Embry (Now Karen Keeley), 2015: "Gary and I met in the summer of 1980. My friends and I were on a day trip to London, and were standing outside London Weekend Television. I recognized him instantly from *Metal Mickey*, but my friends had no clue who he was. Gary was with a photographer from My Guy Magazine documenting "A day in the life of Gary Shail". We asked for his autograph and the photo appeared, with the article, a few weeks later. I was so excited.

Gary was very charismatic and flirted with me outrageously. He arranged for us to see a taping of *Metal Mickey* a few weeks later. From that moment on I was smitten! We must have exchanged phone numbers because we stayed in touch. I would call him from school and arrange to meet him at LWT to watch more tapings of the show. We'd hang out in his dressing room and the LWT bar with the cast and other TV show celebrities. He even introduced me to Micky Dolenz, who was the producer/director of *Metal Mickey*.

On my 16th birthday Gary and his friends, Mike Needleman and David John, came to my mum's house in Farnborough (Kent) for my birthday party. He arrived at the front door with a bottle of champagne wearing a black silk

shirt, white jacket and black pegs (remember those?). After I blew out the candles on my cake, we danced to my mum's record collection.

I will never forget Gary singing and dancing with me to Ringo Starr's "You're Sixteen" (You're beautiful and you're mine). He was an expert at playing air guitar too.

A few months later I passed my driving test and bought a little light blue Austin 1100 for about £200. The world was our oyster and we were riding in style. I would drive up to Hendon (following a map- no GPS or cell phones in those days) and pick Gary up so that we could go out clubbing. I wasn't old enough to drink or get into the clubs, but that didn't seem to matter. We never had to wait in the queue to get in. We had my little car valet parked and walked straight in the door. All the bouncers knew Gary. We sat at the best tables, were greeted by the club owners and got special treatment.

Peppermint Park was where we usually started the night, then next door to Stringfellows, where Gary was always the life and soul of the party. Then we'd head off to the VERY exclusive Bootleggers club on Margaret Street. Gary knew the secret knock and password to get in.

Halloween night, 1982, was such a fun night. I rented costumes from the Beckenham Theatre. A black lacy "Bride of Dracula" dress and veil for me and a black Dracula style suit for Gary. I arrived at Gary's mum and dad's house in Hendon and we got dressed in our outfits. We looked awesome. Complete with scary makeup. Gary's mum, Winnie, was so lovely to me. She emptied her jewellery box and gave me lots of diamante jewels to wear.

Gary drove my car to the West End. We valet parked at Stringfellows, were welcomed by Peter Stringfellow, had some champagne then headed down the road to the Hippodrome where we ran into Julian Lennon (John Lennon's son).

Of course Gary knew him, and we had a nice little chat. Later we headed to Bootleggers. We usually ended up there, along with so many other celebrities like John Entwhistle from The Who and the actor John Hurt.

We got home in the wee hours. Gary was a little worse for wear. I remember us giggling as we crept up the stairs, trying not to wake up the whole house. I slept in Gary's sister Julie's room on the top bunk. The next day Gary's mum cooked lunch for us. I remember eating corn on the cob for the first time in my life.

Another night Gary took me to someone's party at an empty house. There was no carpet or furniture. I could hear someone playing guitar upstairs and went to investigate. It was Joe McGann, all alone, playing "No Woman No Cry". Later that night we were all bundled into the back of a van and got pulled over by the police. We all had to line up on the pavement whilst the police searched us for drugs. I think what anyone had on them had been thrown out of the window. Gary talked to the officers and thankfully they let us go.

Gary was always very protective of me. I remember him telling the police that I had nothing to do with it, and did not know anything.

I was exposed to drugs quite a bit when I was around Gary. It just seemed like everyone was doing it. When lines of coke were being passed around, Gary always made excuses for me and I was never made to feel like I should take anything. So I didn't.

Gary and I lost touch for a while, but years later in the midst of my modelling career I heard that Gary was appearing in a play called *Poppy* at The Half Moon Theatre along with Josie Lawrence. I decided to go and surprise him. I turned up at a pub close to the theatre. He couldn't believe his eyes!

Another time, in the 90's, we were catching up over some Chinese food at a restaurant in Bayswater W2. I was chatting away whilst Gary was enjoying his spare ribs and chicken chow mein, when suddenly he started going red in the face. He was choking and couldn't breathe! I didn't know how to do the Heimlich Manoeuvre, so I hit him really hard on his back. So hard, that a piece of chicken came out of his mouth and flew across the room. He will be indebted to me forever. If it wasn't for me, he wouldn't be around to write this book. I saved his life! Love ya Gary. X"

Rosemaris Chanie. 2015: "Walking on to the set of *Metal Mickey* I had no idea I was going to meet a special person who would remain in my life for the next 35 years as one of my special loves.

I believe the month was late August- early September, 1982, when my agent called me for a walk-on part for the children's T.V. series *Metal Mickey*. I had no idea who, or what this was at the time (having finished watching kids T.V shows some years prior) until I arrived on set and basically understood that the director was the lovely Micky Dolenz from one of my favourite pop groups as a child, The Monkees, and Metal Mickey was a robot of sorts.

Even at the age of 22 I was quiet and shy. However, with my theatrical drama training it had helped me to 'get lost' in other characters, and as long as I wasn't playing myself, I felt just about okay. As we were directed around the main characters of the show, I heard this cheeky voice coming from Steve, the main character, who, as I learned, was always up to some antic making the cast and crew roar with laughter. I had watched him from the corner of my eye, thinking he had not seen me. How wrong was I? As I glanced at him, he winked at me. I immediately looked away, feeling my face flush with embarrassment. To my utter horror, his next move was to walk over to me and ask me my name, after he had said "Hello darlin' of course." My smile gave me away completely and I was immediately taken with his whole persona, his personality and confidence was enough for both of us to feel we could conquer the world.

Gary and I became inseparable over the next couple of years. We knew many of the same circle of people, and enjoyed meeting new people at the same time. We fell head over heels with each other's' fun loving personalities, but as is the nature of the business, work caused us to drift apart. We didn't see each other for a long time, on and off, until we met up again at 'Stringfellows', a nightclub where I worked when I wasn't working on T.V.

Inseparable . . . Gary Shall and his fiancee Rosemaris Robins

Robot's pal to wed

METAL MICKEY star Gary Shall's bachelor days are numbered.

He has become engaged to actress Rosemaris Robins, 25, whom he met last autumn on the set of the kids' TV series.

Gary, also 23, plays prankster Steve in the show, which ends a three-year run tomorrow.

He said yesterday : "I was riveted the moment I saw her. Then work kept us apart until this week when we knocked into each other again in a London nightclub.

"I popped the question that night — and we haven't been apart since."

Rosemaris, who has a Red Indian grandmother, said : "I didn't hesitate for a moment, but we've had no time to make wedding plans yet."

Picture : TIM CORNALL

Gary popped the question there and then and the 'Paps' loved it, putting our engagement news in all the next day's tabloids. We were wild and crazy, spontaneous and young. We had a wonderful time together until work, once again, kept us apart.

Although our lives took very different paths over the coming years, ultimately we met up again a few years ago at a charity function in London. It doesn't seem to matter how much time passes between us, there will always be a special place in our hearts for each other. Gary will always make me smile."

I knew that Metal Mickey's shelf life had been reached when one of the Tabloids ran an article questioning how long we were expected to be believed as teenagers. When the end came, though, it was still sad for me. I'd been at LWT for four wonderful years, and had met some great people. Not only my fellow actors, but other people that I formed strong relationships with. I bought cards and choccies for all the dinner ladies and a bottle of scotch for my dresser Matt, who insisted on drinking it on the spot. Micky Dolenz and I vowed to stay connected and planned to meet up in L.A, where he promised me the grand tour of his old haunts. Georgina Melville would be a mate for life as would Lucinda Bateson, but the person I would miss the most was Irene Handl.

During the final rehearsals of *Metal Mickey*, I received a phone call from Irene's agent Jonathan Alteraz informing me that she was going to be surprised by Eamonn Andrews and his big red book for *This Is Your Life*. Knowing Irene as I did, I told Jonathan that I didn't think she would comply in the slightest, and probably tell Eamonn Andrews to fuck off. Never the less, I promised to keep the secret, and agreed that if they did manage to get her on the show, I would appear. About two days later, whilst she was combing my hair, she whispered like a Vampire in my ear that she knew something was being planned, and I should tell whoever was planning it to stop. How the fuck she knew was beyond me, but I knew then that there was absolutely no way they were going to get her on that couch, so I let Jonathan know, and it was called off.

Irene may have spent her life making others laugh, but she was a fiercely private woman with many dark secrets. Apart from working with her, which was a constant pleasure, I also valued her opinions, and my days around her tiny flat, eating cake and listening to Elvis on her old record player, are the moments I still miss the most.

She always told me she was the president of the Elvis Presley appreciation club of Great Britain. Who knows? Who cares? I must admit though, I would've loved to see her tell Eamonn Andrews to Fuck Off!

TOP HOT 100 HUNKS! 52

GARY SHAIL

The hunk in Metal Mickey was born in London and his birthday is 10th November. He's a very active lad 'cos he'll be working on another series of Metal Mickey soon, and at the moment, he's getting his own group together 'cos he's a fab musician and can play nearly every instrument there is! He's a trained gymnast and he's also the youngest stunt man in the country! He loves whizzing about on his motorbike and his ambition i to have his very own radio station. Whew!

12

The principal message in the TV series *Johnny Jarvis* is a thinly veiled attack on Prime Minister Margaret Thatcher's Britain and the wasted resource of schoolchildren emerging from education to find no jobs and precious few prospects awaiting them

(No change there then!).

My audition for *Johnny Jarvis* was held at the old BBC Television Centre in White City. Sharon, my delectable agent, told me I was up for the part of a young racist schoolboy who bullies one of the leading characters in the show.

To be honest, I didn't really want to go at all. The BBC was a horrible place to get to from where I was living, and I had a hangover the size of Harrods.

If it hadn't been for the fact that Nigel Williams had written it, I think I might've pulled a sickie that morning. Nigel Williams had written some great stage plays, including *Class Enemy*, and was now trying his hand at TV Drama.

The story centred on Johnny Jarvis and Alan Lipton, who are two teenagers in their final year of secondary school at a comprehensive in Hackney. Energetic, anxious and occasionally naïve, the pair are on the brink of entering the adult world where things get complicated.

It was great to see Nigel again and also to meet the director Alan Dossor, who also come from a theatrical background, having been the artistic director of Liverpool's Everyman Theatre back in the late 70's.

After reading for the part of a skinhead called Manning, it was plainly obvious that I was completely wrong for the part, so to avoid any embarrassment, I just stopped the audition and told them both what I knew we were all thinking. We all laughed, and just started chatting.

Nigel wanted to know what I was doing musically, if anything, so I told him about the failed recording career, the hypocrisy within the music industry and my intentions to continue to try and be taken seriously as a musician. (Nigel had once seen me playing the piano after a show one night at the Young Vic theatre, and remembered my impromptu performance well enough to "big me up" in front of Alan Dossor.)

Alan suddenly got very animated and reached for the script of Johnny Jarvis, saying that my part had already been written. The part of Guy Raines, who was a narcissistic egotistical musical genius, would have to be played by a narcissistic egotistical musical genius (which is pretty much what I thought I was anyway) and I was sitting right in front of him.

I wasn't quite sure how to take this, but then Alan Dosser asked me the million dollar question: would I also like to have a go at writing the theme tune? This was the moment I had been waiting for my whole career, so I had to think quickly. Nigel Williams had already written some lyric ideas down, and they had the first three scripts, so I asked if there was anywhere in the building that had a piano in it.

The producer Guy Slater was called, and within half an hour a room with an upright 'joanna' was found, and I started working.

I actually wrote the song "Johnny Jarvis" before even thinking about the theme tune. My reason being, if it worked as a whole song then theoretically it would, without the lyrics, work just as well as a recurring theme at the beginning, and throughout the show. Nigel's words were fantastic. Putting them to music was going to be a joy.

Nigel was writing from the point of view of a narrator, basically telling the story of Johnny's plight. It was straight and to the point, so it would need straight and to the point music.

I started with the minor chords to create the feeling of bleakness, but ended with the majors to suggest the possibility of hope. The lyrics went:

> Johnny gets a Giro Monday morning
> Johnny gets a government cheque
> Johnny gets a fix from the politicians
> That is turning Johnny into a wreck
>
> Johnny reads the paper, Johnny reads the news
> and he's hoping it's going to get better
> It's like waiting for a lover who's a long time dead
> to write you a begging letter...etc.

I knew it was good whilst I was playing it to them, and they all seemed really pleased with my effort, so pleased in fact, that they asked me to write not only the signature music, but also all of the music for the original songs that my character Guy Raines would have to sing "live" with a full backing band of really good musicians. I couldn't fucking believe it!

I had gone to the BBC, with a hangover, for a part I wasn't right for*, and ended up not only in it, but also the composer for a six part major drama series for Aunty Beeb.

There was a lot of work to do, and I actually shat myself once the reality of my situation hit home. There were basically two different bands playing all original songs, but with varying degrees of musicianship. I insisted, for the first band, that all the actors cast should be able to play the instruments they were supposed to be playing. It could then be filmed live on set as we were actually playing it. Also, trying to recreate the same acoustics in a studio seemed pointless to me. If you hired actors who could actually play it, then all my problems were little ones. Of course, I had to actually write the music first.

---

*The part of Manning, the bullyboy skinhead, eventually went to the actor Jamie Foreman.

As I hadn't actually got anything to write on except a bass guitar, I asked Guy Slater the producer if the BBC could provide me with some equipment. Today I could've done it on a laptop, but back then it was still done the old way, i.e. writing it all down, or in my case, remembering everything. To my absolute shame, I have never learnt to read or write music, but the BBC didn't know that. This would not be a problem for the early compositions which were supposed to be rough around the edges, but for the later songs, they would be performed by professional session musicians, so the score would have to be written down.

I ordered a Fender Rhodes Piano and the newest drum machine on the block, The Linn. What I also got was my very own Musical Director.

My shock at having another John Altman in my life was short lived. This wasn't the girlfriend stealing, gold shorts wearing, soon to be the Dot Cotton related John Altman, but the Oscar, Emmy and Bafta nominated composer and arranger John Altman.

This guy had worked with everyone from Monty Python* to Van Morrison, from Eric Clapton to Bob Marley, and now he was going to work with little old me. Of course, I had no idea about any of John's past credits, thinking that he was just another BBC employee from their music department. These days, with the aid of a search engine you can pretty much find out all you need to know about someone, but back then in the dark ages all you had to go on was what people told you. Bullshit was so much easier in the 1980's.

John Altman spent all day in my little attic flat, sitting on the sofa writing his little black dots, whilst I played what I'd written. Thank fuck I didn't know of his incredible reputation as I probably would've been far too nervous to have even turned the piano on, let alone tell him (which I did constantly), how I wanted the songs to eventually sound. John just took it in his stride, assuring me that once we were in the studio (Advision) with his musicians, I would be happy.

*In 1979, John Altman arranged the song "Always Look on the Bright Side of Life" for the film *Monty Python's Life of Brian*, voted the greatest comedy song in movies by the viewers of Channel 4 in the UK.

I also told him that I wanted to be the bass player for the studio sessions which, even though he'd never heard me play, he readily agreed to. If I'd known who John was, I would've asked him to get Aston 'Family Man' Barrett.

John was right, of course, and I was more than happy with his arrangements for my simple (but brilliant) music. For the theme, he used a beautiful combination of guitar, played by Mitch Dalton, and a flute, played by Andy Findon*. He had also arranged little musical indents that could be woven into the story, and help link the scenes. They were brilliant! When we got to the band songs, it was fucking amazing!

John had actually been listening to me back at my flat, and had arranged the songs perfectly. We recorded all the songs as a rock band should (in the same room), and all my well —rehearsed bass lines worked a treat.

With Pete Van Hooke* on drums, Mitch on guitar and John on the saxophone, it sounded like we had played together for years. Someone also played some beautiful piano overdubs, but neither I nor John can remember who it was that played them. It could've even been me. Or John.

The two leading actors in Johnny Jarvis were Mark Farmer and Ian Sears. Mark had also, like me, once been a child actor, appearing regularly in the popular children's drama series *Grange Hill* as Gary Hargreaves from 1979 until 1981. This would be his first major leading role as an adult actor.

Johnny Jarvis was portrayed as a thoroughly decent young man, just trying to do his best for everybody. His youthful optimism though is slowly destroyed by the harsh realities of Thatcher's Britain, and he finds himself on the scrapheap of life before it has even started. Mark played the role beautifully, injecting comedy and pathos in equal measure.

Ian Sears was playing his best friend Alan Lipton, whose life couldn't be more different. Unlike Johnny, whose parents (played by the wonderful John Bardon and Catherine Harding) were loving and supportive, Lipton's home life was far from happy.

With an alcoholic drug-addicted mother and questions over who his real father is, Alan Lipton is only too aware of the crap life can throw at you. He starts writing his thoughts down as songs, using Johnny's life as a template. Alan Lipton's songs would ironically make him rich and successful, whilst Johnny's life spirals into depression and despair.

With Nigel William's lyrics, my music, and John Altman's arrangements, the songs would inter-run as an alternative narration device, commenting on everything from drug addiction to life on the dole. They were hard subjects to tackle, but fantastic as a song writer to do.

*Andy Findon is an English woodwind player. He was educated at Harrow County School and The Royal College of Music. He has been baritone saxophone and flute player in the Michael Nyman Band since 1980.

*Peter Van Hooke was the drummer in the English band Mike & The Mechanics (from 1985 to 1995) and also drummed for Van Morrison's band, Headstone, and Ezio. During the 1980's he co-produced (along with Rod Argent) many of Tanita Tikaram's hits.

By the time I arrived on set for my 2nd job as an actor I was confident that all the work I'd done would stand up. All I needed now were actors who could play. I needn't have worried, as the casting was brilliant. All the boys in the original first band (Rock against God) were supposed to be the residents of a homeless hostel with very basic instruments at their disposal, so all the arrangements were made up on the spot. I taught everyone the songs on the guitar, and we just jammed it for the cameras. It worked a treat, looking and sounding just like a real band rehearsing.

We recorded all the music live for the sound department as a wild track, but did all the vocals live for every take. All the other actors involved in that first day's filming had a fucking ball.

Back in the 80's, there were loads of other actors who, like me, could play music to a professional standard, so I wasn't surprised in the least. It was just a matter of who wanted to play what really. I know that Dorian Healy* played drums, Lauren Hayes the piano, Nik Corfield and Kevin Allen did percussion and backing vocals, John Goodrum played guitar and I sang and played the bass like a sexy muthufukka!!'

On another day's shoot, we were supposed to be playing a gig at a local pub. The management and regular customers objected to the act, and turned off the power. The song I wrote for this scene was called 'We're Coming To Get You'. A total punk-rock thrash of a song, with a football chant chorus that would piss-off anyone over the age of 18 and pretty much guarantee no further bookings.

The story so far...

Guy Raines forms a new band (The New Wastrels) playing all of Alan Lipton's songs, which are still based on Johnny Jarvis' mundane life. They now have a record deal, and are starting to appear on TV.

"My Friend Johnny from across the road
he works in a factory,
he manages his lathe & some days he studies
no he never lives lazily.

He never would argue with the dark machines
crowding out the factory floor
And I never heard him argue at the end of the week
what it was that he was working for."

*Dorian Healy is probably best known for his roles as Jimmy Destry in *Capital City* (1989) and Major Kieron Voce in *Soldier Soldier* (1991-94)

In the final episode where The New Wastrels have hit the big time, they play a concert. These scenes were to be filmed on location at the BBC Theatre in Shepherd's Bush, and we would now be using the backing tracks recorded at Advision Studios by John Altman. Now all the instruments would have to be mimed.

As with anything that was musically connected to the show, I was always consulted by the producer Guy Slater as to how I thought it should sound and look. Even though we would now be miming to the music, I still wanted the vocals to be performed live, so I suggested Joe McGann. We had always worked well together vocally, and he would have no trouble with miming the guitar, so Joe was in.

Dorian Healy was back on drums, of which there was never any doubt. Dorian was (and is) a fantastic drummer who could've made it big in any band, if he'd wanted to. Earl Rhodes was miming to John Altman's Saxophone and a young actor called Martin Phillips played, sorry...mimed the keyboards.

Playing the songs in a proper theatre with proper sound and proper lighting for a screaming, appreciative (specially invited) audience was brilliant fun to do. I may not have been able to do this in the real world, but as my character Guy, I was a bonafide rock star with the world at my feet. It looked and sounded brilliant.

The first episode of Johnny Jarvis was aired on the 10th November, 1983. My 24th birthday.

In 1983, most British households were still getting to grips with VHS machines, and DVD was still a decade away, so there was never any talk about the future of *Johnny Jarvis*, if any. After its first airing, it was never shown again.

Over the years there have been rumours that the BBC erased the tapes by mistake, but I don't think that is true. I think the BBC probably knows that I would sue for more publishing money if they should ever give the show an official DVD release. At the time though, I was just happy to have two credits for *Johnny Jarvis* so I would've signed anything, but I am a lot older and a little wiser now.

The theme music was eventually nominated for an Ivor Novello Award. It didn't win, but at least it proved that I wasn't wasting my time. I had proved a point as far as I was concerned and thought the doors to superstardom would be flung open wide. It didn't happen.

Many years later, I started getting emails from complete strangers asking if I'd been responsible for a tune that had remained in their heads for over 30 years.

Johnny Jarvis had been bootlegged, and was now being sold (illegally I thought) on Ebay for about £7. Clips were also starting to appear on Youtube with comments on how it had changed young lives for the better, and how the show had transported people back to their schooldays. I even got a message from the bass player of The Manic Street Preachers who told me the show had been his inspiration to join a band.

Like everything else in my career, *Johnny Jarvis* become a cult. And like the late great Kenneth Williams* once said, "You'd be hard pressed to find a bigger cult than me in the room". I know how he felt.

Friday nights, once the clubs had closed, I would often stay in town and grab a wonton noodle soup from The Lido restaurant in London's China Town. It was open 24hrs and always busy.

The waiters were not known for their patience, and if you didn't know immediately what you wanted to order, they would just fuck off, never to be seen again. I always ordered the same thing. The Lido's wonton soup was better than penicillin. Some Friday nights I wouldn't bother going to sleep at all, and instead headed over to West London early Saturday morning to the capital's oldest Turkish bath house, The Porchester.

If one needs to completely eradicate a hangover from one's memory, then a couple of hours in a hot steam room, followed by a dip in an icy pool normally does the trick. Follow that up with a soapy massage, then egg on beans on cheese on toast, and you are more than ready for whatever trials and tribulations Saturday night might throw at you.

The Porchester became a regular Saturday hangout for many people in the entertainment and sports world. Quite often, Frank Bruno would be in there doing press ups in the hot room, whilst Terence Stamp sipped nonchalantly on his earl grey tea. No one ever hassled anyone whilst in the baths, plus it's just plain rude to ask a naked man for his autograph, I think.

One Saturday morning, I got chatting to an Australian film director called Russell Mulcahy. Russell had been commissioned to direct a video for a band and casually asked if I would help him out on the following Sunday by shooting a few cut-away scenes in Brighton. He'd pay me £100 cash and buy me lunch.

It was a fun day out, with me just sitting on the beach gazing mournfully out to sea, and then just wandering about looking lost and lonely. At the end of the shoot I asked Russell who the video was for, and was pleasantly informed that it was for a band called Spandau Ballet.

The song was titled 'True'. 'True' was a huge worldwide hit, peaking at number one in the UK Singles Chart on 30 April, 1983, for four weeks, becoming the sixth biggest selling single of the year, and charting highly in 20 other countries. It is Spandau Ballet's biggest hit and their most remembered song in the U.S., reaching number four on the Billboard Hot 100 in the autumn of 1983 and topping the adult contemporary chart for one week.

*Kenneth Charles Williams (1926 –1988) was an eccentric English comic actor and comedian. He was one of the main ensembles in 26 of the 31 *Carry On* films, and appeared in numerous British television shows and radio comedies, including series with Tony Hancock and Kenneth Horne, among others.

The video was eventually re-cut without me in it, apparently because I was too well known. But I heard many years later that Gary Kemp just didn't want that silly C*NT from Metal Mickey in his video. £100 and lunch? Gary Kemp is lucky that the rest of his band weren't the only ones who sued him.

I had always loved working in London, and Johnny Jarvis meant I could now afford to pay off six months' rent on my little flat in West Hampstead. I would've been quite content to do bugger all for a while, and just hang out at the Kings Arms Pub every afternoon talking bollox and getting plastered, but then I was offered a role that I couldn't say no to.

Alan Dossor, who directed Johnny Jarvis, was a great friend of the director and playwright Chris Bond. They had been the driving force behind the Liverpool Everyman's extra-ordinary success in the 70's, with the likes of Willy Russell and Alan Bleasdale*.

Chris Bond's then-wife, Clare Luckham, had written a play called *Trafford Tanzi* that had first been performed in Manchester in 1980, and had since been performed in London with Toyah Wilcox in the lead role. It was also at the time playing on Broadway, starring Debbie Harry from Blondie.

The play is set in a wrestling ring where the story of the title character Tanzi is told. Tanzi's parents bring her up to be feminine, but she refuses to conform to traditional femininity and is labelled a tomboy. She marries a professional wrestler named Dean Rebel and supports him in his career. Eventually, she becomes a champion professional wrestler herself and finally challenges her husband Dean to a match, with the loser being required to do the housework.

In keeping with the wrestling theme, the play is divided into ten rounds, each of which ends with a bell. All of the cast members participate in wrestling during the play, and the audience is welcome to cheer and boo the characters as though they were at an actual wrestling match.

Thanks to Alan Dossor, I had been offered the role of Dean Rebel on a plate. Only problem was that it would mean relocating again. This time to Leeds.

*During the 1970's and the 1980's works of Liverpool playwrights, including Willy Russell and Alan Bleasdale, received debuts in the theatre: these included Shirley Valentine and John, Paul, George, Ringo…and Bert. During its time, the theatre has been involved with the careers of Julie Walters, Bernard Hill, Jonathan Pryce, Pete Postlethwaite, Antony Sher, Bill Nighy, Barbara Dickson, Matthew Kelly, and Cathy Tyson.

Dean Rebel

The Leeds Playhouse (now the West Yorkshire Playhouse) was situated in the centre of town, so I found a cheap little flat to rent on my own. It was within walking distance from the theatre and had a fully functional kitchen. The last time I'd been working up north, I had survived on fish and chips and Indian takeaways, but this time I wanted some home comforts.

The sheer physicality of playing Dean Rebel was daunting, to say the least. All the actors in the play would have to learn how to wrestle to a certain degree, but Dean (Chris and I agreed) would have to be something special.

Before we even started rehearsing, Chris and I began discussing how Dean Rebel would make his entrance. The show was to be performed in the round, with the audience on all sides. So whilst pondering this question in the theatre, we both looked up. Yes, Dean would bungee from the ceiling directly down onto the stage. This would mean crawling 50ft up along a thin plank attached to a safety harness before launching myself off at the given cue. My adrenaline levels would be off the scale before I'd even opened my mouth for the first line.

All the wrestling had to be authentic, and as we would not be getting any understudy's in case of injury, safe.

The biggest name in the UK female wrestling world at that time was Mitzi Mueller, who started her professional career in 1963 at the age of just 14. Trained by her father Joe Connolly, Mitzi won the British Ladies Championships in 1972 and held the title of European Ladies Champion from 1975 to 1990. Mitzi was drafted in to train us.

With my gymnastic and martial arts training background, I wanted my Dean Rebel to be fast and deadly, not relying on just brute force. My leading lady (Tanzi) was a lovely actress called Linda Rooke who was absolutely brilliant at faking getting a backward roundhouse or scissor kick in the chops. The timing of these moves had to be spot on for every performance, or serious injuries would be incurred by Linda and the rest of the cast. We choreographed every move, as one would a dance routine, until we could do them in our sleep.

The referee was played by an actor called George Costigan*, who was another of Chris Bond's cohorts from the Liverpool Everyman days. He was a fantastic actor, but a complete nightmare to work with. I have always been a terrible giggler, and unfortunately, so was George.

---

*George rose to fame in 1986 as adulterous businessman Bob in the comedy film *Rita, Sue and Bob Too*. He has since starred or featured in many television productions, including *The Adventures of Sherlock Holmes, Kavanagh QC, Coogan's Run, Murder Most Horrid, So Haunt Me, London's Burning, The Bill, Holby City, Dalziel* and *Pascoe, The Inspector Lynley Mysteries, The Beiderbecke Connection, New Tricks* and *Casualty*. His film work includes *Calendar Girls* and *Shirley Valentine*. In the theatre, he created the role of Mickey Johnstone in Willy Russell's musical *Blood Brothers*, originally at the Liverpool Playhouse, and later at the Lyric Theatre, London. In December 2009, it was announced that he was to join *Emmerdale* as a friend of Rodney Blackstock. He made his debut in the soap in March 2010 and his last appearance was shown on 23 July, 2010.

I was always more nervous of him than I was from jumping 50ft onto the stage from the rafters, with only a length of rope to stop me from becoming a permanent stain on the theatre floor.

I recently read Julie Walter's autobiography where she writes that whilst she was with The Everyman Theatre in Liverpool, Alan Dossor and Chris Bond would make the actors perform their shows in public houses. I wish I'd read that earlier, because when Chris told me that's what we were going to do, I thought he was taking the fucking piss. He wasn't joking. Before actually opening the play, we performed bits of it in some of the most unpleasant boozers in the north. I fucking hated it!

All my fellow actors were relatively still unknown, but I'd been in Metal Mickey for Christ's sake. Mind you, it certainly prepared me for the abuse that I was about to receive in the theatre when the play actually opened.

The audiences for *Tanzi* were brilliant. They had been actively encouraged to get involved, as it were, and this they certainly did with gusto. On one night, after Dean Rebel makes yet another of his misogynistic remarks, an old lady sitting ring side got up from her seat to batter me with her handbag. I came off script, and told her to shut the fuck up and tie a mattress to her back! The blokes in the audience loved it.

Now that the play had opened, I yet again had all my days free, and I was bored shitless. This was one job that I had to do totally clean and sober. It wasn't really a problem *per se*, but alcohol is a great boredom crusher, as any alcoholic will testify to, and Leeds in the early 80's wasn't exactly known for its daytime cultural activities. I decided to move to Liverpool.

During one of my many escapades in Liverpool with Joe McGann, I had stayed at an old run down hotel owned by an old queen who professed to be Father Christmas. Apparently, if any child in Liverpool had written to St Nick and posted a letter, the post office delivered them all to this bloke who would then answer every one personally. These days he would have probably been investigated by the police for grooming, but he was a lovely old geezer with a heart of gold who would gladly cook you breakfast at three in the morning if you requested it.

The hotel was a lot cheaper than my rented flat, so with the money I was saving I could now afford to commute by cab the 75miles back to Leeds for the evening performance. After the show, I would leg it out of the theatre to an awaiting car and head back to Liverpool's entertaining night life before going home for a nightcap with Father Christmas.

The reviews for *Trafford Tanzi* were great, with the Yorkshire Evening post mentioning me personally for my "unbelievable athletic abilities" and also stating that I could probably take up professional wrestling as an alternative career, if I so wanted to. The press were always urging me to give up acting…

I recently watched a movie on Netflix starring Micky Rourke called *The Wrestler*. It was about an old washed up grappler down on his luck with drink and drugs problems who wants one more moment in the spotlight before he retires or dies. I thought, 'Fuck me! That sounds familiar'.

13

"The biggest name dropper that I know is Paul McCartney"

After the outbreak of World War I, the Defence of the Realm Act was passed by Parliament in 1914. One section of the Act concerned the hours pubs could sell alcohol, as it was believed that alcohol consumption would interfere with the war effort. It restricted opening hours for licensed premises to lunchtime (12:00 to 14:40) and evenings to 18:30 to 21:30. So if you wanted to drink in comfort without breaking the law, you would have to become a member of a private drinking club. London in the 1980's was full of them.

Crispin Buxton, who owned The Tin Pan Alley Recording Studios, introduced me one afternoon to a tiny place at the top of some rickety stairs above a record shop just off Oxford Street called 'Troy's'. It was run by a completely alcohol-fuelled lady called Helen (Geddit) and a mad Polish bird called Yolanda, who would flash her stockings and suspenders at anyone who asked her politely. It was about the size of a small living room, with a small bar at one end and a clientele that mainly consisted of out-of-work advertising execs and depressed, suicidal novel writers. I absolutely loved it.

Troy's would open for business at three in the afternoon, and wouldn't close again until Helen either fell over, or the club ran out of booze. Helen of Troy was the undisputed Queen of Soho and everyone knew it. She knew everybody from the Chief of Police to the local hookers and everybody knew her. I once met her at midday for a drink in The French House* and then walked with her through Soho, stopping at almost every pub on route for a quick drink and a chat with the locals. By the time we actually reached Troy's I was slaughtered, but this was only the beginning to Helen's normal daily routine.

Helen never married, and at the time I would've put her age at somewhere between 50 and 60, although I was far too polite to ask. She was a whisky drinker and never drank the cheap stuff. She even named her cross breed terrier 'whisky' after her favourite tipple, and the dog was almost as well known in the area as its owner was. Helen was a living legend.

*The French House is a Grade II listed pub and dining room at 49 Dean Street, Soho, London. It was previously known as the York Minster, but was informally called "the French pub" or "the French house" by its regulars. It sells more Ricard than anywhere else in Britain and only serves beer in half-pints, except for on April the First, when a recent custom has been that Suggs from the band Madness serves the first pint of the day.

Troy's became known as 'The Office', and even my agent, Sharon, had the phone number in case I needed to be tracked down for an audition or casting. It's remarkable to think that we managed our lives and careers without the aid of mobile telephones or pagers, but there seemed to be an unseen telegraph system in place which meant you could always find out who was looking for you, and sometimes who you were looking to avoid.

Troy's was a place full of dreams and aspirations. Some were dashed on to the rocks of failure and others resulted in champagne celebrations. None of it really mattered though, as in retrospect, just being there was what really counted.

I had never been a fan of the Beatles when I was a kid, so when they broke up in 1970 I was just 11 years old and it didn't even register that anything momentous had happened at all.

My first real acknowledgment of Paul McCartney really only came three years later, when he released the critically acclaimed album "*Band On The Run*" with his new group Wings. There was no getting around the fact, though, that Macca was a bonafide musical legend and the most successful song writer on the bleeding planet. So when I got a phone call saying that he'd like to meet me for lunch, I thought it would be rude not to accept his invitation.

I met Paul and his wife Linda at Elstree Film Studios, where they were busy filming a project called *Give My Regards to Broad Street*. It was quite a surreal experience. One minute I was sitting in my flat pondering what to do with my day, and the next, I was eating sausage, egg and chips in Elstree's cafeteria with the world's most famous married couple.

Paul explained that his 6 year old son, James, was a massive *Metal Mickey* fan, and that they all used to sit down together as a family to watch the show on

Saturday afternoons whilst eating their tea. Apparently their daughter, Heather, (from Linda's 1st marriage) was also a huge fan of mine, but at 21 was far too cool to admit it.

Paul thought that I would be perfect for a scene in the movie and it would involve choreography, live music and getting smacked in the mouth by Linda. How could I refuse an offer like that? Oh, and the money was brilliant.

The choreographer for the scene was a guy called David Toguri, and my fellow dancers were David Easter, with whom I'd worked with before on the film Music Machine, and a beautiful doll-like creature called Lowri-Ann Richards, whom I'd seen performing at The Embassy Club in a group called Shock. I think we spent about a week rehearsing the dance routine, where in fact we could've actually done it in a day, to be honest. It certainly wasn't Swan Lake. Nothing could've prepared us for the sheer scale of this production when we arrived on set though.

The production designers had transformed Elstree Studios into a perfect replica of the old Lyceum Ballroom in its 1950's heyday, complete with stage, lights and balcony. It was certainly impressive, but nowhere near as impressive as the band Paul had put together for this movie. I think the term "supergroup" has been grossly over used over the years, but there was no other way of describing this bunch of musos that I was forced to share a dressing room with.

I suppose if Paul McCartney gives you a call to come and have a play, you'd have to be pretty damn busy not to turn up. Either that or you'd have to be a Tibetan Nose Flute Player living half way up Mount Everest not to. In this one scene alone the band he used could've sold out Wembley Stadium for a week.

The song that they would be performing, whilst I was doing my stuff, was called "Ballroom Dancing", and for this the line-up the band was:

Paul McCartney…Vocals & Piano
Linda McCartney…Vocals & Piano (they had two upright pianos back to back)
Ringo Star...Drums
Dave Edmunds & Chris Spedding...Guitar
and John Paul Jones from Led Zeppelin on bass.

There was also a complete brass section made up from members of Manhattan Transfer.

Paul wanted all the music to be recorded live every time, so he hired The Rolling Stones Mobile Recording Studio, which I would have gladly moved in to, and the music producer for the project was someone Paul McCartney probably owed his entire career to, George Martin.

By now I'd made a few films, but this one was like nothing I'd been used to. This was the director Peter Webb's first movie, and I wasn't quite sure if he, or for that matter anybody else, quite knew what the fuck was going on.

We had a couple of rehearsals with the band and all the extras who were all professional ballroom dancers, and then nothing for the next three days whilst Paul and Peter Webb set up for other scenes. I didn't mind though, as it meant I got to hang out with all the musos.

There was one musician who Paul had flown in from America who I couldn't wait to chat to, his name was Louis Johnson*. Louis Johnson was someone I had admired for years. I'd spent hours listening to his work with The Brothers Johnson, and thought his song 'Strawberry Letter 23' was a work of complete and utter genius. Paul McCartney had flown him all the way from the states for just one scene in the film (Silly Love Songs) and he'd been (just like me) hanging about for days.

It seemed that what he needed was a good night out, and as Elstree wasn't exactly known for its wild hotspots, I suggested that we head into London's West End for the evening, with the promise of a few ales and maybe some attractive female company to help us along.

He seemed very keen on the idea, so I made a couple of calls, arranged a car, and off we went. When we got to Munkberrys, he turned into a Bible Bashing maniac, telling me that he was a Christian who could not be swayed from the path of righteousness, and that all the girls at the club were temptresses. I put him back in the car and sent him home. Louis Johnson sadly died on the 21st May, 2015.

Heather McCartney was the most unaffected child of a superstar I had ever met. I knew that she wasn't Paul's biological daughter, having been adopted by him when she was 6 years old, but still, being the daughter of a Beatle couldn't have been easy for her. We got on really well and started hanging out together.

One night, Heather and I had been out on the razz, and she decided to stay over at my flat. In the cab on the way back, she said that she'd like to pop home first to pick up an overnight bag, and some other girly shit. We pulled up outside this fuck-off gaff in North London, not a stone's throw away from the Abbey Road Recording Studios. Of course I was curious, so we tiptoed as quietly as we could around the side of the house to the back door, and let ourselves in.

*As well as The Brothers Johnson, Louis's work appears on many well-known records by other prominent artists. Johnson also played bass on Michael Jackson's albums *Off the Wall*, *Thriller* and *Dangerous*, and hit songs "Billie Jean" and "Don't Stop 'Til You Get Enough". He also played on George Benson's *Give Me the Night*. He was one of three bassists on Herb Alpert's 1979 album *Rise*, which included its top-10, Grammy-winning disco/jazz title-track.

Heather crept upstairs, leaving me waiting for about ten minutes. All I kept thinking was that at any minute Paul McCartney was going to come down those stairs in his pyjamas, and wonder what the fuck Gary Shail was doing there at three o clock in the morning in his kitchen.

I think Paul probably knew that I was taking drugs. After all, he was hardly whiter than white when it came to the recreational use of narcotics, was he? In March of 1973, Scottish police made a discovery on Paul's Highland farm. It seems that Paul was growing marijuana plants in his garden. An arrest was made, which would lead to a conviction for "illegal cultivation" and with it a £100 fine.

At the time of the arrest, McCartney famously stated that a fan had given him the seeds, and he didn't know what would blossom from them (Good one Paul!). Due to this particular arrest, McCartney was denied a visa by the US government. This was not Paul's first, or last, brush with drug laws. The previous year he had been fined in Sweden for possession of marijuana, and in 1975, he was arrested once again for the same thing, this time in Los Angeles.

Most famous perhaps was his bust at the Tokyo airport in 1980, when customs officers discovered cannabis stashed away in his luggage, and bunged him in the slammer for a couple of days.

What Paul didn't condone though was the use of pharmaceuticals, telling me that he'd seen many of his friends' lives ruined by what they thought was a manageable coke habit. I really should've listened to him, but of course, I thought I knew better. What I never did though was encourage anyone else to take drugs—the last thing I needed was someone wanting to share mine!

Ringo Starr was great fun on set, and so was his wife Barbara Bach, who was a stunner. In 1977, Barbara's role as the Russian spy Anya Amasova in *The Spy Who Loved Me* gained her recognition as an international Bond Girl Sex Symbol, and I'd also remembered her from an old copy of 'Playboy' that I must've casually flicked through in my youth. She was much prettier in the flesh though.

Zak, Ringo's son from his first marriage, was also on set for a couple of days. He was about 17 years old at the time, and very, very cool. Ringo told me that Zak had taken up the family business and was a rock drummer. This was hardly surprising given that his Godfather was one of his dad's best mates, Keith Moon.

One afternoon, after lunch in the cafeteria, I wandered back on to the set to have a cheeky play on Paul McCartney's piano. I must've got carried away 'cos I never heard him sneak up behind me whilst I was playing to join me in a duet of "Twenty Flight Rock."*

*"Twenty Flight Rock" is a song originally performed by Eddie Cochran in the 1956 film comedy *The Girl Can't Help It*, and released as a single in 1957. The good first impression of McCartney's performance led to an invitation to join The Quarrymen. On July 6, 1957 in Liverpool, the barely 15-year-old Paul McCartney used "Twenty Flight Rock" as his first song when he auditioned for John Lennon. The 16yr old Lennon was impressed by the young McCartney's ability to play the song on the guitar during their first official introductions at St. Peter's Church Hall, prior to a church garden fete

Paul McCartney and Gary.

Even though I'd never been a Beatles fan, I'd always loved the song "The Long and Winding Road". Over the years, whenever I've played it for anyone I've always said, "Yes it's a great song...Paul McCartney taught me that." Because he did!

When the film was released in October 1984, it was universally panned by the critics, although the soundtrack album did get some good reviews. I have never seen the film, but I did buy the album, mainly because there is a great picture of me doing a backward somersault on the inner sleeve.

The song "No More Lonely Nights", graced by a terrific David Gilmour guitar solo did well though, reaching no 6 in the U.K chart, and also doing well in America. Rolling Stone magazine said…

"No More Lonely Nights" is one of the most solid pop tracks McCartney has recorded in years. With its delicate melody and instant-hook chorus, it's a song worthy of the man's unquestioned talents."

Almost all of my performance in *Give My Regards to Broad Street* is featured in the accompanying video.

Peter Stringfellow had been expanding his nightclub empire in London, and acquired the old Talk Of The Town theatre in Leicester Square, renaming it The Hippodrome. He completely refurbished it with an amazing lighting rig, new bars and a flashing dance floor. It was nowhere near as exclusive as Stringfellows, but what it lacked in taste it certainly made up for it in other ways. Namely the tall gorgeous blonde girl that worked the reception. Her name was Rian.

Over the following weeks, I spent more time and money at the Hippodrome than at any other pub or club in London. I'd been smitten by Rian from the moment I saw her, and pursued her relentlessly. She was so cool that even if she had known (which she didn't) that I was on the television, she wouldn't have cared less.

My persistence eventually bore fruit and Rian agreed to go out with me, although I knew she wasn't going to put up with any of my shenanigans, and that this would have to be an exclusive relationship. This suited me fine, as I was getting bored of having to remember who I'd been with, and where I'd been. Some nights I had three different girls waiting for me in three different clubs, and it was getting tricky. Rian was now my girl, and I wanted everyone to know it.

Rian wasn't a big drinker and, apart from the odd social spliff, didn't take drugs. This was good for me and it certainly calmed me down a great deal. Also, she sometimes didn't finish work until four in the morning, so if I wanted to see her before she went home to sleep I had to be sober and awake. For a long while we rarely saw each other during the daytime at all.

Rian had a little top floor studio flat in Bayswater, and some of my best memories of those early days in our relationship were lying in bed watching Blockbusters, making love and eating pizza. I loved Rian with a passion!

Workwise, things couldn't be better. I made some cameo appearances in a few TV shows, did a short horror film, and made a commercial for the Milk Marketing Board, which everyone thought was hysterical, with the most witty remark being that "the only reason Shail drinks milk is to line his fucking stomach before he goes out on the piss!"

I got to do an episode of a popular TV cop show called *Dempsey and Makepeace** where I had to drive a truck. My agent had thought it best not to tell them that I didn't actually have a driving license as this, she reckoned, might cause them some concern.

As I was a registered stuntman at the time, no one even thought to ask me. In the last scene I get shot trying to stop arms smugglers from stealing the truck, and had to fall from the speeding vehicle into a strategically placed flower stall. All this would happen before the opening credits had even rolled.

Since *Quadrophenia,* Sting had become a worldwide superstar with his rock band Police, so it seemed logical that he would have the same success as a movie star. Franc Roddam, who had given Sting his first break into films, took full advantage of this fact and had raised the cash to finance a project called *The Bride.*

Based very loosely on Mary Shelley's Frankenstein, the story centres on Baron Frankenstein who creates the perfect bride for his not-so-perfect monster. Apart from Sting, who was to play The Baron, the film would also star Jennifer Beals as Eva (The Bride), and Clancy Brown as Viktor The Monster*.

Jennifer recently had huge success in a movie called *Flashdance,* and the hope was that hers and Stings on-screen chemistry would set cinemas alight across the globe.

Dempsey and Makepeace was a British television crime drama made by London Weekend Television for ITV, created and produced by Ranald Graham. The leading roles were played by Michael Brandon (Dempsey) and Glynis Barber (Makepeace), who later married each other on 18 November, 1989. The series combined elements of previous series such as the mismatching of British and American crime-fighters from different classes as seen in *The Persuaders* and the action of *The Professionals*

*Clarence J. "Clancy" Brown III is an American film, television and voice actor. He is known for his live-action roles as Captain Byron Hadley in *The Shawshank Redemption*; The Kurgan in *Highlander*; Brother Justin Crowe in *Carnivàle* and Career Sergeant Zim in *Starship Troopers*.

The supporting cast was interesting, to say the least. Quentin Crisp, the flamboyant homosexual for whom Sting would eventually write "An Englishman in New York" was cast as Dr Zalhus, Alexei Sayle, the well-known Bolshevik stand-up comedian, was cast as the cruel circus owner Magar. The dwarf Rinaldo was played by David Rappaport, who'd achieved great success for his portrayal of Randall in the hit Terry Gilliam movie *Time Bandits*. Cary Elwes, known for his stable-boy turned swashbuckler Westley in Rob Reiner's fantasy-comedy *The Princess Bride*, played Captain Josef Schoden. And Timmy Spall, the well-known Levis-Filler, (Quad in-joke) played a maniac called Paulus.

Oh yes... Me and Phil Daniels were in it too!

Actually, Phil had a really nice part playing Bella, an evil nasty piece of work who would've gladly sold his own granny for the price of a beer (Typecast again eh Phil), but me?

Franc Roddam called me to ask if I'd like to be in the film, but couldn't elaborate on what I'd actually be doing in it. He just said that it would be fun, nice to have me around, and it would be shot in the South of France. I told Franc that I'd make the tea. My scrumptious agent Sharon wasn't sure I should do it, but I had already packed my bucket and spade, and was heading for the airport.

"Nearly every actor I knew had made at least one film abroad. The furthest I'd been was Wembley!"

There was no way that I was going to let a little thing like not having a script, or even a definite part to speak of, stop me going to a Medieval Castle in the south of France in the middle of summer, and get paid for it.

I didn't give two flying fucks if I appeared in the film at all to be Franc (Geddit)

A Brief History of where we were going.

Carcassonne history goes back as least as far as Roman Gaul; parts of the city's fortifications date from 1st century AD. Located at the strategic intersection of two historic trade routes, from the Atlantic to the Mediterranean and from Spain to the centre of France, Carcassonne's defences were strengthened by successive owners. In the 5th century the Visigoth's extended the Roman defences, and for many years after Carcassonne Castle proved impenetrable to invaders.

One legend from Carcassonne history is the attempted siege by Charlemagne in the 9th century. According to the story, a Madame Carcas cunningly fed the last of the city's wheat to a pig in full view of the invading army. Believing that the besieged townspeople had an inexhaustible supply of food, Charlemagne retreated from the walls and the town was renamed in honour of the ingenious lady. Carcassonne took its name (or a version of it) even before the Roman conquest of Gaul.

From the book: 'Carcassonne's Bloody History'

It really was an amazing place, you could actually taste the history embedded within the ancient walls that surrounded this town. Some serious shit had happened here!

Apart from the main and supporting cast, there were also hundreds of extras, stunt men, horse wranglers, wild animals and speciality performers that all had to be housed and fed.

I was billeted about 20 minutes away from the main town in a little family-run hotel with an actor called Carl Chase, who I knew from Liverpool. Carl had been very involved with the Liverpool music and theatre scene, and I met him socially on more than one occasion whilst out with the McGann boys.

The film unit for *The Bride* basically took over the entire town, which pleased the local shops and businesses so much that they were almost polite to us. We were getting *per diems* of about 50 francs a day, more than enough to get fed and watered sufficiently without having to touch your fee. We were required on set early so as the make-up and wardrobe departments could do their magic. Everyone wanted a wig. I ended up with blonde hair extensions and knee high leather boots. I really did look like something out of a Spandau Ballet video.

Clancy Brown, on the other hand, had to be in the make-up chair three hours earlier than everybody else. Poor Clancy, as The Monster was required to wear prosthetics which had to be moulded to his face and stuck on with glue. When it got hot (which was most days) Clancy would sweat under the rubber prosthetics because his skin could not breathe. It was not nice for Clancy at all. He knew what he was letting himself in for though, and I can't ever remember him losing it, or complaining to anyone. Clancy was a true professional and a bloody good bloke as well.

I would be involved in the circus scenes (I eventually discovered) with Alexei, Phil and Carl. It was a real working (politically incorrect) circus, with elephants, lions and tigers. It was fantastic to be so up and close to these magnificent beasts, but they didn't look happy at all. Let's just say that the way the French and Spanish handlers treated them was harsher than I would have liked.

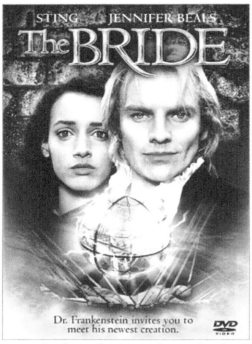

Dr. Frankenstein invites you to meet his newest creation.

There were also the speciality acts which were a law unto themselves and were all famous in their own circus community and their own minds. We had a strong man, a bearded lady, a tattooed lady (who I quite fancied) and a sword swallower called The Great Stromboli.

One day I was chatting with The Great Stromboli (real name Danny Lynch) and I asked him if the sword he used was for real. He let me have a hold of it, before taking it back and shoving it down his fucking throat!

I got friendly with one of the horse trainers called Petre (I called him Pete) and he let me ride with him if I was up early enough. They were magnificent horses that didn't need bits and reins to guide them. Just a thin rope placed across the horse's nose determined which direction you wanted it to go. These animals were fast! Again, it was the training methods that I didn't like. The horses had little scars all over their noses where they had been whipped with a swish cane so that when the guiding rope was placed over its face, it reacted and headed in that direction.

The Lion Tamer was the worst, though. In one scene Phil Daniels had to be slammed into the lion's cage. Phil was never in any real danger, as the poor lion was just too fucking bored to react. When the cameras started rolling though, and at the desired moment, the tamer stuck an electronic shocker through the bars of the cage and right up poor Leo's arse!

Of course the lion reacted violently, wouldn't you? Phil was outraged and had to be restrained from grabbing the shocking stick and giving the trainer a taste of his own medicine.

Clancy Brown's skin problems were starting to get worse. Days would pass when we could not film anything at all. For insurance purposes though, we were still required to go through the motions of getting made up and into costume every day. After about a week it was decided that Clancy needed some proper medical attention, so he was flown back to London to see a skin specialist in Harley Street. There was no point keeping us all on stand-by for days on end, so the whole production was put on hold, and we all flew home.

It felt strange being back in London, knowing that I could get a call at any minute summoning me back to France. Of course it was great to see Rian and the family, but I felt like I was sitting in limbo. Alexei Sayle, on the other hand, was already planning his journey back.

Alexei hated flying! So much so that he decided that he wasn't ever going to do it again. He called me and asked if I fancied driving back to Carcassonne via Paris, which would be celebrating Bastille Day on July 14th. This is the day that the whole of France celebrates the beginning of The French Revolution and the storming of the Bastille. We would be making the journey in Alexei's classic 1962 Rover 80 and he would be bringing his wife Linda to navigate.

I didn't know Alexei at all before making this movie, but of course I'd seen him at the Comedy Store in London's Soho where he was the Master of Ceremonies. He was also in one of my favourite TV shows of all time *The Young Ones* playing the entire Balowski family. His on-stage and TV personas were absolutely nothing like the man himself though. He was so much more intelligent and funnier in real life, as was his wife Linda.

The journey back to Carcassonne was brilliant and I'd love to elaborate, but I spent most of the journey drinking Scotch through a novelty straw.

Once we were back in Carcassonne, things started to move more quickly and I was actually given some lines to say. Any one of the extras could've handled them, but I really didn't care as I'd already had a great adventure and a fine time to boot. The only time I remember there being any trouble, of course I was bang right in the middle of it.

Victor Drai, (one of the producers), had thrown a massive wrap party to which we were all invited. He'd just finished producing a film called *The Woman in Red* and had invited the star Kelly Le Brock and her new husband Steven Segal over to France for the do. The entertainment, though, was totally inappropriate. Someone thought it had been a good idea to hire a local stripper who proceeded to strut her stuff through the visibly embarrassed guests, discarding all her clobber along the way. When she got to me, I picked her up and threw her head first into the swimming pool.

As I was attempting to help the now bedraggled young lady out of the water, her boyfriend and his mates attacked me with Gaelic Gusto.

They managed to get a few punches in before the entire cast and crew of *The Bride* stepped in to back me up. Even little David Rappaport, who was only 3ft 6, was giving these hot-blooded locals the evil eye, and they all backed off. No sign of Steven Segal though…

I have never actually seen *The Bride* all the way through. And if you have ever seen it, it's a blink and you'll miss the performance from me. I had a fantastic time though, and met some amazing people such as David Rappaport, who I stayed in touch with when we were back in England.

David and Clancy

With Pete

With Phil Daniels

David had such a lot of crap to deal with in everyday life. I remember once taking him to The Kings Arms for drinks one day and I had to physically lift him so he could reach the cash machine. There was so much more to David than met the eye though. He had a first class degree from the University of Bristol in Psychology and also played the drums professionally.

His career seemed to be headed in the right direction, with offers of work coming from America where he appeared in shows such as *L.A Law* and *The Wizard*. He had married his college girlfriend and had a son, so when I learned that he had apparently gone into Laurel Canyon Park in California and had shot himself to death, I was devastated!

I don't think America did any favours for David at all. It had cost him his marriage and he had lost contact with all of his friends- including me. Over here, his size (or lack of it) was rarely mentioned if at all, and he'd led a relatively normal life. But in the United States he became the object of curiosity and fun.

Talk show host Arsenio Hall, for example, began his interview with David by making fun of the term "little people" as a more socially acceptable way of referring to people who are dwarfs, and then he are asked how he could possibly make love to a full-sized woman.

That remark alone would've devastated David if you knew him, and if I ever get to meet that unfunny Twat Arse, or whatever his fucking name is, I will give him a slap!

It's in the bank David!

David Rappaport 23/11/1951 – 2/5/1990

14

"What's the difference between a nine-month pregnant woman and a glamour model?
-Nothing, if the pregnant woman's husband knows what's good for him"

I was back in London, had a gorgeous girlfriend who worked in a top nightclub, and had a few quid in the bank. Life was good. Stringfellows was now in its zenith and the place to see and be seen. I took full advantage of my minor celebrity status and partied like there was no tomorrow. Of course, other women were completely out of the question as Rian was working just down the road at the Hippodrome. She knew all the waitresses at Stringies and took great pleasure in letting me know that she knew who I'd been talking to during the evening. These girls had their own hot-line for fuck sake, so I was well aware that I was under constant surveillance. I really was behaving myself though, yes really!

It's hard for the younger generation today to know what a real celebrity is (or was) back in the mid 80's. Today kids will line up for hours to get a selfie from an industry-created star, but believe me, you certainly wouldn't be able to get that up close and personal to any of the real stars in my day.

Stringfellows was a safe haven for the rich and famous to let their sometimes questionable hair down. John Entwistle was almost part of the furniture, as was John Hurt. The lads from Status Quo were often seen propping up the bar 'till the wee smalls and Rod Stewart always passed by when he wasn't avoiding tax in L.A. Of course the new breed of superstars was well represented too. Madonna always looked great strutting her stuff on the dance floor and Duran Duran could often be found touching up their eyeliner in the gents. Sometimes though, a real fucking star would grace us with his presence.

Peter Stringfellow was great with me. He knew how much I loved soul music and the old Motown classics in particular. Some nights, if it was quiet, he would let me play the piano in the upstairs bar where I knew that anything by Marvin or Stevie would go down well with the punters. One night when I arrived at the club, he grabbed me by the arm and led me through the crowd to the downstairs bar. There was a roped-off section guarded by some seriously large dudes. Once they saw it was Peter, they let us through to where Stevie Wonder was sat sipping on a cocktail.

I was recently at an event in a pub and went to the loo. There was a large sign on the door stating that only one person was allowed in the cubicle at any one time, and any infringement of this rule would result in expulsion from the venue and the police informed. It made me smile.

At Stringfellows, a very well-spoken impeccably-dressed valet would not only open the cubical door for you (and whoever), he would also brush you down, give you a dab of aftershave and check your nose for any residuals. The valet at Stringies must've earned a fortune in tips.

One night Rian had some news. We were pregnant. Rian and I never even considered the alternative to us starting a family. We were both over- the-moon but cautious about letting our families and friends know the news until all the relative scans and checks had been done. One thing was for certain though; we would need somewhere to live.

My mate, Dave John, told me about a cottage that had recently become vacant in North London, so I signed a year's rental agreement, and we set up our little nest. Rian would continue working for as long as she could, and I promised not to leave London unless it was for a decent part in a movie that would enable us to buy our own house. It never happened though, so I joined a rock band instead.

I was drinking one night at The Embassy Club when a very dapper young Asian dude called Tariq cornered me, telling me that he was the manager of a rock band called Traitor. He thought I'd be the perfect front man for the group, and asked if I'd consider joining the band. He seemed like he had a few bob, and was very enthusiastic, so I went to watch them in rehearsals at a studio in The Elephant and Castle. Fuck, they were loud! They were also very good. Think Black Sabbath meets Bon Jovi and you get the picture.

I started rehearsing with Traitor and really enjoyed it, but when it actually came to playing live, I hated it. Some of the dives we played were awful, and in some we were lucky if we even got a proper sound-check. We were often the support band for some other acts that were, quite frankly, crap, and I would just get pissed and insult the audience. One night we were playing to a bunch of wannabe Hells Angels who threw an Alsatian dog onto the stage. I stopped mid-song and asked if the dog had paid.

I decided to take matters into my own hands, and arranged a proper showcase for Traitor at The Embassy. The gig was a sell out and attended by some of the rock world's biggest luminaries. Motorhead's Lemmy and Filthy Animal were there, as was John Entwistle and Gary Moore. We got a great review in Kerrang, and even Julie Burchill* liked us.

I actually thought that Traitor stood a good chance if we could've recorded the songs down on to tape, but Tariq insisted that we should continue with the live gigs and every time I pressed to get us into the studio, there was always some excuse why we couldn't.

I felt that Traitor wasn't my band anyway, so why was I bothered so much. It's a real shame though, as I think the band had at least one good album in them. I did make two lifelong friends though. The exceptionally gifted lead guitarist John 'sweety-boy' Glykys and his lovely wife Karen became very close to Rian and I during our pregnancy, and I was even best man at their wedding.

I started spending more and more time at the Tin Pan Alley studios, working and recording on several different projects with Crispin Buxton and the house engineers. Crispin signed a band from Scotland called The 30 Footers, who all hailed from Aberdeen, and he asked me to play some piano on some of their recordings.

The lead singer and main songwriter was a guy called Neil Cairney, who lived the life and philosophy of a Rastafarian. All of his songs were reggae influenced and tinged with African mysticism. I loved the songs, so when I was asked if I'd like to join the band as the keyboard player and play some live gigs, I jumped at the chance.

Neil Cairney, 2015: "The second Dingwall's gig. So we knew the dressing room wasn't big enough to swing a gerbil in, and with 7 peeps on board it was gonna be a tight squeeze. But out we popped all clad in tartan rags and kumina face masks, all set for another whiplash set. Then Ross smacks his guitar against a pillar inconveniently placed in the middle of the stage. What a sound!

Ross went mental and had to use mine. Whose idea was it to have a club in that dump? And I was out of my box after being up all night shagging the daughter of a Columbian Diplomat. Anyhow, first chord of the night, "Karamba Man" and I fell over Davy's drum kit backwards and disappeared under his snare drum. What a twat!

*Julie Burchill is a British writer. Beginning as a journalist on the staff of the New Musical Express at the age of 17, she has subsequently contributed to newspapers such as The Sunday Times and The Guardian. Describing herself as a "militant feminist", she has several times been involved in legal action resulting from her work.

"I think I left my body guys....sorry guys...can we start again...ha ha ha ha.....ooops...so unprofessional...aaagh...fuck it....who gives a shit!"

It went down well though...and my memory of the rest of the night is blank!"

I don't remember it either!

Rian and I settled into our new home and informed my parents of their impending first grandchild. I think they were pleased, but a tad surprised, as I hadn't really introduced Rian into the family like I had with previous girlfriends. They were, as always, very supportive though, and helped with the furnishings and all the other crap you think you don't need until you need it. Dad also spent a day tidying up the garden, where he swore he found a Japanese soldier hiding in the undergrowth who didn't know that the war was over.

By Christmas 1985 we were as settled as we could be. The only thing missing was a dog. I had never had a dog as a child, as my little sister Julie had suffered with eczema since birth and was highly allergic to animals. We did have a cat called Plodder before she'd been born, but the only other animal I remember us having was a tortoise called Tootsie who'd mysteriously disappeared one morning just after the dustman had been. I knew nothing about dogs.

Rian wanted to get a rescue dog from The Battersea Dogs Home, so up she got one morning and left me at home, promising not to come back with a Rottweiler. By tea time that evening I was sat on the sofa being stared at by a German Shepherd that looked like he wanted to eat me. We named him Tramp.

Tramp loved Rian but hated me. He ate my bass guitar, my ceremonial Japanese sword and would've eaten my headphones if he hadn't shat in them first. I fucking hated that dog. I swear if he'd had fingers, he would've stuck two of them in my face every time Rian's back was turned. Whenever I had to take the little sod out for a walk which, as Rian grew larger, became more and more often, Tramp would run off whilst I stood like a twat waiting for the little bleeder to come back—which he never did. I'd end up chasing the little fucker all over the park trying to get him back on his lead, whilst he took the piss. One night, I'd had enough.

Tramp was up to his old tricks, and wouldn't come back as usual. It was fucking freezing, so I just left him to make his own way home. He knew where he lived by now, and I was sure that he'd probably be at home before me, and very possibly eating my dinner. He wasn't.

After about half an hour we were worried, so I went back out to find him. As I was heading back to the park, some local kids ran towards me yelling that Tramp had been hit by a car on the main road. As I was about to run towards the road, Tramp appeared limping heavily towards me, and as I reached him he collapsed into my arms, covered in blood. He was injured badly and barely alive.

Luckily we lived almost opposite the local police station, and a lovely female copper helped to get Tramp into the back of her squad car, and she drove us to a local emergency vet where he was rushed in for emergency surgery. It didn't look good though.

The next few hours were the longest of my life. Then at about three in the morning the surgery door opened, and out limped Tramp with one arm in plaster and minus a fang. The vet told me that Tramp had completely refused to die, and although he'd suffered some internal injuries as well as the obvious, given time and care, he'd make old age.

If a dog could talk, then I'm sure Tramp was saying, "Sorry Dad I won't do it again," But it was me who was saying sorry!

Have you ever seen a movie starring Gwyneth Paltrow called *Sliding Doors*? It's quite a simple story of how one, seemingly random action such as missing a train by a few seconds, could change your entire life and your destiny forever. It happens every day. Just getting up an hour later than usual in the morning could have a catastrophic effect on the rest of your life. We just don't think about it. Shit happens. But if I hadn't left Tramp in the park he wouldn't have got hurt, and if Rian had got a pair of shoes instead of a dog then I'd still have had that bass guitar, and we wouldn't have got an eviction notice from our landlord for having a dog.

It became clear that our landlord was not going to back down when it came to Tramp. We started getting nasty letters from his solicitors and although I was up for the fight, at the end of the day the contract for the house did state 'no pets'. Tramp was pensioned off to Rian's mum's house up north, and me and my pregnant girlfriend started packing. It didn't take long.

Neil Cairney and the other members of The 30 Footers had rented a massive dilapidated house in the arse end of Brixton- right opposite Brockwell Park. They had a small spare room at the top of the house, so Rian and I were invited to join the commune. The boys in the band brought their girlfriends down from Aberdeen, so Rian would have some much-needed female company.

One of the girls called Robbie was also a trained nurse, and this was ideal, given Rian's condition. They were also all vegans, which I'm sure had its health benefits, but beans and lentils can eventually become boring as fuck no matter how you cook them. Thank God for the Prince Regent Pub that was only two doors away and did a fabulous steak and kidney pie on most days, and a roast on Sundays.

The basement of the house had been turned into a band rehearsal room where most days were spent writing new material and smoking ganja. No one had any money to speak of, and what little money I had saved from the last couple of years of working was dwindling fast. It didn't seem to matter though and as long as we had gigs lined up there was always enough cash for food, beer and ganja.

Brixton in the 1980's hadn't always received glowing reviews in the British press. Apparently there were no-go areas where if you were white you could almost be sure of getting mugged or raped, or if you were extremely unlucky, both. This certainly was not the Brixton I experienced. Of course we all heard about the rich idiots from Golders Green who thought it was cool to buy their weed at The Frontline and got ripped off, but I found the locals to be as friendly and helpful as anywhere else I had lived. There were no massive cultural divisions to speak of, and everyone just got on with it.

Our immediate neighbours were a noisy bunch of dreadlocked young men, who were busy renovating what looked like an old warehouse. They were, to my absolute delight, building a 24 track recording studio with a speakeasy bar on the top floor and a fully operational live room and control suite with offices on the ground area. The studio, to be called Sparkside, was the brainchild of a guy called Eaton Blake who had been the bass player in a band called Matumbi*.

The whole of Brixton's Reggae Music Royalty started working and socialising at Sparkside Recording Studios. It was an amazingly creative place to be, and a lot of fun just to hang out at. All of Eaton Blake's immediate family were involved in the running of the studio, from the bar, which was always fully stocked with Red Stripe and Guinness, to the fab home-cooked oxtail, rice and peas, which if you didn't get ordered fast enough, would be gone as soon as you were thinking about having any. Considering what my childhood musical influences had been, this was a dream come true.

Dennis Bovell and Linton Kwesi Johnson also recorded here. They had been responsible for one of my favourite albums of all time.

The 1979 *Forces of Victory* had been the perfect marriage of Linton's poetry and Dennis Bovell's dub backing tracks. I always thought that this album had been recorded in Jamaica, but I was wrong. In fact, many of the records I bought in my youth, thinking they were Jamaican imports, had actually been recorded in London but then been pressed and distributed by a Jamaican company. The reason was pure musical snobbery.

*Matumbi were one of the top British reggae bands of the 1970's and early 1980's, and are best known as the first successful band of guitarist and record producer Dennis (Blackbeard) Bovell.

In the 70's and very early 80's every pure reggae fan wanted the imports, and I think that even I would have questioned the authenticity of a home grown reggae band. Bands like Matumbi and Birmingham's Steele Pulse went a long way to changing these attitudes, but even then the credibility of British reggae music was brought into question. It would take a primarily white band called UB40 to really put the music on the map.

Of course, reggae wasn't the only music being recorded at Sparkside. A young soul singer called Noel McCoy* was recording with a band that were way ahead of their time. I got chatting with Noel one day and sold him on the idea of doing something a bit more rock and roll.

I had a song called 'Red Light' that had originally been recorded as a B Side for the McGann boys, but I thought Noel and the band would do a much better job. And I was right. I co-produced the song with Eaton Blake, and after that I was no longer just the little white keyboard player from next door with the pregnant girlfriend.

Rian was getting bigger by the day, and had been told by the doctor to quit smoking. I actually asked the doc if smoking pure ganja would be better for her, and he said that he'd rather she didn't smoke anything at all, but marijuana was by far the preferable alternative, given the choice.

We made good friends with an old Jamaican guy called Ben who lived on the same street. Ben was a London bus driver, driving the number 3 from Brixton to Oxford Street from morning to late afternoon. He used to come over in the mornings for a cuppa and a spliff before starting his shift. Before he left the house, he would roll Rian a huge joint of pure weed which would then last her all day long. It was known as Rian's spliff and completely out of bounds to anyone else on pain of death.

One night, I took Old Ben and a few of the guys up to London for a night out which ended up in Troy's drinking club, where I then proceeded to drink an entire bottle of scotch, and then quite literally died…

*Noel McKoy is a British-based soul music singer. His music is a collection of soul, gospel, funk and Northern soul. He also currently owns the Dutch Pot, a nightclub located in London. Born in South London, he fronted the James Taylor Quartet in the early 1990s and has duetted with Juliet Roberts, Mica Paris, Vanessa Simon, Beverley Knight and Ebony Alleyne.

15

"Alcoholics go to meetings — us drunks go to parties!"

The information available today on the dangers of misusing alcohol are a little bit different to when I was a young man in my twenties. I still don't know precisely what a unit is, or why anyone can be bothered to count them. If you like to drink, you are not going to let a warning label stop you, are you? And if you do count your weekly or monthly or yearly alcohol consumption, why not quit? 'Cos you obviously don't love alcohol the same way that I did.

I never had any set of rules when it came to drinking. I always knew that if I was drunk and drove my bike, I would fall off. I also knew that if I got drunk and tried to play the piano whilst attempting a back-flip, I would probably look like a twat. So here were at least two rules I had set for myself where drinking was not appropriate. Flying an airplane was another, and climbing a mountain after a few ales is probably not advisable, ooh…and brain surgery is a complete no no!

As long as none of these activities were being attempted, then I saw absolutely no harm in drinking steadily from morning 'till bed time if I had nothing better to do. I discovered Wray & Nephews Jamaican Over-proof White Rum one evening whilst playing pool in the bar upstairs at Sparkside. It was just the kind of drink I'd been looking for. Short, neat and straight to the point.

I found out that a local off-license was stocking this rocket fuel, and what was even better, they sold it in miniature form. I bought a box of 24 and drank two in the morning and another couple in the evening, then had Sunday off, 'cos I was usually in the pub that day anyway.

One week had been particularly heavy. I had been out for three nights in a row. I hadn't seen any of my friends from the clubs in ages, so I was on a bit of a mission. I'd been to Stringfellows, Bootleggers, The Embassy and a few bars in Chelsea too. On the third day, Helen from Troy asked me to help with a charity event at the club, raising money for kids with Cystic Fibrosis*.

Helen had been planning this event for months, and I promised to spend the day helping entertain a coach load of ill kids and their carers who were coming down from somewhere in the north of England for the day. I thought it would be a great idea to take the band and the girls with me, as well as old Ben. So when we arrived at about ten in the morning, I'd already been up and drinking steadily for 24hrs. The only thing keeping me upright was the cocaine I purchased from a dealer the night before at The Embassy Club.

*Cystic fibrosis, also known as mucoviscidosis, is a genetic disorder that affects mostly the lungs but also the pancreas, liver, kidneys and intestine. Long-term issues include difficulty breathing and coughing up sputum as a result of frequent lung infections.

The day was hectic but great fun. The 30 Footers did a brilliant acoustic set, whilst Old Ben helped out with the sausage rolls and the egg and cress sarnies. Every so often Helen would pour me a large scotch, which I would then knock back when I thought no one was looking.

Of course, I then needed some cocaine to keep me going. All was going fine until I ran out. I managed to keep it together until all the kids had gone, and then everything went black!

What happened next, I only have other people's testimonies to go on, but according to Helen, I'd drunk an entire bottle of Glenfiddich whisky during the day, and fallen asleep in the corner of the room where some kind soul had covered me with a coat. After about an hour, Robbie (the trained nurse) decided to check on me and found that my pulse was weak and my pupils were dilated. An ambulance was called and I was put on oxygen and a trolley and then carted off to a hospital.

I awoke to a cacophony of sounds and smells that were unfamiliar and all around. It took a few seconds before the pain in my chest registered, closely followed by the realization that I was definitely not in my own bed. I tried to raise myself up, but the pain in my chest restricted my movement to such an extent, I was forced to roll on to my side, so as to see the cause of the pain. Fuck!!

I looked and felt as if I had been in a car crash. Both sides of my chest were the colour of a Van Gogh painting during his depressive period. Had I been attacked? The realization that I was in hospital was reinforced somewhat by the long tube sticking out of my arm and the crisp white coats that were heading in my direction. There was no getting away from the fact that I was not getting out of this one any time soon.

The doctors were doing their morning rounds, and I was next on the list. I tried my best to look interested and concerned as it was explained to me that I had very nearly drunk myself to death, and that my heart had to be reset with the aid of CPR and an electrical defibrillator. All this treatment had been administered in the back of the ambulance, and was the cause of the bruising on my chest. I'd been put on a saline drip to flush out my system, and had been monitored throughout the night. The doctor asked if I had any questions. All I wanted to know was when I could leave, and where were my clothes?

He answered both questions, but all I could hear was that my clothes had been incinerated after being cut from my drunken body due to the fact that I had soiled them somewhat during my brief but rapid journey to the hospital. Oh! This was not good! I was in a hospital ward with real ill people. I felt like a fraud that had no right being there and had brought all this on myself. I had to get out as quickly and as quietly as possible. But with no clothes or money, it would take ingenuity and stealth.

There was a ward telephone, so with the ten pence acquired from my neighbouring inmate, I phoned the only man I knew who could get me out of there without any fuss, Stephen Hyer.

Stephen arrived within the hour with a completely new set of clobber, including socks and shoes. He then helped me, complete with saline drip, to the bathroom where I had to painfully unfasten the intravenous line and get dressed into my new outfit. I emerged from the bathroom and Stephen and I casually wandered past the information desk, down to the reception area, and out of the main entrance to the car park, where Stephen's white Rolls Royce Corniche Convertible was parked. "Lunch?" asked Stephen.

We parked the car back at Stephen's in Hyde Park Street, and caught a cab back into Mayfair where we went to one of Stephen's favourite fish restaurants, Stocks. Before the menus had even arrived, I had ordered a beer with a large brandy chaser. After the night I'd just had, I needed a fucking drink!

John Entwistle and I had become quite good friends over the past couple of years, mostly due to the clubs that we both frequented. We found it amusing that people were always surprised that John and I had known each other from way back. Remember, most people we socialised with had no idea about any 'Mod Revival' or Quadrophenia. Most people only knew me from Metal Mickey, which bemused people even more.

John had a flat in London which he shared with his fiancé Maxine, who was an American lass. He also shared it with a large tarantula spider called Doris, who sat in a specially heated tank devouring live locusts. Every now and then John would let Doris out for a little play, and Doris liked nothing more than crawling up your arm to sit on your shoulder, where she would then sit motionless for hours—me included...

John even wore a spider around his neck. He'd had this amazing onyx and white gold arachnid made, which rested (just like Doris) on his chest just below the neck line and I rarely (if ever) saw John without it. John was actually scared of spiders though, which is why he bought Doris in the first place.

John's job was being a rock star, and he did his job very well. He was always working on other musical projects when not performing with The Who, and he took his bass playing seriously. You don't get voted onto the best ever bass players of all-time lists by sitting on your arse playing rock-band.

There were always brand new guitars all over the flat that the manufacturers wanted John to endorse, and I was lucky enough to get to play them all. He was a musical genius, in my humble opinion, who'd known all about arrangement and harmony from a very early age.

His style of bass playing was totally unique to him. Ask any other bass player, especially those who are in Who tribute bands and they will tell you the same thing. Fucking special! Yes John was a proper fucking rock star. And he had a proper fucking rock star's house in the country too.

It was New Year's Eve 1985, Rian was four months pregnant, and we were planning a quiet one with friends at Troy's club. I had arranged to meet an actor friend of mine called Ken Sharrock* and his girlfriend for a few light ales before seeing the New Year in, and then getting a cab back to Brixton for just after midnight.

We arranged to meet early so we could be assured of somewhere for Rian to park her rapidly expanding arse, and also get some much needed food. When we arrived, Helen informed me that a girl called Max had been trying to contact me all afternoon, and I had to call her back as soon as possible.

Quarwood

It was Maxine Entwhistle who had been trying all afternoon to get hold of me. The only other number she had was my mum's, so Mum had given Maxine Troy's number as a possible place I could be contacted. John and Max were having a party and I had to go.

I explained that I had guests and that it might be a tad strenuous for Rian, but Max was insistent that we would all be well catered for, but should leave right now if we were going to get to Stow-On-The-Wold (wherever the fuck that was) before midnight. She told me the house was called Quarwood, and that was it. All I had was Quarwood, Stow-On-The-Wold, and we were going.

I went back to the table and asked everyone what they thought we should do. Ken and his girlfriend thought I was joking, but Rian knew that I wasn't, and started checking her bag to make sure she had all her essentials. Ken's girl had a map and a Mini, so we downed our drinks, bade everyone a happy new year, then jumped in the car and headed out of central London into a blanket of thick fog towards Gloucestershire.

*Ken Sharrock was born 11th December, 1946 in Liverpool and died 29th November, 2005 in London. He was an English actor who played Derek Taylor in *EastEnders*. He played Den Booth in the 1980 BBC TV series of Angels. He was also a lead actor in Steven Berkoff's *West*, premiered at the Donar Warehouse theatre in London in 1983. He appeared in several films including *Prayer for The Dying* and *Shirley Valentine*. He died on the 20th November, 2003.

We must've been driving for a couple of hours in what we thought was the right direction, when we eventually came to a little place called Lower Slaughter, which had a pub. Ken and I went in to ask for directions to Quarwood and were relieved to find out that the house was only a couple more miles further up the road. We knocked back a couple of large brandies (just to be sociable of course) and got back in the car with the ladies.

Just the outside entrance to this house was imposing, with a large Gothic Gate flanked either side with huge stone lions that looked hungry but stately. I rang the intercom and the gates slowly opened onto a driveway that led (after about five minutes) to the door of the main house where John and Max were waiting to greet us.

"You made it," John said. "Let's get pissed!"

Walking into his bar hung with the lifeless bodies of shark and marlin that he had caught himself, we were confronted by some of the other guests that included actors John Hurt and Robert Powell, drummers Kenny Jones and Zak Starkey, Midge Ure and Jim Diamond, the Glaswegian singer of the worldwide number one hit 'I Should've Known Better'.

John was behind the bar mixing drinks. His favourite, the Link-Up, went down rather well; being three parts Stolichnaya vodka to three parts Southern Comfort. He'd created it, he said, to commemorate the joining of Russian and American space modules.

He also made Traffic Lights, with Crème de Menthe and cherry brandy, and the Good King Wenceslas, a recipe that he claimed to have stolen from Paul Young, so lethal you didn't need to know what was in it, just where you would be spending the next four days after drinking it!

The house was a cross between an eccentric country pile and a museum, and contained all sorts of random stuff. Toys, teapots, suits of armour, weaponry, (especially guns), train-sets, lighters, porcelain Disney figures, rugs, fine art and photography. There were also a couple of life-size skeletons and a space invaders and pinball machine.

There were also two blokes dressed in police uniforms, who turned out to be the actual local village cops just popping in for a quick New Year's Eve drink. Once they had left, Party!

The following day Rian and I woke up to a crisp January morning and the smell of bacon. I managed to manoeuvre my alcohol-sodden, drug-addled carcass down to the kitchen where John's mum Queenie was preparing breakfast for any early survivors. Apparently, according to Queenie, the party had been a huge success because nobody had been arrested or found running naked in the grounds, yet.

Queenie had witnessed a few of John's parties over the years, I think, and she just seemed to take all this rock n roll stuff completely in her stride. I couldn't even remember going to bed. According to Rian, I fell into most people's bedrooms (all fifteen of them) until I found the one with her in it, and then just passed out.

After breakfast, John showed me around the house. I had been completely pissed from the moment we had arrived the evening before, but now I wanted to see everything. Quarwood House stood in 42 acres of parkland which included numerous fish ponds, paddocks, woodlands, 7 cottages, and a host of garages to accommodate John's fleet of cars.

John also collected cars: Cadillac's, Thunderbirds and even a Rolls-Royce that he'd had converted into an estate car to drive his Irish wolfhound 'Fits Perfectly' around. John had never learnt to drive though, and said he liked the cars just to drink in.

John had built two recording studios in the house, one upstairs and one downstairs. The downstairs studio was set up for live playing and recording, whilst the upstairs was for new ideas and mastering. The real joy for me, though, was seeing John's unparalleled collection of bass guitars. He had everything! Fenders, Gibbons, Deans, Alembics, Wals, Status', and a few that had been designed just for him.

John asked me if I could have any bass guitar in the world, what would it be? I had to think for a few minutes as that was like asking what your favourite cake of all time was. I settled on something classic and personal. A 1959 Fender Precision. John said "What colour?" I said "Powder blue", he said, "Hang on a minute." He then went rummaging through the many cases littered around his bass room and eventually pulled out a dusty old hard case that looked like it had been in a war zone. "There you go," he said. Funny Fucker!

John and Maxine

Spending the short time that I had in John Entwistle's company had been incredible, but I couldn't help thinking that he was always looking for the ultimate high that could never be achieved. Waking up to a line of cocaine and a large brandy just makes you look at life in a different way, I suppose, especially when money is no object. Customizing a Rolls Royce to fit an Irish Wolfhound dog should give you some idea of the way John spent his days when he got bored.

Quite out of the blue, I started getting some production work. The first singer I worked with was a lady called Christina whom I'd been introduced to at Stringfellows. She had no real talent at all apart from being rich, which suited me fine. It was a strange time musically, with lots of new machines to play with. For the amount of money that she was paying me I decided that she would be better suited recording in London's West End, so I hired Tin Pan Alley.

By now, I was used to the studio and the engineers and Crispin Buxton always gave me a good deal, so I wrote Christina a funky little ditty, and apart from the drums, played everything else myself. There was one piece of equipment that everyone was talking about called The Fairlight Series 111. It cost about £20,000 and needed its own truck to deliver it. It had about three seconds of sampling time, which was a bit of a novelty at the time. We hired one for the session, and spent two days trying to work out how to turn the damn thing on. Funny to think that an average mobile telephone now has more processing power than The Fairlight ever had.

The next project was for a DJ called Mike Anthony who was living in Belgium but wanted to record in London. He had a manager and everything. They all came over on the ferry to spend a week recording at Tin Pan Alley. I was a little surprised to find out that he didn't actually have any material, but the budget was good, so I hired some musicians and we wrote the song as we recorded. Two of the musicians I'd been recommended were incredible musos. They were identical twins called Paul and Jeremy Stacey who would go on to work with the likes of Oasis, amongst others. Once the song had been recorded, Mike Anthony's management felt that the song should be mixed and mastered in a digital studio that they had in Belgium. Rian was getting larger by the day, but she insisted that I wasn't going anywhere without her, so we packed a couple of bags and headed to the ferry port. I had also roped in my old pal from Portland Studios, Andy 'Killer' Miller, to take care of the engineering duties, and my London contact from the record company Brian Allen would also be joining us.

As soon as we docked into the ferry port of Ghent, we very quickly realised that we were completely unprepared for the weather. It was the worst winter on record, apparently. It was so cold that the fluid in your face froze, which was an interesting sensation, but we all huddled in the back of Mike's manager's little Fiat, which had snow chains on the wheels, and made the slow journey to Brussels.

They had rented us a house that looked like it should've been in a magazine. It was incredible, with a fully stocked fridge and bar and all the bedrooms had en-suite bathrooms. This was a bit different to the little attic that Rian and I were used to in Brixton, and I was really glad that Rian had insisted on coming with me. This would be a little holiday for us before we would have to get down to the impending job of parenthood. The recording studio was equally as impressive. They even had a chef and waiters. Lunch was ordered daily from an extensive menu, and gin & tonics were on a regular supply. The song didn't sound too shabby either.

I had to record three versions of the song, which was called "She's so Fine," one for radio, one for a club mix, and one for a twelve inch. For anyone under the age of 50, a twelve inch was basically just an extended version of the radio edit. I'd recorded plenty of stuff back in London, so re-editing was a joy. The record did really well in Belgium and reached number three in their hit parade. So we sold about 50 records then.

On May 16, 1986, I became a father. I wish I could say that becoming a father changed me into a responsible human being, but it didn't. In fact, I actually got worse. Work seemed to have dried up just when I needed it most, and of course being totally unqualified to do anything other than act or write music meant that I was at the mercy of my mum and dad. They, of course, were incredibly practical and somehow found us a council flat on the worst estate in North London. I hated it with a vengeance. I become a snob, looking down on my fellow estate dwellers from my self- appointed lofty perch, whilst in reality I was just another out-of-work dole scrounger like everyone else. Whilst I should've been enjoying being a new dad, I resented it, and when Rian said she would go back to work to support us, I resented that even more.

I was definitely not a natural father in any sense of the word. I missed my lifestyle and my friends in Brixton. Even though I loved the idea of being a dad, in reality, it was too much for me to cope with. I started drinking at home.

I never tried to hide the fact that I liked a drink, everyone knew that, but I had never been a secret drinker. Now, though, I started to drink in private. Looking back, this should've been the happiest time of my life, but it was hell. I was so bored and lonely and drinking seemed to stem the pain and resentment that I felt. It was a magical cure. These days everyone has fucking depression. Every morning someone is sitting on a TV couch prattling on about being pissed off. Back then, depression was not something to be talked about, or even discussed.

I wasn't fooling anyone. Even my closest friends stopped coming over to see me, so I made new ones from the local pool of petty thieves and criminals that seemed to be in abundance. Rian was not living with the person that she'd met at The Hippodrome anymore, and when I looked into her eyes she just looked trapped and disappointed. Then, all of a sudden, I received a lifeline.

My agent Sharon (who I thought had left the country) called me one day to ask if I'd be interested in doing a play at the Edinburgh Festival. At this point I would've been interested in doing a training film for the Klu Klux Klan, but I played the game and agreed to meet the producers of a piece called *Sleaze and Dreams*.

The play had been written by a feminist writer who obviously was not a fan of the male gender, but what made it interesting for me was that it was being produced by the drummer from a band called Dire Straits, Pick Withers.* Pick had commissioned the play as a vehicle for his wife Linda, who had ambitions of becoming an actress, but until now was only paying for private acting classes with a tutor.

I met them in their London flat to discuss the role (the male lead) and we all got on well enough, so when the money was agreed (which was brilliant for the Edinburgh Festival) I made plans to leave London for rehearsals to be held at Pick's main house in Monmouth, Wales. After the first day I knew the Director, who was Linda's acting coach, had to go. I think it was the cravat that did it.

After about a week of rehearsing with a director who thought he was Orson Welles, I told Pick and Linda that it was either me going, or him, but if they trusted me I would secure the services of a great director who I knew well. Trevor Laird had been a founder member of the Black Theatre Cooperative and had directed many of their plays, some of which I'd seen. Trevor was also a good friend from when I'd started my career in *Quadrophenia,* and I knew that at that moment he wasn't working. I arranged a meeting and Trevor was hired.

Trevor started by making some radical cast changes, bringing in Carl Chase with whom I'd worked with on *The Bride*, and a very scary black girl called Pauline Black who I knew from the Ska band The Selecter. Pauline was on a sabbatical from the band, and she was now trying her hand at acting. Also in the cast was an Italian/American actor called Dondi Bastone that Linda and Pick had flown specially over from Los Angeles to play the part of a cross-dressing magician (don't ask). It really was a strange show.

---

*David "Pick" Withers is an English rock drummer. He was the original drummer for the rock band Dire Straits and played on their first four albums, which included hit singles such as "Sultans of Swing," "Romeo and Juliet" and "Private Investigations."

Ask most actors what their first experience of doing The Edinburgh Festival was like, and most would say that it meant having no money, crap accommodation and hardly any audiences. Well we certainly had money (due to Pick Wither's massive royalty cheques for selling a zillion records), plus we had beautiful flats rented on the outskirts of Edinburgh, but yes, we had sparse audiences due to the fact (in my opinion) that the venue for the show wasn't central enough. Most festival goers will attend a show on a whim if you make it easy for them, but to see *Sleaze and Dreams* meant getting a bus or hiking, which American and Japanese tourists are just not programmed to do. It was a real shame as the show was actually very entertaining and fun to watch.

I loved Edinburgh and the whole festival atmosphere. Our show wasn't on until late evening so I spent the days, if I didn't see a show, exploring the city which spreads at the foot of Edinburgh Castle in multiple directions. Of course I missed Rian and the baby, but this was the break that I needed to see if I could fathom out what was wrong with me, if anything. I loved being away so much that I felt guilty as hell, but as long as I was earning some money for my family, I justified my pleasure. One night I think I took my pleasure-seeking too far.

One night after the show, Dondi Bastone and I went to a late bar to try some rare Edinburgh whisky. I'd gone out in a beautiful suede and leather jacket, but woke up on the steps of Edinburgh Cathedral the following morning in an old donkey jacket. To this very day, I have absolutely no explanation. Oh yes, I was drunk.

Mark Bramble was a successful theatrical impresario, and I didn't give two flying fucks. My amply- proportioned agent, Sharon, had taken me to Joe Allen's in

Covent Garden to meet him for dinner. Mark had produced and directed some serious box office hit shows. He was a legend in the theatrical world, and I liked him on first sight. He'd already written, produced, and directed shows called *Barnham* and *42ⁿᵈ Street*, but for his next production he required actors who could sing, dance, juggle, stilt walk and be prepared to work like slaves for very little pay, get sweaty, tight rope walk, do gymnastics and not ask questions. I wasn't asking any. The show was called *Fat Pig* and was about an extremely large pig who sings and dances whilst trying to lose weight to avoid getting the chop from a farmer that no one ever sees. I thought it was a rubbish idea, but it didn't matter. All I wanted was to be away from the nightmare world that I had created for myself in London.

The rehearsals started at the Leicester Haymarket theatre at some ridiculous time in the morning when I really should've been waking up in a rehab unit. Of course, I arrived late but looked fantastic in a silver-grey, two piece suit with matching tie and shoes. Everyone else in the cast were already dressed in warm-up clothes, ready to start rehearsals. As I walked into the room, Mark Bramble introduced me to the assembled cast of fresh faced performers who were limbering up.

(American Drawl) "Ladies and gentlemen, this is Gary Shail, he is late, and he doesn't care!"

Fat Pig was an expensive production to mount. The costumes were ridiculously heavy but beautifully made and must've cost an absolute fortune to make. I was playing a wild boar called Snorter and I had my own show-stopping number, which I had to sing through a piece of gauze that restricted every orifice in my face.

I hated it so much; I spent the whole time in rehearsal lusting after the girls dressed as chickens. There were three of them, and one of them was called Lindsey. Henry Krieger had written the music, which for me was the best thing about this show. I cannot express just what a genius this bloke was. Henry had previously written the music for a show called *Dreamgirls*, which was loosely based on the fictitious (Motown) story of a megalomaniac manager who forms a girl group with three very attractive black girls (Sound familiar?). Apparently the recorded music for *Dreamgirls* had been a huge hit in America, but due to the objections of a certain superstar who liked to be touched in the morning, it had been put on hold whilst all the lawyers sorted out alleged libel allegations.

Eventually, *Dreamgirls* was made into a movie starring some of Hollywood's finest A-listers, and would win an Oscar for the newcomer Jennifer Hudson. Henry Krieger got there in the end though, winning a Grammy for the original album and three Academy nominations for the songs in the movie.

I shared a dressing room with a guy called David Morris, who was quite frankly insane. He was playing an Elvis impersonating duck and had to perform one of the opening numbers. He'd been given his duck-head to rehearse with and started talking to it regularly. At first I thought he was doing it just for my amusement, but I once heard him arguing with it whilst I was on the other side of the door. "You want to go on my head don't you? Well you fucking can't, you stupid fucking head," etc. He also loved shagging inanimate objects such as tables and chairs, but nothing was out of bounds for David, including a couple of the local girls who'd been brought in as dressers for the show. Funnily enough, it was David's insanity that helped me cope with a show that I clearly should never been a part of. I wanted out.

David Morris 2015: "I have to say, that job was three months of sheer unadulterated HELL! Gary played a pig and I was a duck and everyone in the show wore a fucking animal head, which no one fucking knew about until we turned up in nobbing Leicester where the show was on for three years. Well that's what it felt like. Leicester, a friendly place? A friend of Gary's came to visit, lovely bloke named Mark Wingett (aka Damage). One night, after two wonderful shows of "fucked up pig", Gary, Mark, me and a few others went for a stroll into town, where we were set upon by a bunch of the locals who just decided, for some reason, to punch Mark Wingett in the face. There was a general fracas, the police came, and we all ended up in the police station. In the end they threw us all out, as I don't think they could cope with mine and Gary's antics and also Gary's continual request for a pint and a whiskey chaser, and of course me shagging all the furniture!! We all ended up in this massive waiting room cab office where unbelievably all the guys that had attacked us a few hours before were. As we walked in the whole place went quiet, and we all stood there looking at each other, you could have heard a pin drop. Then Gary screamed "COME ON YOU CUNTS —which one of you wants to take me on CCCOOOMMMEEE OOOONNNN!!" I, for some reason, put a pair of leather gloves on, did a spin round and we all went outside. Not one of them followed us, so we all jumped in a cab and went home. Just another normal day in Leicester."

I don't know what the health and safety laws were in 1987, but I certainly don't remember being made aware of any. This show was downright dangerous, and that's saying something if I thought so. Doing stilt walking or whatever is bad enough, but doing it in a 50 pound costume with an animal head on and very limited vision was suicidal. Even without the costumes it was madness, as I found out to my cost.

One of the circus performers had to do a stunt called a cloud swing. It involved being hoisted above the auditorium, between two pieces of rope (hence the swing). "Sounds like fun," I thought. What a terribly bad decision that was. I got the rope tied (Unintentionally, I might add) around my neck and very quickly turned a beautiful shade of blue. How the hell was I even allowed to be up there? If it hadn't been for a gymnast called Paul Miller who shot up a safety rope to untangle me, I have no doubts that I would've known what Ruth Ellis's final thoughts were.

Thank God for the beautiful distraction that was a chicken called Lindsey.

16

"Oh, don't you worry about Gary...Gary will always land on somebody's feet."

I never denied that I had a girlfriend and a young child back in London. I was very proud of them, and if mobile phones had been as prevalent as they are now, then I'm sure it would have been filled with photos of both of them. Before leaving for Leicester, I had done a couple of days filming for a new TV cop show, and had a one night stand with the leading lady, who happened to be married. A now-defunct tabloid newspaper called The News of the World had got wind of it and printed the story in the sordid way that the paper was well- known for. Rian had been mortified, embarrassed, and humiliated in equal measure, and I didn't blame her for kicking me out. This had been the reason for me doing this show in the first place, and also the reason why I hadn't walked away from it. Now that I was once again free and single, I saw no reason not to blank my pain with a lovely new relationship, oh yes… and alcohol.

For my 27th birthday that November, Lindsey and the rest of the cast had bought me a litre bottle of scotch, which in retrospect was totally irresponsible, but most appreciated. I kept it in my dressing room and stayed topped up for days.

Mine and Lindsey's relationship started off tentatively, but over the rehearsal period, blossomed into a full-blown love affair with all the excitement and heart fluttering that goes with it. She really was five foot two, with eyes of blue and we had lots in common.

Toto Coelo

Lindsey had been in an all-girl group called Toto Coelo, who'd had a top ten hit in 1982 with a song called 'I Eat Cannibals'. They went on to make a follow up single and album, but it never really hit the big time, which was a shame in my humble opinion, as they really were way ahead of their time. In 1994, a very similar group was formed called The Spice Girls, and they certainly got it right, didn't they?!

As a solo performer though, Lindsey was fantastic. For someone who was so small and petit, she had a voice that could stop a truck in its tracks with a personality to match. She was now singing with a rock band called Call Me Wayne (??) and she'd played me their debut album which I thought was brilliant. Then again, I was biased wasn't I?

Lindsey was also a born-again Christian, which I found a tad worrying, as I thought she might try to save me, but my drinking (which I had curbed dramatically) didn't seem to bother her too much. After all, it had been her idea to buy me the scotch for my birthday.

I had been living on my own in a cheap hotel near the theatre, but now Lil (as I now called her) and I felt our relationship had moved on far enough for us to live together, albeit in some shabby guest house in Leicester, but as far as I was concerned it might as well have been The Ritz. I had fallen completely in love with this girl and couldn't imagine another minute without her. One evening after rehearsals, Lindsey asked me to marry her. We had known each other less than a month!

Our engagement caused quite some excitement amongst our fellow cast members, and the management wasted no time in using the news to publicise the show. The local paper ran the headline "PIG AND CHICKEN TO TIE THE KNOT", and we did a few local radio shows where we talked about our whirlwind romance. All this made doing the show bearable for me and as Christmas 1987 approached, I felt that at last this could be a new beginning for me. Oh yes…and Lil.

We had a few days off for the festivities and headed back to London to break the news to our families. Mark Bramble's assistant, a lovely guy called William Butler-Sloss whose mum was the high court judge Baroness Elizabeth Butler-Sloss*, drove me back to my parents where he had been invited to spend Christmas Day. After lunch, I broke the news about my future intentions, whereupon my mother carried on with the washing up and my dad continued playing with his new toys. To them this was normal Gary behaviour and certainly not to be taken seriously. As for my two sisters, they were already planning their wedding outfits.

In the evening we drove over to Putney where Lil's parents owned a restaurant by the river. They were holding a family party which, by the time we got there, was in full swing. It was fantastic.

They were all so theatrical. Lil's dad was an actor, her beautiful mum had once been an actress but now ran the restaurant, and her brother Tommy was a musician and DJ. They played brilliant Christmas party games, and the wine flowed like there was no tomorrow. I was going to love being a member of this family, I thought, so after a while, and when we gauged that the time was right, we announced our engagement.

To be completely honest, I thought they'd have begged Lindsey to run a mile, but they all seemed really happy at the prospect of having me as a son-in-law, and I was made to feel so welcome that I actually thought that this wedding could actually happen.

*Ann Elizabeth Oldfield Butler-Sloss, Baroness Butler-Sloss, GBE, PC, is a retired English judge. She was the first female Lord Justice of Appeal and, until 2004, was the highest-ranking female judge in the United Kingdom. Until June 2007, she chaired the inquests into the deaths of Diana, Princess of Wales, and Dodi Fayed. She stood down from that task with effect from that date, and the inquest was conducted by Lord Justice Scott Baker.

Lil had a little attic flat just a stone's throw from the restaurant that she actually owned. It was tiny but bijoux. She had made a table out of bricks and a pane of glass that I found particularly aesthetically pleasing, and she had a knack of making everyday objects look like works of art, which by its very nature is an art form in itself.

Lil was actually a year older than me (which I found strangely comforting), and she'd had some broken heart stories of her own. Her very being seemed to be about caring for others though, and when she talked about life, her eyes flamed. I truly believed she believed that she had been chosen by God to help people with their pain and suffering. She was without a doubt the nicest woman I had ever met. What the fuck she wanted me for though, well only God himself could've answered that one. But with Lindsey at my side who knew? Maybe I could get to know God too. Or at least get an introduction.

To say how guilty I felt at finding such happiness in such a short time after leaving Rian and the baby was an understatement. And I drank on it whenever that pain of guilt got too much. It was a constant battle of emotions. One minute I was enthusing about something and the next moment I'd be in a complete fucking mess. After a few ales though, life once again would be sweet. It was like being on the scariest ride in Disney World. I find it incredible that no one, not even Lil, thought that I might need help. Maybe they did, but just didn't think I'd listen. They were right.

Back in Leicester, *Fat Pig* thundered on to its tragic but inevitable demise. On some of the matinee performances all the audience consisted of was a few toffee chewing grannies and their carers. It was soul-destroying for the cast who would have to spend serious time getting into the costumes, and then risk life and limb for an almost empty theatre. I argued with the management about cancelling some of these shows, but my protests fell on deaf ears. The show had already lost thousands of pounds, so any money coming in, no matter how little, was a bonus. We were the last of their concerns.

One brief moment of levity though was when we were asked to appear on the children's factual BBC TV show *Blue Peter*. We all travelled down to London on a coach to perform selected *Fat Pig* scenes live. It was like a school journey, with packed lunches, fizzy pop and sing-songs.

After the show we all had to get back on the coach back to Leicester to perform again that evening. One good thing though, I got a Blue Peter Badge.

Being back in London, I felt a mixture of emotions. I certainly didn't have enough money to buy somewhere for Lil and I to live, so it was decided that I would move in with her. This was certainly not an ideal situation for me, and must've been a real strain for her. Lil had been used to living on her own, and although she told me to make the flat my own, I knew it never would be.

Of course I tried to send money to Rian and the baby whenever I could, and my mum and dad helped out enormously, but still I felt like a complete failure. Funny that I always managed to find enough money for wine though.

Being in Putney was refreshing. The flat was two minutes from the river, which I loved, and very often I would sit on its banks reading or just watching the world float by. For the last few years I had been living out of a suitcase, so it was nice to feel grounded for a while.

Lindsey subsidized our existence by working in her mum's restaurant, which was great as there were no travelling expenses, and as her dad was an actor he knew what it was like to be out of work, so I wasn't put under any pressure to get off my drunken arse to find a job.

It was decided that we would have an August wedding (certainly not by me) and it would be the full-on church affair. Meetings were held upstairs in the restaurant about colour schemes, invitations, catering, entertainment, venues, menus, and anything else that could be remotely missed that might scar the perfect day. This was going to be the wedding of the year as far as Lil's family were concerned. I only requested one thing; I got to choose the minister who would marry us.

John Arrowsmith had been the Chaplin at The Arts Educational School, where he also taught Religious Education. For most young people this could be classed as the most boring subject on the fucking planet, but not with John. He made the Bible come alive, especially the Old Testament, with all the fire and brimstone, pestilence and Wrath of God stuff. He'd been an actor in his youth, so he knew how to tell a story. I got in touch with John, and Lindsey and I visited him in his little flat in Brighton to discuss the wedding service. With John at the helm, I knew it wouldn't be boring.

It is funny, that in only one day, one's life can change completely. This is why suicide should never be an option in my opinion. I'm not saying that I haven't thought about it, and even threatened it on occasion, but I am far too curious about tomorrow to actually go through with it. One particularly fine day, I got a call from my old Stunt Gaffer Peter Braham.

Within two hours, I was in the west end of London sat in the plush offices of a certain David Wickes*. David Wickes and Peter Braham had worked together for many years on some classic British TV shows, and this sounded like it was going to be another one. The story of Jack the Ripper had been already done to death over the years, but this new version promised something new.

*David Wickes is one of the UK's most renowned producer/directors and an early pioneer of UK-American television network co-productions. He has also made several successful theatrical feature films.

I listened incredulously as David told me that in his film the identity of the most famous murderer in the history of time would be revealed. He had to be joking, I thought, but no, David was deadly serious. The production had started the year before, but was halted in December 1987, after the American television network CBS became interested in the project and most of the original cast and crew were paid off. They thought that with more money they could acquire the services of a much bigger star to play the leading role of Inspector Abberline. Now, with an $11 million budget they did just that, and stars didn't come any bigger than Michael Caine.

Whilst I was sitting (open mouthed), listening to David, Peter kept smiling and winking at me. David said that Peter thought I would be perfect for the part of an integral character called Billy White who was the East End Pimp in charge of the murdered prostitutes. It would involve some stunt work that Peter had assured him I could handle effortlessly, and if I wanted it, then the part was mine.

I hadn't had to read or anything. This amazing opportunity hadn't come from my agent, but an East End Jewish stunt man, whom I'd first met down in Brighton a decade earlier when I was just a baby with stars in his eyes. I wanted to scream the fucking house down.

After leaving David Wickes' offices, and promising wedding invitations to everyone including the receptionists, I walked the short distance to my full-bosomed agent Sharon's office to tell her the news. As I walked down Regent Street everyone seemed to be smiling at me as if they knew my news. Even the London pollution smelled sweet. I stopped off at a hot dog vendor at Oxford Circus and treated myself to lunch.

Sharon was her normal bubbly self and happy to see me, as usual. In all the years she's represented me, I had never had to make an appointment to see her. She'd come a long way since our first encounter in the bar at The Arts, and we were much more than just agent/client. I helped her out when her ceiling collapsed in her dingy Maida Vale flat, and we never missed each other's birthday. I met her parents and her little brother whom I'd taken on a tour of Soho's sex district when he was a curious thirteen year old. I'd even suggested new clients for her books. Jonathan Caplan, David John and Trevor Laird were all now making money for her. Sharon to me was far more than just my agent. She was my friend.

Jack the Ripper began filming in February, 1988, at Pinewood Studios. I'd been picked up for my first day's filming early in the morning by a unit car that would then stop off in Fulham to pick up another cast member. Her name was Lysette Anthony. I'd never met Lysette, but knew her from the television show Three Up, Two Down, in which she had starred with my old mate Michael Elphick. She was devastatingly beautiful even at that time in the morning and with no make-up. I, on the other hand, had been told not to shave or worry about my appearance, as the character of Billy White was a completely unwashed scumbag. It didn't make me feel any better though.

I already knew from the cast list that I would be meeting some old friends whilst working on this film. Jonathan Moore, with whom I'd worked with at the Young Vic on *Class Enemy*, was playing a newspaper reporter called Benjamin Bates, and Gary Love, playing a young police officer, was the son of a good friend of mine Allan Love*. The most exciting prospect for me, though, was that I would be teaming up with my old mate Lewis Collins.

The last time I had seen him was when he had thrown us out of a plane, so today would be payback, as on my very first day we would be shooting a fight scene. I already knew from the script that I had to lose, but thought I could probably get a sly dig in his ribs before I went down.

I will be honest and say that the thought of working with the legend that is Caine did make my heart skip a beat slightly. I have never been that easily impressed (I had worked with McCartney, for fuck sake), but it's hard not to be in awe of an actor who has made films like *Alfie, Zulu, The Italian Job, Get Carter, Educating Rita, The Swarm, (Sorry Michael), A Bridge Too Far, The Eagle Has Landed, The Ipcress File, Dressed To Kill, Hannah And Her Sisters* (Academy Award Winner) OK you get the point. Yes you could say that I was slightly nervous…

Pinewood Studios had been completely transformed into the Victorian East End of London, but was far less filthy than I thought it would be, for some reason. This, I was told, was because the film was also being aimed at the Americans, who wouldn't believe that British people, even in 1888, could possibly live in such squalor. Ahh I thought, that must be why all the whores in my charge look so incredibly gorgeous. And the most gorgeous of the lot was the actress playing

Catherine Eddowes, Jack's fourth victim. To be played by Susan George.

When I was about twelve years old, mum had let me stay up late to watch, what in the old days was called an X film, called *Straw Dogs*, and it had scared the shit out of me. Its star was Dustin Hoffman, but all I could remember, when I went to bed, was the 21year old blonde girl whose name was Susan George.

---

*Allan Love is an actor and composer, known for 'Gregory's Girl' (1981), 'The Apple' (1980) and 'That Sinking Feeling' (1979)

As I was sitting in the hair and makeup wagon having my teeth discoloured, I heard a familiar voice. "Well there goes the fucking neighbourhood." It was Lewis Collins, and he looked fantastic. He had lost loads of weight and looked fit and lean. He had grown a little moustache, which really suited him, and he looked dapper in his period suit and fedora.

I couldn't answer as I had a paint brush in my mouth, but then I heard a voice that was instantly recognizable. Michael Caine wanted to know if Lewis and I wanted to run some lines. I so wanted to say, "Sorry Mike, but I'm a bit busy at the mo". I held back, but Lewis could already see that today was going to be a bloody good laugh. He was not wrong.

Normally if an actor has to do anything remotely risky, it would usually be left until the end of the day- for obvious reasons, but because I was on the Stunt Register, Peter Braham felt that we could push the boat out and shoot the scenes from multiple angles. Peter would be directing the bar room brawl as the 2nd unit director. Before that though, David Wickes wanted to shoot the establishing lead-up scenes. This would involve me having to talk to Susan George.

They say you should never meet your heroes, and I have always tended to agree with this statement, as I have met quite a few arseholes in my time that I had previously admired. Here is the list. Hahahaha…are you mad? But it's true to say that the bigger the star, the less the ego. Susan, by my calculations, was now 38 years old, and I still would've. She was absolutely stunning and charming in equal measure. She was word perfect, as was I, and we did the first scene in two or three takes.

During a break, whilst the crew were setting up for the next scene, I looked around to see who else was about. For the fight sequences there would be chairs and tables flying around as well as bottles, so Peter would surround the actors with stunt performers. One of these was an old warhorse called Jazzer Jeyes.

Jazzer was a true legend. He had performed stunts in every James Bond movie since 1967 and one of his specialities was fire. I asked him in all seriousness how he'd avoided being burnt in all these years, and he casually replied "You Don't." He then rolled up one of his sleeves to reveal an arm that looked like it had been on the barbecue for an hour.

Lunch on a film set can be spectacular, and on this one the food was incredible. Lewis and I knew that after lunch we would be throwing each other around, so we decided not to go for the fantastic homemade steak and mushroom pie, and settled with the salad selection instead.

The other thing that you will not find on a film set these days is alcohol, but back then trying to stop actors having a tipple at lunchtime was unheard of. I drank fruit juice. It has always been a mystery for me how I can just quit drinking when my mind is occupied. It just isn't an issue at all. I don't get the shakes or anything. It's like the booze saying, 'There you go Gazza…have some time off and enjoy yourself…don't worry son…I will still be here when you get bored!'

After lunch, we got down to business. As I would be the one doing all the flying about, Peter wanted to pad me up. Obviously these pads couldn't be seen, so we put one around my lower back and one for each elbow. I always hated having to do this because the restriction in movement can often cause more problems than the benefits. Peter was adamant though, as I would have to do this scene multiple times, and with more action stuff to shoot the following day, he didn't want to take any risks. You never argued with your gaffer, and you most certainly never argued with Peter Braham, so I put them on. Lewis Collins called me a poofter.

The scene begins with me shouting at Mary Jane Kelly (Lysette) and Susan's character Catherine Eddowes. Sgt George Godley (Lewis) intervenes to ask questions, and is met with a tirade of abuse from Billy (Me). Whereupon Sgt Godley attempts to arrest Billy, leading him away from the table. Billy takes great exception to this and retaliates by breaking a beer bottle against the bar and tries to stab poor Godley in the face. On his third attempt Godley parries the lunge and gives Billy a right hander, which sends him crashing into the bar. All hell breaks loose and Godley finds himself having to fight off multiple assailants. Billy, seeing his chance to escape, manoeuvres himself through the melee towards the door. Godley catches him though, grabs him by the scruff of the neck, and throws him through the closed door and out into the street. Take 1, ACTION.

The first time we did it, everything went like clockwork until Lewis threw me through the door. The carpenters had put it on the wrong way round and I just bounced back into the room. Everyone burst out laughing, and we had to do the whole fucking thing again. Now I knew why Peter had insisted on the pads.

The rest of the day was spent doing pick-up and reaction shots, and then it was a wrap for the day. My next call was for the following evening where the action would take place on the other side of the door and where I would be sprawled in the mud at the feet of Inspector Abberline, played by Sir Michael Caine.

On the drive back to Putney I took stock of the day and how my life had completely changed once again. I didn't know what to think, to be honest. All I knew for certain was when I was being collected the following afternoon, what lines I had to learn and what bruises had to be tended to, oh... and I was getting married in six months..."HI HONEY, I'M HOME!"

I love night shoots, I think there is something very romantic about filming at night. I find the same with making music. Normal everyday distractions just seem to melt away, and I have always found it easier to concentrate when the sun goes down.

As I was sitting in hair and make-up with Lewis and Michael, David Wickes came into the trailer to tell us that he had seen the previous day's rushes (What we'd filmed the day before) and they were fantastic. Obviously everything had to be edited together, but as far as he was concerned nothing would have to be re-shot. He then singled me out saying that he thought I was giving a BAFTA award-winning performance and to keep up the good work. All three of us looked at each other and laughed out loud. Of course David wasn't being serious, but it was nice that he'd said it, especially in front of Michael Caine. Trouble was, that now Collins and Caine had heard it, they relentlessly took the piss out of me for the rest of the night.

My first scene though, was with an actor I had yet to work with. Armand Assante was playing the part of a Shakespearean actor called Richard Mansfield who secured the services of prostitutes from my character Billy White in the pub. Armand was from New York City but I suspected that he was from Italian stock as he had the look of a Mafia Crime Boss.

It was only a short scene stood at the bar, but we had to look as if we were doing business as the camera would be cutting back to us for reactions and so forth. I was supposed to be drinking, and they used real beer. It was a fucking nightmare. I hadn't had a drink for three days and hadn't given it any thought at all. Suddenly I had a pint of real ale in my hand, and at the end of the scene had to knock it back in one. Armand Assante was chatting away, but I didn't hear a word. All I could think about was drinking that beer, and what it was going to do to me. I just prayed that we could get the shot in one.

My scene with Michael and Lewis was always going to be tricky. During the fight inside the pub, Inspector Abberline (Michael) is supposed to be outside looking in. As I get thrown through the door, I had to land in exactly the right place for the camera to pick up the action.

Sgt Godley (Lewis) then drags me up, covered in horseshit and mud, and Inspector Abberline casually wanders into the frame to talk to Billy White, who it turns out, is one of the Inspector's informants. Godley then releases Billy, who gives them both 'daggers'. He then spits, furtively looks around, and then walks out of shot. It would all be over in a few seconds, but took most of the evening to shoot.

Now that I was already covered in crap, David wanted to film the scene where Billy gets his comeuppance and takes a real hiding from three unknown assailants. Peter Braham wanted to rehearse this first with the three stuntmen on call that night.

Filming a fight scene realistically can be fraught with danger. I once saw an actor get kicked in the bollox by mistake and couldn't piss for a week. Peter Braham was an expert in this field, so all the punches were rehearsed in slow motion and then steadily speeded up until we knew exactly what we were doing. It looked brilliant, and once the make-up department had worked their magic with the fake blood and bruises, poor old Billy White looked like he'd been in a car crash.

The only thing that blighted an otherwise fantastic and unforgettable experience was the death of Armand Assante's stand-in. These are the people who stand-in for the leading actors whilst the shots are being lined-up and focused. The bloke in question was a lovely man who had been in the industry for years. He'd come to work already feeling unwell and should've been sent home. But such was the nature of the business back then that no one, except the leading actors, ever complained about anything. He haemorrhaged and died on the spot. An ambulance was called, but there was nothing that could be done, and after the body had been taken away, filming continued.

David Wickes was determined that as few people as possible should know who would be unmasked as the killer, and four dummy endings were shot, revealing George Lusk, Inspector Spratling, Chief Superintendent Arnold, and Sir Charles Warren as the Ripper. He also mocked up a scene with Godley pulling William Gull from a coach in a case of mistaken identity, and then edited them all together to produce the end result. Reportedly, only eight members of Wickes' staff knew the truth before the production wrapped.

Of course David Wickes didn't have a fucking clue who Jack the Ripper was, but the publicity certainly didn't harm the viewing figures on both sides of the Atlantic when it was released to coincide with the 100 year anniversary of Jack's first victim.

The series premiered in the UK on 11 October, 1988, and in the USA on 21 October, 1988.

In 2007, an American businessman bought a shawl on the understanding that it had been found next to the body of the fourth victim Catherine Eddowes. After extensive DNA testing and almost seven years of research, it was supposed to have been the definitive piece of scientific evidence that finally exposed the true identity of Jack the Ripper.

A 23-year-old Polish immigrant barber called Aaron Kosminski was "definitely, categorically and absolutely" the man who carried out the atrocities in 1888. However, the scientist who carried out the DNA analysis apparently made a fundamental error that fatally undermines his case against Kosminski.

The scientist, Jari Louhelainen, is said to have made an "error of nomenclature" when using a DNA database to calculate the chances of a genetic match. If true, it would mean his calculations were wrong and that virtually anyone could have left the DNA that he insisted came from the Ripper's victim.

They say the error means no DNA connection can be made between Kosminski and Eddowes. Any suggestion, therefore, that the Ripper and Kosminski are the same person appears to be based on conjecture and supposition – as it has been ever since the police first identified Kosminski as a possible suspect more than a century ago. And so the mystery remains.

On the 27th November 2013, I received the heart-breaking news that Lewis Collins died at his California home. He had been diagnosed with cancer in 2008, but thought he'd beaten it. He was a fantastic bloke and, in my opinion, one of our most under-rated actors from a time when men were men and were not afraid to show it! Whenever I watch my episode of *The Professionals* I always smile to myself. That bastard threw me out of a perfectly good aeroplane.

It was him!

17

I started meeting some of Lindsey's friends. Her 'bestest buddy' was a stunning lady from a Greek/Cypriot family called Eleni 'Boo' Beggs. Everyone just called her Boo. Boo was married to a, and I mean this in the nicest possible way, complete nutjob.

Nick Beggs had been the driving force behind a pop group called Kajagoogoo, and in 1983 scored a number one with their debut single "Too Shy". I loved that record (still do) especially the bass line, the like of which you would only normally hear from funk bands like The Brothers Johnson. Nick Beggs was that bass player, so the prospect of having him in my new circle of friends was appealing to say the least, and they lived locally.

After the demise of Kajagoogoo, Nick seriously thought about giving up playing music. He'd been offered various record company executive A&R jobs which never came to anything, but now he was back playing and writing music with a new band called Ellis, Beggs & Howard. Lindsey and I attended their first live show at The Greyhound in Fulham and I thought they were fantastic! Their first single "Big Bubbles" was a hit all over Europe but only reached 41 in the charts back here. This was the time of "Acid House" which had been developed (if that's the right word for it) by DJ's in Chicago and travelled like an infected rat on a ship to pollute the sensibilities of anyone trying to make decent music. I fucking hated it.

Lindsey's brother, Tommy, though, had embraced this new form of sound pollution, had started wearing his baseball cap back to front and was now having huge success in the various clubs he DJ'd in. I just could not get it, or wanted to! What made matters even worse was when Lil left her fantastic rock band to collaborate with Tommy, and I was now forced to listen to this electronic drivel at home. It was the first time Lindsey and I had fundamentally disagreed about anything. It was enough to turn me to drink.

Lindsey, Nick and Boo professed to be born again Christians and on Sundays attended a church in Notting Hill called The Kensington Temple. On occasion I went with Lindsey as I thought that 1, it would get me out of the house, and 2, I really did want to share in my future wife's interests. It was truly an amazing spectacle. The Church was Pentecostal, which meant it was predominantly black and extremely vocal. Lots of hand raising and swooning and "can I get an amen" was going on all around me as the spirit of The Lord made his merry way through the beautifully dressed congregation, making them all look like stroke victims. The music and the band were great though.

To say that The Kensington Temple Church Band was good is an understatement as it was run by the husband and wife team of David and Carrie Grant. David had been the singer in a British funk band called Lynx and was now carving out a solo career. I didn't know it at the time, but I would be working with these two Christian singers on a regular basis within the next ten years.

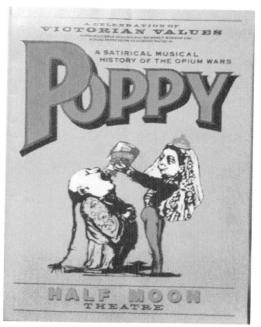

Chris Bond, the director, with whom I'd worked with on *Trafford Tanzi* in Leeds, had been back on the telephone to ask if I'd be interested in appearing in a new production of a musical called *Poppy*. I was doing fuck all, so I thought why not. *Poppy*, written by Peter Nichols with music by Monty Norman, was a musical comedy set in the first Victorian Opium War of 1840. The play takes the form of a pantomime, complete with Dick Whittington (played as a principal boy), a pantomime dame, and a pantomime horse. I was to play a character called Idle Jack.

On the first day of rehearsals, I was pleasantly surprised to see an old school friend cast as one of the chorus. Scott St Martyn had been one of the first people I met when I attended my college course at The Arts. He was always dressed outrageously, surrounded by woman, and very, very, camp. It was so lovely to see him again. Also in the cast were two women that I hadn't met, one I knew from the TV, and one other who would eventually hardly be off it.

Josie Lawrence was the biggest star in this show (although I begged to differ); having regularly appeared on the Channel 4 improvisational comedy series *Whose Line Is It Anyway*? She was a fantastic singer, and her speciality on that show was her ability to improvise songs on the spot. We got on immediately.

The other young lady, that I hadn't met, was an actress called Siobhan Finneran*. She had already starred in a saucy film called *Rita, Sue and Bob Too*, which also featured Chris Bond's old mate George Costigan. This, I suspect, is how she ended up doing this show in the East End of London. Siobhan was a northern lass, in fact, everyone except Scott St Martyn and I seemed to be northern, and she was brilliant fun to be around. Siobhan was playing the top half of my pantomime horse, Randy.

---

*Siobhan Finneran is an English television and film actress. She is known for her regular roles in the BBC drama *Clocking Off* (2000-2002), ITV comedy *Benidorm* (2007-2015), ITV drama *Downton Abbey* (2010-2013) and BBC drama *Happy Valley* (2014).

Another member of the cast was an actor called Ayub Khan-Din, who was playing Lin Tse-Tsii, who was the Commissioner to the Emperor. Ayub was born in Salford to an English mother and a traditional Pakistani father. Ayub was such a great laugh and yet again I had found someone that I had to avoid making eye contact with whilst on stage. Ayub's dad owned a fish & chip shop whilst Ayub was growing up, and some of the stories from his childhood made me weep with laughter.

Ayub would eventually write all these stories down and write a stage play about it. Called East Is East*, the play was first performed at the Birmingham Repertory Theatre Studio on 8 October 1996 before enjoying three sell-out London runs and an Olivier Award nomination for Best New Comedy.

All in all it was a happy company, and when the play opened in late July that year it got great reviews and reasonable box office returns. I enjoyed doing Poppy immensely, even if I did sometimes get a bollocking from Chris Bond for being completely unprofessional. There is a moment in the play when, because of starvation on board the ship heading to China, it is decided that Randy the horse has to be eaten. Obviously, Idle Jack isn't very happy about this but needs must. Before dispatching poor Randy with his revolver, Jack sings him a lullaby to put him to sleep, then very quietly puts the gun to his head and pulls the trigger.

*East is East went on to be made into a BAFTA award-winning film of the same name released in 1999, launching the careers of many of the play's original cast members.

If I got it right, you could hear a pin drop in the theatre. One night though, and just as I was about to pull the trigger, a woman in the front row coughed and completely broke the tension. So I shot her instead. The audience loved it, but I had to run for my life from Chris Bond.

The other bonus for me doing the show was that I had absolutely no time to get roped into the wedding planning that was going on all around me, and I rarely, if at all, took any notice. Even my impending stag night was being meticulously organised for me, by the man I had chosen to take the title of best man: John Caplan. Obviously, I had introduced Lindsey to family and friends. We'd had a family meal at a steakhouse in Hampstead where mine and Lil's mum and dad discussed the final arrangements. I sat at the end of the table drinking lager.

All my friends loved Lil. Jon Caplan actually told me that she was far too good for me and for once I was in complete agreement. I have no doubts whatsoever that she loved me, as I did her, but I felt like I was playing a part in a show. Gary Shail the actor, musician, joker whatever, was far more interesting than me. If I wanted anyone to like me at all, I would have to keep up the performance 24/7. I could never let my guard down, not even for a minute. The reality was too horrible to contemplate.

The stag night would be held exactly one week before the wedding, which had been booked in at the All Saints Anglican Church in the parish of Putney on Sunday 28th August, 1988. Lindsey decided to spend the week down at her grandmother's country retreat in Padstow, whilst I endured what promised to be a re-working of *Sodom and Gomorrah*.

Jon Caplan had taken his best man duties seriously. He'd arranged the beautiful engraved wedding rings purchased from Hatton Gardens, hired a vintage convertible Rolls Royce, and booked a nightclub called Crazy Larry's in the Kings Road for the gentleman's evening of stag. The club was run by an old friend of ours called Robert Pereno, who'd been on the London club scene in some way or another for years. He had already caused controversy by marrying a 15 year old wild child called Emma Ridley in Las Vegas, but was now back promoting this new club on his home turf. It would be the perfect venue. Jon had 300 invitations printed with a picture of me drunk and unconscious on the front, with the copy "Possibly for the last time, please join Gary for what promises to be a night to remember". They were brilliant, and I wish I still had one to include in this book. Another stroke of brilliance was how Jon planned to pay for the event. He opened a new bank account and had the account number printed on the ticket. Guests would pay £25, but would not have to pay for anything else once they were admitted to the club. That would raise £7500, and in 1988 we could've probably hired Crazy Larry's for a month with that.

Jon planned this event like a military exercise with nothing left to chance. A limo was hired for the entire night for a few choice friends which included Trevor Laird and David John, and security was privately hired from Big Fuckers R Us. The evening would start off at our local, The Kings Arms, where Lil O'Brien (Landlady) had prepared a cold buffet for the initial guests. These guests would include my father, my future father in-law, my two future brother in-laws on my family's side, and Lindsey's brother Tommy.

This was the dummy stag party. All would be invited to the next stage, but were warned that it might cause irreparable damage to their reputations and relationships if word got out. They would have to carry the memory of this night to their graves, never to divulge, even under torture or pain of death what was about to be witnessed. No one dropped out. I knew that Jon had been planning this for weeks. He'd even kept his plans secret from me, but I knew that at some point it would involve me being stripped naked and molested by some scantily clad totty. This, I vowed, would never happen. I had made sure that some of my Brixton friends had been invited who had been very well briefed to stop any girl, no matter how scantily clad, from getting within ten yards from me.

Outside Crazy Larry's the paparazzi were lurking. I recognised a couple of them from outside Stringfellows where they usually camped. Someone (probably Jon Caplan) had tipped them off, but what they really wanted was to be inside. This was never going to happen though, and our security guys were under strict instructions to pat every guest down for any hidden cameras. Can you imagine trying to keep something like this out of the public domain today? It would've been on Youtube within minutes, closely followed by a raid from the vice squad an hour later.

Most of my guests, including Peter Braham and Lewis Collins, were already there tucking into the pre-show Hor d'Oeuvres that were being passed around by some very nubile young ladies in gold bikinis. A huge cheer went up as we entered the club, and I was led to a table where a bottle of champagne was on ice already waiting for me. As soon as I sat down I was surrounded on all sides by my friends from Brixton. They really were well-briefed. I wanted no one to be under any illusions. I was not going to be compromised in any way, shape or form. If anybody was disappointed with this decision, then they obviously didn't know me at all. I have absolutely no problem with guys who like cavorting with strippers, as it is their choice if they want to behave like a twat. But if you are stupid enough to think that girls who do this for a living actually enjoy being put into these kinds of situations, then you are more of a twat than I thought you were.

My friend Greg, on the other hand, became the unofficial Master of Ceremonies. I'd always known from our days at Stephen Hyer's flat in Hyde Park that Greg swung both ways, and now he was in his element. He really was like the proverbial dog on heat. Most of the guys were reasonably well behaved, slipping the odd £5 note into the girls' knickers whilst they danced, but Greg thought he was directing a fucking porno. At one stage it was announced that a volunteer was required to come up onto the stage and Greg was there like a shot. Within seconds he had his kit off, with one girl sitting on his face whilst another did unspeakable things to his genitals. My normally well-behaved friends had turned into animals, whooping with delight and approval. I couldn't even imagine what my dad and future father in-law must've been thinking. I glanced around the room to see if I could find them, and there they both were, standing on chairs to get a better look.

By all accounts it had been the stag night to end them all. Apparently people were being found in skips and slumped in doorways up and down the Kings Road the following morning. Even to this day, I still meet people who profess to have been there. Only very recently I spoke to Scott St Martyn who still remembers that night as an 80's highlight. And he is gay!

The Limo dropped me back home in Putney at about five in the morning. It was already getting light with the dawn chorus the only sound to break the silence. I sat on the front steps to the flat and lit a cigarette. I had come through the evening unscathed and unblemished in any way. There would have to be no embellishments with the truth when I spoke to Lindsey later on that day, and I had remained relatively sober throughout. I wasn't sure if the same could be said of my dad and future father in-law though.

The night before the big day, I stayed with Jon Caplan and his girlfriend Nikki at his little flat in Wandsworth. We had a quiet evening, just chatting over old times, reminiscing past glories and spectacular failures with equal glee. Jon had been a good friend and there had never been anybody else in the frame when it came to choosing my best man.

The following morning, after a hearty breakfast, we started to get ready. Jon's girlfriend Nikki, who was quite a liberal sort of girl, stood topless next to me in the bathroom chatting as I brushed my teeth. I remember thinking that this was probably the last chance that I would get to see another semi-naked girl for a while. It was a sobering thought.

Because I was still doing the show (Poppy) I still had long hair and a beard which I tried to smarten as best I could. It wasn't the best look to go with top hat and tails, but hey, I thought, I was a working actor so I could pull it off. The only other contradiction to this otherwise formal attire was my choice of footwear. I'd bought a spectacular pair of black suede cowboy boots from R.Soles in the Kings Road. Jon had written GET ME OUT OF HERE in black felt tip on the soles, which we both agreed would give the congregation a good laugh when I knelt to take my vows, but apart from that, I thought I looked the part.

When we got to the church I noticed the surrounding gardens had been spruced up. Unbeknown to me my dad had gone round the day before with his strimmer. This was so typical of my father, he always thought ahead. The guests started arriving in all their finery. A lot of them adhered to the top hat and tails request and it was brilliant watching my Brixton family trying to balance top hats on dreadlocks. Obviously not everyone wore the tails though, Nick Beggs, for instance, wore a metallic green suit, and Greg turned up in full Scottish Highland attire complete with sporran and dirk.

Lindsey's old band mates from Toto Coelo were the maids of honour, all looking like super models, as did all the girls from *Fat Pig*. My mum looked resplendent in powder blue and my grandmother wore her new hat. My younger sisters looked funky, and my even younger brother, who we'd given the job as an usher to, looked smart, awkwardly ogling the girls. Everyone had risen to the occasion, and as I surveyed the scene it brought a lump to my throat that I had such wonderful family and friends.

The inside of the church looked like an advert for Interflora. There were flowers everywhere you looked, with a scent that was incredible. Jon and I stood at the front of the congregation awaiting the arrival of the sweetest flower of them all. All of a sudden, and apparently from nowhere, John Arrowsmith appeared looking like a medieval bishop in his ceremonial garb. He gave me a wink, raised his hands to quieten the congregation (who were already partying), gave a theatrical glance to the organist, and then the unmistakable sound of Mendelssohn's Wedding March filled the rafters. All eyes flew to the door.

There are no words to describe how beautiful Lindsey looked, so I won't even try. The service was lovely, the choice of hymns inspired and lots of tears of happiness were shed. As John Arrowsmith pronounced us man and wife, he raised his cassocks to reveal a pair of Union Jack boxer shorts. I knew he wouldn't let me down.

The reception was held at The Kings College in Chelsea, just a short vintage Rolls Royce drive from the church. On the way there, Lil presented me with a gold pocket watch with the inscription 'Good Times Ahead', I gave her nothing. I didn't know that I was supposed to. Once inside, Lindsey and our respective families had to stand in line whilst a very loud Master of Ceremonies announced our guests. A classical string quartet accompanied him in the background. I sent Greg to the bar to get me a beer. Some of the guests I didn't know at all, but others I was glad to see. My oldest and best friend Milton Jaghai from Hendon was there with his girlfriend Kim, whom I'd also been to school with and so was his mum and dad, Fredrick and Avis. Other old school friends were also in attendance. Jacqui Bischoff I had known forever. Her mum and mine had been great friends back in the day and Jacqui and I were like brother and sister. I had always secretly fancied her though, but I didn't think that this was the time to confess that little snippet of information. She did look cute though.

After about three hours of welcoming guests, it was time for lunch. I don't remember eating a damn thing, although I was told it was fantastic. Everyone had been given a glass of champagne on arrival and there was plenty of booze on each of the tables, so by the time it came to the speeches and thank you's, most of the guests were already very merry. Jon's speech was inspired, with the biggest laugh coming when he said that there were probably easier ways for me to join a golf club. Lindsey's father was a keen golfer, you see. You had to be there, I suppose, but it was very funny. After lunch, it was time to get changed

For the evening's festivities, I had chosen a white Stephen King suit with blue accessories. This would prove to be a disastrous decision, but for the moment I thought I looked the epitome of 80's chic! Lindsey, on the other hand, got it perfect! Her fantastic hand-made pearl studded wedding dress split into two parts. Once the bottom half had been discarded, the top half transformed into a mini dress which she complimented with black leather calf length platform boots. It was a stroke of fashion genius.

We'd had a cool jazz band playing throughout lunch, but for the evening's entertainment a backline of drums, amplifiers and various instruments had been set up for the jam that would inevitably happen once all the musicians in the room had got pissed.

Before all that though, the official photographer wanted some more shots outside on the lawns. We went out into the gardens for some more photos. By now most people were well on the way to being arseholed, and the photographer was having a hard time getting the poses he wanted. He wanted a shot of all the girls sitting on the grass, but couldn't get them all to look his way at the same time. Greg had the solution. As the photographer was about to attempt another shot, Greg raised his kilt, proving that age old question of does he or doesn't he. Well Greg wasn't. The look on the girls' faces was priceless.

So far, we'd had a classical string quartet, a very cool jazz band, a Punch & Judy show for the kids and a firework display. But for me, and something I don't think I will ever forget, was when Lindsey and Tommy performed the classic Aretha song "I Say a Little Prayer."

Lil had changed the lyrics somewhat.

> The moment I wake up
> Before I put on my make-up
> I'll make sausage, egg & chips for you.

By the time they'd finished performing I, and everyone else for that matter, were in floods, it really was such a beautiful thing to do. It was my fave song and meal combined and a lot of thought had gone into it. Everyone was telling me how lucky I was, but strangely I don't remember anyone saying that to Lindsey.

As predicted, an impromptu band was formed and the evening rocked on. I can't remember exactly who played, apart from my old friend Charlie Grima who was the drummer in a band called Wizzard. He seemed to be playing for ages. I know that there were plenty of other drummers in the room who could've played, but Charlie was a hard act to follow and drummers are a strange lot. At some point in the proceedings I was roped in on guitar. I vaguely remember playing "I'm So Bored with The USA" by The Clash, before ripping a fingernail off and spraying my very expensive white Stephen King Suit with blood. Went well with the song, I suppose.

At one point there was a real danger that the alcohol would run out. An old neighbour of mine who now ran an off-license in Putney came to the rescue. He jumped in his car, which was a brave or idiotic thing to do- depending on which way you look at it, and was back within the hour with more supplies. I asked him how much I owed him, but he said to consider it a wedding gift.

All of a sudden Lil and I were told we were going. Apparently it was traditional for the bride and groom to be the first to leave, usually for the honeymoon. As we both knew I would be working the following day, nothing had been arranged. Scott St Martyn and his lovely boyfriend Jean had booked us the suite at The Royal

Horse Guard Hotel on the banks of the Thames as a wedding present, so we spent about an hour saying our good byes and then we left for the hotel, with me covered in blood and Lil carrying her platform boots under her arm. It had been a fantastic day.

With Milton's mum, Avis

18

"A woman worries about the future until she gets a husband. A man never worries about the future, until he gets a wife."

In 1989, Lindsey secured a nice little part in a new musical called *Metropolis*. Based on the Fritz Lang movie, it was to be staged at The Piccadilly Theatre in London. It was just as well, as since finishing *Poppy* I hadn't earned a bean. There was always money owed to me of course, but usually only just enough for a decent night out or two with maybe a Chinese takeaway thrown in. I was bored shitless, and desperately needed a project to keep me occupied. No one I knew was making music. Even the Brixton boys at Sparkside Studios were struggling to make ends meet, so I decided that Lindsey and I should move. It was yet another decision made on the spur of the moment that I would live to regret.

I had completely forgotten that I was playing with Lindsey's money. She had worked so hard to buy her little attic flat, and here I was attempting to play the property market. All Lil's family lived only a walk away, but I convinced her that we could secure our financial future by selling high, and buying low. I'd been completely suckered by Margaret Thatcher's promise of profit in property. I wanted her family to see that I was taking control to secure their only daughter's future happiness, when in fact I was just showing off.

Of course it didn't take long to sell Lil's flat; it was in a very desirable area close to the river and within walking distance of Putney tube station, which made commuting into central London easy. I moved us to a grade 3 listed, one bedroomed flat, in a house in West Kensington that the estate agent assured me could not lose money, when in fact we started losing money on the very first day. I, of course, buried my head in the sand and used the ensuing worry as an excuse to drink.

As no one was hiring me to produce music at this time, I decided to go on the offensive. I met a lovely Irish guy called Gary Hurst in the Kings Arms. Gary had been one of Kate Bush's dancers, appearing in most of her early videos and rarely performed stage shows in the early 80's, but now, with Kate's encouragement, Gary wanted to become a recording artist in his own right.

I also met a budding songwriter, another Irish lad called Jim Henning, who was also trying to break into the recording industry. Jim had been hanging around Sparkside Studios waiting for the right project to get his teeth into, so I put the two of them together to see what they would come up with. It was a magical pairing. They never stopped writing. They eventually came up with the track that I and Eaton Blake thought was the hit.

The song, "Suzy's Got A Gun", went into production shortly afterwards with all hands on deck. Everyone at Sparkside loved Level 42, and more recently Go West, whose 1985 debut album was rarely off the Sparkside bar's playlist, so when we learnt that the guitarist, Alan Murphy, had been responsible for the axe work in both bands and Gary Hurst knew him well, we had to have him. Alan Murphy turned up on time with just a tiny little amp which he then surrounded with microphones to give us the sound that we'd hoped he'd give us, stayed to check, got paid, and then fucked off. Brilliant. All that was needed now was the final vocal to be recorded the following weekend.

Gary, Jim and I met back at the Kings Arms to discuss the boring contract stuff, but we all agreed that the project had legs. Gary looked tired, but there was no doubting his commitment to this venture, and was already planning the video shoot.

On the following Saturday we were ready to go. I was in the bar upstairs when I got the news that Gary wasn't feeling well. I rushed downstairs and into the studio where I found Gary hunched over holding his head in his hands and moaning like an injured animal. This wasn't just an average headache in my opinion, as Gary was completely incoherent and couldn't focus on anything at all. I decided to call an ambulance which arrived within minutes. I went with Gary in the ambulance where he was put on a ventilator to The Westminster Hospital. Once there, Gary was rushed away leaving me to wait in the corridor. I was there for only a couple of hours when a doctor came out to inform me that Gary died. It had been meningitis.

To say I was in shock is an understatement. It nearly shocked me sober. I was told much later on, the meningitis had been brought on by the HIV Virus, although this was never confirmed. What was even more shocking was that only a few months after Gary's death, I received the news that Alan Murphy died from an aids- related illness at the age of 36. These two very talented guys had been major players in Kate Bush's career*. So I can only imagine how sad she felt. Actually, I didn't have to wait that long to find out just how sad Kate Bush felt about losing Gary. At his funeral Kate gave a very moving eulogy where she spoke about his wonderful Irish charm and zest for life. The church was packed, with many of the dancers and choreographers that he'd worked with in attendance. I knew most of them, including my old Kings Arms drinking buddy Charles Augins.

After the funeral, Charles invited Lindsey and I back to his place for nibbles and drinks. Charles had moved house since I last saw him and now lived just up the road from our new place. Also at this impromptu wake were Sinitta's mum, Miquel Brown, and an American singer called Maurey Richards.

*In the music video for Kate Bush's version of "Rocket Man", released as part of the 1991 *Two Rooms: Celebrating the Songs of Elton John & Bernie Taupin* tribute album, she performs with her band but there is an empty chair, a guitar and a candle where Alan Murphy would have been and cross-faded footage of him playing in the closing choruses. "This is one of the last tracks that he did with us," Kate told BBC Radio 1, "and it's particularly nice for me to feel that it's not only keeping him alive, but I know he would be really thrilled to know that the single was doing so well. And it's nice for all of us that loved Al to know that he can be a part of this now."

Maurey, Miquel and I got chatting about Gary and the project that I had been working on with him before his untimely death. Maurey at the time was singing with a vocal group called The Platters, but was clearly bored shitless with having to sing "Only You" to an audience of Chicken 'inna' Basket wankers every night and told me he was more interested in writing some original material. Miquel Brown was also interested in working with me. She had gone into management and had found a very young singer/songwriter she wanted me to hear with a view to producing some demos.

As a very wise man once said, when one door closes another is opened. Or maybe he just lived in a drafty old house.

Miquel Brown was an absolute joy to be around. At the time I didn't have a piano in our new flat, so Miquel bought me a state of the art workstation keyboard to compose and arrange on. The youngster she was managing was a precocious fourteen year old called Hannah Clive, whose father was a famous actor. I recognised him immediately as one of the stars of *The Italian Job,* and also *Roberts Robo*ts, which had been a childhood favourite of mine. He'd also starred in the movie *A Clockwork Orange, Yellow Submarine*, where he featured as the voice of John Lennon, and a couple of *Carry On* films as well.

Miquel would be dealing with John when it came to the contracts and all the boring stuff, whilst I would be in charge of production. This suited me fine, as you can talk and enthuse all you like about a project, but until it was actually in your hand, as it were, it was all just bollox as far as I was concerned.

Hanna's songs, and especially her lyrics, were remarkable and she fucking knew it. She was wise beyond her years and had it all going on. She flirted with me outrageously when she thought no one was looking, and I suspected that once in the studio I would have trouble with her. In fact, when we did eventually start recording, she was a total professional and listened intently whenever I suggested something to her.

The studio was in the annex of a private house in a place called Southfields and was owned by a strange bloke whom I always tried to avoid. He kept coming into the control room to listen to the playbacks, nodding his approval—as if I gave a fuck. I had to get Miquel to have a word with him and after that he started to complain about the volume. The house engineer, a lovely scouser called Pete Hurst, on the other hand, was a diamond. I'd always been used to recording onto tape, but now everything was digital. Pete was brilliant at filtering my ideas to suit all this new-fangled trickery and I found this new way of recording music to be much more creative than I'd thought it would be. I would try to use real instruments whenever possible, but it was liberating to know that I could have a 42 piece orchestra at my disposal if I'd wanted it.

Hannah and I were definitely on the same wavelength when it came to arranging her songs and I loved the fact that she wanted to be regarded as an artist and not a pop star. I'm not so sure that Miquel Brown was as enthusiastic though. Miquel wanted a hit record, I suppose, but I had no idea how to do that as I didn't have any real reference points. Hannah's voice was certainly not conventional by any means, so I wanted the backing tracks to reflect that. I started sculpting the sound around her voice instead of just getting her to sing along. It was very time consuming, and some nights we'd work until it got light, which pissed off the owner somewhat, so I had all the clocks in the room removed, which pissed him off even more.

I loved working on Hannah Clive's songs. It was a very intense time for me, as I felt responsible for her. I wanted so much to set a good example, and make her memories of her first recording experiences to be good ones. I really think she knew that. She trusted me, and that is a great feeling, especially when the trust comes from someone so young. It was just what I needed.

Unbeknown to Miquel and Hannah, they had probably saved my life.

Hannah Clive 2015: "If I were asked to describe Gary Shail in one word it would be 'lightning bolt'. Well alright, technically that's two words, but as he'd say, "fuck it". I first met Gary at the tender age of just fourteen. He carries the accolade of being my first Music Producer and we met after my father, the actor and author John Clive, had orchestrated what was to be my first music deal.

As a budding singer/songwriter, Gary was to be my first initiation into the pulsating world that was the British music industry, and it's fair to say, it was as illuminating and useful an introduction as one could've hoped for, living up to all expectation.

I remember turning up at a small recording studio in deepest, darkest Southfields, a place hitherto beyond my geographical area of knowledge (she lived four miles away) and being introduced to what was this crazily enthusiastic electric individual, with a shock of blonde spikey hair, who to me, a hormone-driven teenager, was just about the coolest looking dude I had ever met, with a personality to match. I remember I hadn't felt so forbidden-ly drawn to someone since I walked out of a cinema on air, having just watched Michael J Fox in *Back to the Future*! Only, Gary was taller.

But of course, setting my jailbait sexual desire aside for a moment, Gary was, and is a great producer, always listening to my ideas, he interpreted them in exactly the right way. He gave me room as an artist, complementing instead of dictating, which is rare, unlike so many other producers at that time were

prone to do. My subsequent career experience singing with the likes of Ray Charles has taught me just how important that quality is in both the producer and as a creative. I had struck gold.

Gary understood about motivation, when to step back and let the artist just 'do' and when to direct. I remember telling him how I wanted a sort of electronic Twin-Peaks-y type vibe and his enthusiasm when he subsequently played me the backing track he'd painstakingly built; his energy such that I thought he might spontaneously combust when playing me the reverse drum sound he and the engineer had created, using what was of course fairly new technology at the time. And he was spot on. This was a new nuance and contemporary nod to what had been happening on the British electronic music scene only a few years before. Gary was bang on the money with it, but in a completely new way.

Then there was the attraction between us, which surely played its part in eliciting previously undiscovered energy when it came to performances and song writing. I must add that Gary was completely above board and had the decency not to do what many others would subsequently try and do and take advantage of the slim, blonde haired, full mouthed, long legged, gawky girl who strayed into his path. No, that came later. By then I was well over the legal limit and, quite frankly, I don't think Gary had any choice in the matter. No, during those sessions, and exploring my newfound sexual power, Gary had to content himself instead with me flirting outrageously and regularly sitting on his lap, in black leggings. Poor sod.

I recall how, years after these sessions, I must've been late teens, early twenties, pre internet and mobile phones, when if you lost someone's number that was it, somehow I found him. Now single and living in a flat above a bank, of all places, he promptly took me off to the pub.

Off to the local we went and proceeded to get outrageously drunk at lunchtime, this followed I think- and here's where it gets a bit hazy, by a further two days of non-stop music recording, drinking, illicit partying (by now at least I could roll a joint) and he and I getting down to business. It was passionate, and well, let's just say, that was a helluva lot of energy to hold back for the intervening years, but we certainly lost no time making up for it. Not sure my dad would've approved of the last bit, but hey- he sure loved them recordings, and to coin a modern phrase...it was worth it! My Baptism was now complete. Thanks for the education Gary... Love ya!"

During the Hannah Clive sessions I hadn't drank on the job. Obviously I drank before and after, but never in the studio. At this point I still had some measure of responsibility and still thought that I was in control. Where others would reward themselves with a well-earned pint after work, mine was a medical necessity.

I don't know what happened between Miquel Brown and John Clive. One minute they were best buddies, and the next not talking. Apparently John wasn't happy with Hannah's contract and negotiations had broken down blah, blah, blah! I stayed out of it. Miquel then wanted me to work with her daughter Sinitta, who'd gone from being a sweet little thing to becoming a fully-fledged diva. She'd had a couple of hit records with Stock Aitken and Waterman, but Sinitta wanted to write her own stuff too. I met with her at her house in Chelsea to listen to her ideas.

Sinitta bought some basic recording equipment which was set up in one of her spare rooms. Just a keyboard, Atari computer and an Akai S1000 sampler, but more than enough to get some basic ideas down. Trouble was I couldn't get Sinitta to work. She was obviously busy carving out her career, but she was treating me like one of the fucking staff! I would spend all fucking day putting a backing track together with no input from her, and then she would schedule when she could fit me in to do the vocals. It's a real shame, as a couple of her songs could've been hits in my opinion.

What I needed was a new project where I could combine together my two favourite pastimes: writing music, and drinking alcohol. Thank God for Maurey Richards.

Maurey Richards

19

"Those in power write the history, while those who suffer write the songs."

Maurey was from Chicago but had been living in England for some years now, and he settled in a little two bedroomed flat in Notting Hill Gate with his boyfriend Craig, who was an Australian. Lindsey and I invited them over for dinner one evening where we got very drunk and ended up jamming around my electronic keyboard until the early hours. Maurey's voice was incredible.

I'd been working on some new song ideas of my own and played Maurey some of the music that I had been writing, with a view to adding lyrics and hopefully some vocals to in the near future. Maurey started scribbling ideas down immediately, and by the following morning we had written our first song. I hadn't worked like this since the old days with Joe McGann and Dave and I was excited that I had once again found someone to work with who was exactly on my wavelength. I started spending most of my days at Maurey's flat writing and drinking.

For our first wedding anniversary Lindsey bought me a push bike, with a view to me getting fit and saving money on train fares. It had been a lovely idea, but completely impractical. I was okay getting to Maurey's flat in the morning, but after a day's song writing and two bottles of vodka, I couldn't ride the damn thing home.

Although Maurey was earning good money from singing with The Platters, who were basically just a tribute band now considering all of the original members had long since died of old age, it wasn't regular work. This meant that he had lots of time between gigs for us to write. We started recording our new songs as we were writing them, which was wonderfully creative and lots of fun. By now, I was well up to speed with all the new technology that was available and we started buying state of the art recording equipment so that we could record ideas at home. Actually, this proved difficult. It's not easy trying to get a vocal down whilst someone is banging on the ceiling with a broom handle, so we re-located from Maurey's flat to a mutual friend's house in South London to finish the recordings. We set up a midi-digital recording studio in the living room, and used the bathroom as a vocal booth. A couple of the songs required backing vocals so, as well as Lindsey, we drafted in Ami Stewart, Miquel Brown and Charles Augins to give us (once multi-tracked) a gospel sound that sounded both immense and authentic. The neighbours were actually really friendly as long as we kept the music down after dark, but got a bit pissed off with us for re-designing their beautiful garden.

One afternoon we decided to take some promo photographs in the back garden. There was a huge brick wall that ran the whole length, and the photographer asked us all to stand with our backs against it whilst he snapped away. As we all lent back onto the wall the whole bloody thing collapsed with us on it. We couldn't stop laughing it was so funny. We delegated Maurey to make the apologies to the neighbours, 'cos he was the oldest.

Apart from our own stuff, we also started writing songs for other people. One evening at a Platters gig I attended, the support act was a black soul singer whose stage name was Pearl Star. She only sang covers by the likes of Randy Crawford and Gladys Knight, but I thought that, given some original material, she could actually live up to her stage name. We had a meeting with her manager (who was also her husband), and then Maurey and I went to work. We wrote an epic song called "Who'd Have Thought I'd be Loving You", that we knew would show off Pearl's incredible vocal range, and then we started touting the idea around.

An old friend of mine called Errol Kennedy, who'd been the drummer in the band Imagination, was now working for a record label called 'World Dance Music' and he thought, just as I had, that Pearl was a star just waiting to explode. All of a sudden the whole fucking project went into overdrive, but not in the way I'd wanted. Errol and his record company lost their nerve, in my opinion, and instead of putting the original song out, a cover version of a Robert Palmer song, "Every Kinda People" was recorded and put out on the A side instead.

I am not saying it was a bad version of the song, just that it was incredibly boring. Errol even wanted to include a rap section and hired some backward-hat-wearing white person with a speech impediment. It was atrocious. The B side (our song) on the other hand was interesting, and fucking rocked in my opinion, but hey, what did I know? What also added insult to injury was when the record was eventually released, Errol Kennedy had given himself a production credit above mine, and they'd spelt my name wrong. The record sunk without trace.

We also wrote a very belligerent song for an incredibly versatile singer, and actor called Scott Smith Pattison called "Just Tryin' to Live my Life", which was another one that never saw the light of day. I loved hanging out with Scott though.

Scott Smith Pattison 2015: "O.K, so it's sometime in the year 1992, when bands like Simply Red and Erasure rang loud from commercial radio stations with the biggest selling record of the year being Whitney Houston's cover of "I Will Always love You" and Gary and Scott or Gaz and Skazz couldn't give a fuck.

I was, at the time, a cast member of the Andrew Lloyd Webber musical *Starlight Express* and had the pleasure of meeting Gary at a bar called Mcready's on a boat that was docked and floated up and down with the tide on the River Thames, on The Embankment under the shadow of Blackfriar's Bridge, that opened when the pubs closed, and closed when the last person had left. We were, more often than not, the last people to leave and were tight as thieves from day one.

With a multitude of extra-curricular activities at our disposal, this particular evening we decided to chew on some acid and walk home at 2 a.m. But to whose home we could not decide. After debating the contents of the river, we sat on a wall, dangling our feet over a fifteen foot drop to the water and asking a policeman that moved us on very politely if his head went all the way to the top of his pointy hat.

We walked and walked, acquiring a bottle of Tequila along the way to Sparkside Recording Studios in Brixton (about a one hour and forty minutes' walk when sober) smoked a few joints, and then moved on. Falling out of the door of the studio, we headed straight across Brockwell Park, and after about, who knows how long of hilarity, found ourselves on a lovely little street overlooking the park close to, what is now, The Peabody Trust Estate. Tired, drunk, stoned, tripping and still savouring the last of the Tequila, we suddenly came across a truly beautiful house, which Gary decided, in his infinite wisdom, to enter. After very little persuasion, I also thought that this was a brilliant idea. So we walked up the front path, dimly lit by the dawn of yet another shitty day in London, and unbelievably turned the handle, and pushed open the door. We were now faced with what in my current state looked like Mr Higgin's house in *My Fair Lady*, with a huge staircase that wrapped around a grand entrance or foyer.

At the bottom of the staircase, on a beautiful parquet floor, was a baby grand piano. Gary immediately sat down, flung the lid upward and began playing classical music with reckless abandonment. This was, at that exact time in our lives, the funniest thing that could ever happen, happened!! After hearing sounds from the upper levels of the dwelling, I ran to the front garden, and looked behind to see lights turn on, one room at a time, as Gary stumbled and fell down the six steps that lead to the entrance, and then we ran back through the park and back to Sparkside Studios, where we both slept in the upstairs bar until well into the next day, at which point we brushed ourselves down, and started all over again, and again, and again.

This story doesn't even begin to scratch the surface of the stuff we used to get up too, but the childlike activities that took place that evening/morning were, and still are, a reminder of how precious life and its endless bonds are. People say you can't choose your family, they're wrong. Gary is more than a brother to me. We both wear the physical and emotional scars of the time we spent together that I know that we are both happy to have, and would not change for the world."

My immediate neighbour was a lovely, very attractive, lady called Johanne, who was a northerner. We all became great friends, often staying up late into the night listening to music, smoking dope and drinking wine. She was out of work, so I suggested her to a mate of mine called Mark Fuller, who had just taken on the lease to a restaurant in Greek Street in London's West End. Mark had once been the owner of the Embassy Club, but was now starting to build his restaurant empire in

Soho with the financial help of his landlord Paul Raymond. Johanne went to meet Mark and was given the job of bar manager within five minutes of their meeting.

Simon Ellis, who'd been in the band 'Ellis, Beggs & Howard' was a regular at this new restaurant and took an immediate shine to Johanne. Once he'd found out that she was my neighbour he started spending more and more time 'round my flat hoping to bump into Jo. They eventually started dating, then got married and had two kids. They have now been married for over twenty years. I am very glad it all worked out for them, as I am without a doubt totally responsible for their children's lives, and one day I am going to tell them that.

It was now the early 90's, and I hadn't had any acting work for almost a year. Lindsey's lovely mum helped me out financially by giving me a little job baking vegetarian lasagne for her new outside catering business, but the money I earned barely kept me in vodka. As the mortgage bills mounted up, I did my well-rehearsed impression of an Ostrich.

Since *Jack the Ripper*, I'd only been offered one day's filming work, and that was courtesy of Peter Braham and David Wickes. Due to the huge success of 'The Ripper', David and Michael Caine had decided to tackle another classic tale, *Jekyll and Hyde*. I was cast as a young sailor coming to the rescue of a young damsel in distress who gets thrown down a flight of stairs by Michael Caine (playing Hyde) for his trouble. Even though I'd been padded, the shock of the stair fall caused severe bruising all over my upper body and I could hardly move the following day. It had been nice seeing the lads again though.

It became obviously clear that I was heading for some kind of breakdown. I stopped answering the phone and lost interest in almost everything, including sex. Now I knew that I was ill! An appointment with a doctor was arranged for me and he diagnosed depression. Of course I was fucking depressed! I was out of work, had no money, was drinking a bottle of vodka a day and couldn't satisfy my gorgeous wife. Wouldn't you be depressed? The quack had given me some green jellified tablets to take, but they just made me feel worse, so I flushed them down the toilet with my acting career and started drinking scotch instead of vodka. Like they say...a change is as good as a rest!

Eventually the proverbial shit hit the fan and we were forced to sell the flat at a loss. Once a buyer had been found and our outstanding mortgage payments made, we were left with only a few grand to play with. I had lost most, if not all, of Lil's capital investment, but she never said a word. Our cat 'Marmite', though, looked at me with scorn, and when we eventually vacated, decided to stay on at the flat with the new owners rather than spend another minute in my company. I sometimes think that Lindsey should've done the same.

Our new rented two bedroomed flat (back in Putney) was a penthouse above an office block that once used to be a bank. Situated on The Upper Richmond Road, it had its own private elevator and a living room that you could play cricket in. With the little money that we had left we decided after nearly three years of marriage to have our honeymoon. I had always wanted to go to Jamaica and Lil had always fancied Disney World, so we found a package that combined both destinations, put our troubles behind us, and started packing.

We arrived in Montego Bay on a hot and balmy Caribbean evening in good spirits. Lindsey and I held hands all the way there and I felt so proud and in love with my beautiful, talented and generous wife that it actually hurt. We had to take a coach from the airport to Ocho Rios, which was our final destination, and once on the bus the tour guide went into her spiel.

After the usual boring touristy stuff, the guide got onto the serious issue of drugs. She informed everyone on the bus that even though marijuana grew wild and in abundance in Jamaica, buying and smoking it was still illegal. Lindsey turned to me and whispered that one of the first things we should do once at the hotel was find some. What she didn't know was that I had already bought enough ganja from a baggage handler back at the airport to last us for the entire holiday.

Jamaica was just what I needed, and although Ocho Rios was basically still a construction site (including the hotel), the locals and staff were lovely. Obviously we were not the only package holiday makers there, and some of them I thought would've been better off at Butlins or a caravan site back in England. One night, Lil and I went for dinner to a beautiful local cliff top restaurant overlooking the Caribbean Sea. The menu was fantastic. Fresh platters of locally caught fish and seafood, Jerk Chicken with rice and peas, Oxtail Stew, and of course, baked bananas and dumplings. As we were perusing the menu I overheard the dinners at the next table, who were from Newcastle, asking for steak chips and garden peas, with Heinz tomato sauce.

The tour operators arranged daily excursions to see the local sites and places of interest, but Lindsey and I had already decided that when and if we needed a guide, we would find our own. In fact, one found us. The hotel had its own private beach that had been fenced off on either side from the general public. One particularly hot afternoon, I was floating both mentally and physically on a lilo, when I suddenly saw someone snorkelling towards me. Up popped a local Jamaican dude who then started trying to sell me some ganja, amongst other things. I explained I had more than enough weed, but what I really needed was a boat so we could sail down the coast to Dunns River Falls, passing Ian Flemming's house (Goldeneye) on the way. The local dude, named Kenny, said he had a cousin with a boat and would be ready and waiting for us the following morning on the public beach.

The next morning, at sun up, Lil and I met Kenny and his cousin and we set off. The lads were brilliant fun, regaling us with tales of local mysteries and legends whilst continuously rolling spliffs. We stopped off at The Falls, where Lil and I climbed the 600 feet to the top, and there we bought some local souvenirs for the folks back home. Then it was back on the boat for more spliff and stories, a bit of snorkelling, some freshly picked mangos and then back to our hotel. It had been a fantastic day out. I gave Kenny and his cousin a £50 note which was about $10,000 Jamaican. I think they were happy.

On the final night of our Jamaican trip, and after smoking a last Bob Marley sized spliff, we cast the rest of the weed to the winds off the hotel balcony and started packing for Florida.

The hotel in Orlando was basically their version of a Travel Lodge with a restaurant attached. Pretty basic, but adequate for our needs as we wouldn't be spending much time there anyway. We bought all-day passes for all of the Disney World attractions in advance and wandered around the parks marvelling at all the fat people, which was far more of a spectacle than anything old Walt could've dreamed up. There really are some humungous arses in the USA! I actually spent an entire morning filming some of these ridiculously proportioned posteriors for posterity, and should've made a documentary called 'WOT THE FUCK!'

Lindsey had a good friend called Lisa who'd once been her neighbour in Putney, but had now relocated to Sarasota. They had stayed in touch ever since, so we hired a Chrysler and made the 130 mile journey cross-country down to the Gulf of Mexico. All I can really remember about Sarasota were the fantastic sandy beaches which stretched for miles, and that everyone I met seemed to be talking about a band called Nirvana. America seemed to be in the grip of a grunge epidemic and Nirvana was the poster boys for this seriously depressing music. Of course, songs about addiction and dysfunctional relationships were nothing new; I just didn't want to hear them whilst sitting sipping a beer on the beach.

Lindsey's mate Lisa played the "Nevermind" album continuously whilst we were there and kept telling us how this music had changed her life. I just thought she should get out more.

The flight home was horrendous! After the intense heat of Jamaica and Florida our bodies had become conditioned, I suppose, but the airplane was fucking freezing. We spent the entire journey huddled under a blanket to stay warm. By the time we landed back in England, Lil and I both had sore throats and runny noses. Apart from that, it had been a lovely holiday and I felt rejuvenated and positive about the future. If I knew what my immediate future held though, I think I would've stayed in Jamaica.

There was an office block directly below our flat that specialized in creating software packages for various finance companies. I'd become quite friendly with one of the guys that worked there, originally just swapping pleasantries and the like, but he seemed like an interesting bloke, so I started meeting him occasionally for a drink in the local pub. On one of these occasions Tim (as was his name) asked me if I'd ever had any sailing experience. I told him that apart from the odd ferry trip and boat party... no I hadn't. Tim then asked me if I would like to sail a 35ft Yacht with his two brothers across the English Channel to Cherbourg and then deliver it to his 80 year old father, who was then planning to sail it down to the Bay of Biscay. Apparently it would need a crew of four to do this, which surprised me somewhat, as I had heard of intrepid adventurers sailing boats this size single-handed around the world. Tim assured me that this was going to be more of a pleasure cruise and if I wanted to be the fourth crew member, then all I had to do was say yo-ho-ho, pack something waterproof and climb aboard.

I don't think Lindsey was very happy about me fucking off again so soon after our holiday, but she realized that this was a once-in-a-lifetime opportunity and something someone like me just couldn't pass up. I would only be away for a week, and as I still wasn't getting any acting work, might as well get some new life experiences. That's what I told her, but in reality I just wanted to wear a blazer and cap and drink copious amounts of gin and tonic.

We arrived in Plymouth late afternoon where I met Tim's two brothers in the harbour pub. Peter and his younger brother Nick were both experienced sailors, as was Tim. Peter was a serving Lieutenant Commander in The Royal Navy and had served on the battleships Ark Royal and Invincible as a Sea King helicopter pilot. Peter would be our Captain, Tim the Navigator, Nick the deck-hand, and me? I would cook the Frey Bento's steak and kidney pies and un-cork the wine. The weather was beautiful and the sea smooth as glass.

We would be making the channel crossing at night, so after a couple of pints and a bit of food and alcohol shopping, we made our way down to the jetty where I was introduced to the vessel that would be my home for the next 24 hours or so. Her name was Calliope.

"Man marks the earth with ruin – his control stops with the shore."
Byron

We set sail into a beautiful sunset and I felt exhilaration and trepidation in equal measure. Tim and Peter were busy explaining to me that whilst at sea one has to be aware of every eventuality, as the sea was so unpredictable. To prove his point, Tim threw a coke can overboard and told me to close my eyes for a brief moment and then try to find it again. When I opened my eyes it had disappeared from view completely. What no one saw though was the fucking huge orange harbour buoy that we smashed into only seconds later.

With no damage done, apart from a couple of bruised egos, we motored Calliope out of Plymouth Harbour and into the ensuing darkness that was beginning to envelope us like a shroud. Calliope was fitted with a navigational system called 'Decca' that Peter said was a bit Micky Mouse but should do the job, and I remember thinking 'SHOULD?' but my fears were calmed with another gin and tonic and the promise of fine French wines and pâté at our destination.

After about four hours of sailing with a fine brisk wind in our sails the weather suddenly and very definitely changed for the worse. Up until now the sea had been relatively calm, with only the odd swell to make my stomach churn, but steadily the waves began to swell higher and more frequently. Then it started raining hard. I could tell from Peter, Nick, and Tim's reactions that this hadn't been entirely expected, and when the life jackets were handed out I knew that this was going to get interesting. Peter was busy trying to get some weather information on the VHF radio, whilst the rest of us tied ourselves to rivets attached to the boat. The waves got higher and the rain fell harder. Less than thirty minutes earlier we had been bathing in beautiful moonlight, but now the sky was seriously pissed off about something and was taking it out on us. In the harbour back in Plymouth the boat had seemed sturdy and tough, but now it might as well have been a matchstick sharing a bath with a frisky dog. It had happened so fast that I hadn't had time to freak out, but when we started hearing mayday communications from other vessels in the area it all became very, very, real.

The only advice from the coastguard was that if possible, get to the nearest port and wait it out. But we were half way to France with no land in sight. Now the waves were so high they seemed to reach the sky as they headed towards us in what seemed like slow motion. Once the mountain of water reached us, it lifted the boat like an empty milk carton before slamming it back down onto the ocean like a sack of potatoes. There hadn't been time to reel the fore-sail in and, through the sheet of icy rain, we could see that it had begun to rip and tangle itself around the mast. It had to be untangled before the weight of the torn sail broke the mast in two. Nick volunteered to climb up to free the flapping material but got his foot caught in the rigging, so I carefully manoeuvred myself as quickly as possible along the side of the boat to help free him. It was without a shadow of a doubt the most terrifying thing I had ever done. One slip and I would've never been able to get back onto the boat. I managed to free Nick's foot and he fell to the deck, totally exhausted. We managed to inch our way back to the stern where we huddled together for comfort and warmth, contemplating our watery fate. There was absolutely no point trying to steer Calliope through this, so we just held on tight and left our lives in Poseidon's hands. It would be the longest night of my life.

We had survived a Force 10 storm, which is described in the Beaufort scale as very high waves with overhanging crests. Large patches of foam from wave crests give the sea a white appearance. Considerable tumbling of waves with heavy impact. Large amounts of airborne spray and reduced visibility, with structural damage very likely.

There was an eerie mist the following morning as we limped Calliope towards Brest, which was now the nearest port. We had been blown at least 100 miles off our original course, but with no foresail and dwindling fuel supplies, we were lucky to get there at all. Of course we hadn't been the only seafarers out that night, and as we motored into Brest Harbour we could already see people inspecting the damage the storm had inflicted on their crafts. It was an amazing feeling though. As I disembarked, I could hardly stand, my legs were like jelly as I tried awkwardly to get used to being back on terra firma. I do remember falling to the ground to kiss it though.

Peter and Tim, although physically and mentally exhausted, decided to make the repairs to Calliope as soon as possible and after detaching the damaged sail and enquiring as to where to get it stitched, wandered into the town. Nick and I found a bar with a pool table and stayed there for the rest of the day, and most of the night. The landlord and the locals were wonderful. Almost everyone in the pub knew that we'd been caught in that storm and kept buying us drinks. Every round was a toast to life and happiness. But what we didn't know at the time was that fourteen people had lost their lives that night just NNW of our position where the storm had been at its worst.

We left the bar totally and utterly arseholed and had to help each other stagger back to the boat whilst laughing hysterically. As I tried (unsuccessfully as it turned out) to get aboard I missed the deck completely and fell between the jetty and the boat and into the sea, knocking myself out cold in the process. Luckily, Nick managed to grab my belt and hauled me out to safety before I sank. Fucking typical, I had survived a Force 10 storm crossing only to nearly kill myself coming home from the bleedin' pub!

It took a couple of days before Calliope was shipshape and Bristol fashion and ready to sail once again. Peter would now take the yacht, and his father, down to the Bay of Biscay whilst Tim, Nick and I would catch the train to Roscoff and then a ferry back to Blighty. It had definitely been an adventure and one that I would never forget, but I vowed never to put myself into a situation like that again. The feeling of helplessness is something I will never forget, or ever want to repeat.

The ferry journey home was a right laugh. It was only an overnight crossing so we just sat in the bar drinking all night. There was a large group of French guys heading to England who were all carrying cases that I knew held musical instruments. It turned out they were a Jazz Band heading to Sheffield for a festival. There was a piano in the bar, so I suggested we have a jam. A few ales later, Gary and the Roscoff jazz orchestra were rocking the boat. Forty eight hours earlier, that old saying had meant something completely different!

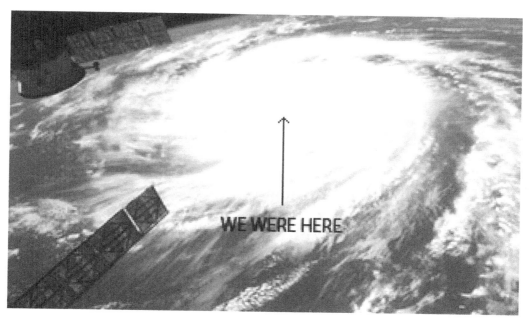

20

**"Well, since my baby left me,
I found a new place to dwell.
It's down at the end of lonely street
at Heartbreak Hotel."**

Apart from a couple of episodes of *The Bill*, which almost every actor in Britain eventually got to do at least once, the work just wasn't coming in anymore. I hid my disappointment behind drunken bravado, and spent more of Lil's money on musical equipment and wine.

I bought a new keyboard (an M1, I think), an S1000 sampler, an Atari 1040st computer, a Gibson 335 guitar (copy), and a silver bass guitar just to cheer myself up with. Lil's brother Tom, who by now was producing hit records, gave me his old 16 track mixing desk complete with cables. I spent two days installing it all in the spare room. I was still relatively new to home recording, preferring to work with an engineer in a studio, but professional recording facilities just weren't needed when recording certain types of music anymore.

Hip-Hop and rap was big now and still very much underground and subversive in the early 90's. I listened to an album called *Straight Outta Compton*, by an entertaining bunch of lads called Niggers with Attitude. This would be abbreviated to NWA for British sensibilities, and I would've loved to walk into HMV in the middle of Brixton, and at the top of my voice, and in a very upper class accent say, "Excuse me young serving person, I wish to purchase that fabulous new record by NIGGARS WITH ATTITUDE!" But I didn't.

The album had been out since 1988 but still sounded fresh to me. I used that record to teach myself how to programme, create beats and sample music together, record vocals and then put it all down onto Digital Audio Tape (Dat) to master from. All I needed was some clients.

I'd met this very middle-class lad, called Mathew, who was the friend of Lindsey's best mate Lisa's ex-boyfriend's best mate (?) who had written some Hip-Hop lyrics. He turned up at the flat with a bag full of weed and a notebook full of words. We smoked a couple of spliffs and started writing a tune about smoking spliffs. This collaboration led me to working with another wealthy white boy called Seb Fontaine.

Seb could've been anything he'd wanted to be. He was highly intelligent, came from a very good family, had a good business brain and definitely knew his music which is why he'd chosen DJ'ing as his career path. Oh yes...he also had a stunningly beautiful girlfriend who would sometimes sit-in on a session or two, which was always very, very, nice.

Seb set up his own label called Spot on Records and we started releasing stuff. We did a track called "Smells like Dope" where I sampled the opening guitar riff from the Nirvana song "Smells like Teen Spirit", added the drum fill from the Phil

Collins track "In the Air Tonight", a murderous hip-hop back beat nicked from NWA, a few random sampled vocal phrases and a saxophone break from the JBs (James Browns Band). It sold really well. We could never admit to ever doing it though, as we didn't ask permission from any of the artists for nicking their work.

Seb* and I actually worked really well together. He had no musical ability whatsoever, but he knew all about beats per minute (BPM) and what his audience were listening and dancing to. I just got pissed and stoned and did what he told me to do. I did enjoy it though, as it was always a joy seeing Seb's face light up when I got what was in his brain down on to tape. I think we made three albums together.

All of this work was independently financed though, so there was never any hard cash available. Plenty of drugs, but very little cash was ever made from financing your own product back then, as the actual cost of making and printing the record always cost more than you could ever hope to make. You would've had to have sold shit-loads of records to make any money worth writing about, but we did get some good reviews in some of the British hip-hop magazines. Bless 'em!

The next project came out of the blue via an old school friend whom I'd been at Hendon High with. Des Ashley, as well as my best friend Milton Jaghai, upon leaving school had done something that had made their Jamaican mothers extremely proud–gone into banking.

Des got himself involved with a stunningly beautiful black lady called Kanya King*, who wanted to stage a live music awards event called The Black Music Awards. I think that Kanya had wrapped poor Des around her little finger, but after listening to her plans and ideas, I too could see what Des saw in her and so I agreed to help.

After many meetings and phone calls with agents, managers, Peter Stringfellow, sound men, lighting men and ticket agencies —to name but a few, we put a brilliant show together. All the awards were given to black artists and all the celebrity award givers were black. I got Charles Augins, Craig Charles, Frank Bruno and Linford Christie, amongst others, to present awards, and the whole thing was produced by me. I don't care what is in the history books; I worked my nuts off putting on that show. During one of the many meetings for The Black Music Awards, I raised an issue about the name of the event. I said that if I held an event called The White Music Awards I'd probably get banned or shot, but Kanya and the rest of her crew didn't, couldn't, or wouldn't get my point. So I just shut up.

---

*Seb Fontaine (born Jean Sebastian Fontaine, (14 July 1970) is an English house music DJ. In 2000, he joined BBC Radio 1 as a specialist dance DJ, hosting a weekly show, as well as broadcasts from Radio 1 outside broadcasts in Ibiza, leaving in 2003.

*Kanya King MBE is the founder of the MOBO Awards. In February 2013, she was assessed as one of the 100 most powerful women in the United Kingdom by Woman's Hour on BBC Radio The annual MOBO Awards has become one of the most televised music shows in the world and showcases the best British and international urban music talent.

This show was the template for future events. Kanya learnt what worked and what didn't from putting that first show together. Maybe what I was trying to say did get listened to though, as when Kanya rebranded the event in 1996, it was renamed The Music of Black Origin Awards (MOBO).

Of course I had been drinking throughout all these projects. I would always keep a bottle of something hidden away in different locations throughout the flat. This wasn't like working with Maurey Richards, which was always booze-fuelled with passion and fun. These people had very different agendas and took very different drugs. Ecstasy was suddenly introduced into my musical world and I took to it immediately. To me it felt like an amalgam of drugs. The colour intensity effects from acid, the feeling of good-will and bonhomie from heroin, and the talking of complete and utter bollox from speed. These little white tablets would make listening to house music and hip hop almost bearable. I also started going to the pub.

I'd never really been a pub person, but now I started frequenting a local boozer that was inhabited by some of the supposed faces of Putney. Some of these guys were downright dangerous, whilst others just thought that they were. But it didn't take too long to find out who to avoid and who to have a drink with, and after a while I was accepted as a regular. I had absolutely nothing in common with any of my new friends, but after a while I became knowledgeable about who sold what, who was shagging who, and where to buy a bottle of vodka at three in the morning. All useful stuff.

My undoubtedly better-half was of course financing my new lifestyle, as I now had absolutely no money in the bank whatsoever and no way of being in any fit state to earn any. Lindsey joined the cast of *Les Miserable* and was rehearsing all day, whilst I just barked at the moon and howled with pain.

Lindsey originally joined *Les Mis* as a swing performer. This meant that she would have to learn multiple roles in case anyone was off sick, but when they came to re-cast the role of Fantine, Lil got the job. It was an amazing moment for her and I was so proud that I thought my heart might explode. On her opening night I just cried with joy at the sheer spectacle of the show that was both moving and tragic, and when Lindsey sang Fantine's lament, "I Dreamed a Dream", at the end of the first act, there wasn't a dry eye in the house.

Lindsey made this song her own, tapping into emotions I'm sure she must've felt personally. The lyrics talk of happy days that were now in the past and how her once content life could've come to this tragic and miserable conclusion. Yes… Lindsey could definitely relate to poor Fantine's plight, I think.

In 2009, a very dowdy Scottish woman called Susan Boyle appeared on a TV talent show called *Britain's Got Talent*. For her performance she sang Fantine's lament to an audience of millions, most of which probably hadn't known that the song was from a show at all. It wasn't a bad karaoke performance, but such is the power of this song she got a standing ovation from the transfixed audience and a record deal from BGT producer Simon Cowell. She didn't actually win the competition, losing out to a dance group, but with the help of social media and massive publicity the song catapulted Susan Boyle to super-stardom.

Her debut album *I Dreamed a Dream* has been declared the fastest selling debut album of all time in the UK, and sold 701,000 copies in its first week in the US alone, breaking the record for the highest debut ever for a solo female artist.

I guarantee if you go down to the Queens Theatre tonight you will hear some completely unknown actress sing it properly.

When the end came—as I knew it would, I cried like a baby and I'm not ashamed to say it. Even though I'd given Lindsey little choice except leaving me, I felt betrayal, anger and jealously all at the same time and I didn't like it one bit. I accused her of imagined love affairs and even attacked her faith, saying that she was a fucking hypocrite for marrying me in a church and taking the 'for better or worse' vow. I threw plates and cups, ripped up shared photographs and even put a guitar through the glass door of the oven. I smashed my Batman alarm clock against the wall, but had to throw it again when the alarm went off playing the theme tune. You can't really be expected to express your inner most agony with nanananananananan BATMAN playing in the background can you?

Now I had the ultimate excuse to drink! No one could reproach me for wanting to drown my sorrows in any way. I would need an audience though, so I invited a few of my new pub buddies back to the flat and threw a party that lasted for three days. People I'd only just met and after only a few minutes were busy swigging vodka in my wrecked little kitchen, telling me that I'd had a lucky escape and could do a lot better for myself.

Once all the booze ran out everyone left, taking all the framed pictures in my hallway with them and for some strange reason most of the cutlery. I was now left alone, with a severe case of alcohol poisoning, serious withdrawal symptoms and no money to get any more.

I took my remaining guitar down to a second hand store in Wandsworth and sold it for £50, half of which I spent on the cheapest booze I could find and the other £25 on a big lump of dope, which I reasoned would help me through the withdrawal once the booze ran out. I put myself into the circle of no return. It would need a miracle to break it, but not for one minute did I think I should seek professional help. And as for God...he could fuck off!

My acute survival instinct kicked in and I managed to sort out some housing benefit that apparently would be back-paid. I had absolutely no idea what this meant, but was pleasantly surprised when a cheque for £1600 landed on my doormat the following week. I gave £600 to the landlord to keep him quiet and went shopping for clothes and a new guitar with the rest. What I really needed now though, was a new woman.

One sunny afternoon, as I was drinking with some friends, an incredibly beautiful and statuesque dark haired young lady wearing hot-pants, stilettoes, and Ray-Bans was casually strolling in the sunlight on the opposite side of the road. Everyone was stunned into silence. Her arms and legs looked like they'd been sculpted from bronze and her tight T-shirt left very little to the imagination. She really was a vision. There was something vaguely familiar about her though...and then it hit me like a bolt between the eyes. It only took me a couple of finger-clicking seconds to realise that it was Beverly Downey, the hottest girl in Hendon High.

It was so lovely bumping into Beverly after so many years. She had been one of the most popular girls at Hendon High and always had plenty of admirers, me included. I'd heard rumours over the years that she'd gone into modelling, which nobody had been surprised about, and I'd seen her back in 1981 appearing in the controversial video for Duran Duran's hit record "Girls on Film" which had been banned by the BBC due to its explicit sexual content. As I still had some cash left from my shopping spree (courtesy of the tax payer), I invited Beverly out to dinner that evening with no other thought on my mind than having a good old catch-up with a girl I'd known since I was five years old.

Beverly had a hard time of late. She'd recently been in an abusive relationship and been regularly beaten the crap out of. It made her feel powerless and worthless, so she'd taken up body building as a way to redeem her self-confidence and was now winning medals for it. We talked for hours about the old days at school before adulthood had been forced upon us, laughing at shared memories and wondering why we'd never stayed in touch. I think she'd forgotten I was never one of the 'cool' people at school, but now things were definitely different. At the end of a wonderful evening, it seemed totally natural that she would be coming home with me.

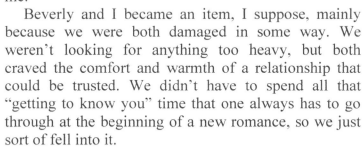

Beverly and I became an item, I suppose, mainly because we were both damaged in some way. We weren't looking for anything too heavy, but both craved the comfort and warmth of a relationship that could be trusted. We didn't have to spend all that "getting to know you" time that one always has to go through at the beginning of a new romance, so we just sort of fell into it.

I'd never gone out with a body builder before, and the amount of attention we got in the local pubs was astounding. Some people were generally interested in Beverly's chosen sport, but others were downright rude and insulting. By now though, I had some seriously heavy mates, who on hearing anything detrimental against Bev would make it their business to have a quiet word with the perpetrators before Beverly heard it and threw them through a window. I thought Beverly was the sexiest women alive.

For a few short months we just tried to make each other better. She would make sure I ate properly and taught me about nutrition, but she never broached the subject of my boozing, although I did stop drinking hard liquor for a while, and she never spoke too much about the future. I think we were both just trying to live in the moment, to be honest, and for us to think too far ahead was a path that neither of us wanted to travel down.

I reconnected with Beverly some years later and she looked fantastic. She now had no need for bodybuilding and she'd had a baby daughter. We saw each other for a couple of casual dates, but we'd both moved on considerably by now, so we went to dance classes and learnt the Tango instead.

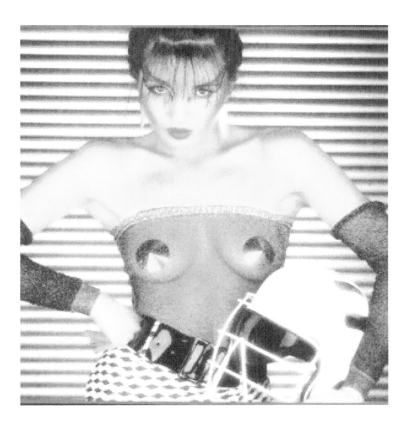

21

"Hey Nineteen—That's 'Retha Franklin, She don't remember
The Queen of Soul"
Steely Dan

I started to meet people I actually quite liked. Chris Casey, who was nick-named Tall Chris (for obvious reasons,) was a trainee chef who lived locally and drank with his girlfriend Vanessa in the local pub. I also become friendly with a total nutter called Jason Gossy, who'd spent most of his life dodging the police. I'd been warned to avoid Jason at all costs, but I found him to be charming and gentle as long as no one pissed him off, also he was always a good source for acquiring narcotics.

One afternoon, Jason, Chris and I were having a beer and shooting the breeze, when for some reason the subject of health and safety came up. The main concern was that if there was a fire in the offices downstairs, I would have no means of escape as I was on the top floor. I said that if the choice was burning alive or diving off the balcony for the nearest tree, I would choose the tree every time. With that, Jason ran full-pelt and leapt off the balcony into the branches of a tree that was about ten feet away. "Yes it's possible," said Jason.

We started drinking in a new pub on Putney High Street that had just been newly refurbished called The Rat & Parrot. The new manager Paul and his wife were very ambitious, creating a fantastic food menu including breakfasts and bar snacks. He also had an extremely pretty daughter called Melanie. Mel was a beautiful, highly intelligent and well-spoken young lady aged just nineteen who'd originated from a place called Woking. She was working for her dad behind the bar of The Rat until she could find a proper job that would utilise her university degree in whatever it was that she had studied. Within a few weeks she had practically moved in.

It was fun having a young girlfriend who also had a car. She was enthusiastic about everything I said or did. I could re-tell all of my bullshit stories over again without fear of contradiction and she would come and pick me up from wherever I was, day or night. Yes, Mel looked at me through puppy dog eyes, and I completely took her for granted. My life, for what it was, was starting to resemble some kind of normality and I started to work again. My life as an actor seemed to be over now and my agent Sharon stopped calling even to just see how I was. I really didn't give it too much thought and started to create a completely new life for myself based solely on creating music.

I reconnected with Sparkside studios in Brixton and started bringing in some new clients. One of these was a fantastic young singer/songwriter called Diana Ray, who was at the time being managed by the woman whom I'd always said I was going to marry one day, Cate Latto. Again, there was never any real money involved, but for Cate I would've done just about anything. Diana was great fun though and would often stay over at the flat just to hang out and write. I had my drinking under control once again and felt confident I could keep it that way.

I knew that to completely give up alcohol was a tall order and in my case probably medically dangerous, so I tried (quite successfully) to stop drinking in the morning and waited until lunchtime before having a few ales with Melanie in The Rat. I would then work in my home studio until I'd finished writing something, and then reward myself with a bottle of vino in the evening. It was a manageable system both financially and mentally. I could now remember what I'd done the day before and I was having fun. I'd done a deal with my landlord to keep the rent manageable and I had some new friends whom I could actually trust. Lindsey popped over a couple of times to see if I was still alive and, I think, quite disappointed to see that not only was I alive but had a brand new girlfriend who was half her age. This was probably only imaginary, but the thought certainly made me feel better.

Some Sundays Tall Chris would cook everyone a roast dinner at my place. He was at catering college now and used me and our friends to practice on. They were always joyous events, with everyone mucking in with the washing up before heading to The Rat in the evening for nibbles and drinks. Even though Paul the Landlord was originally (and quite understandably) concerned about his only daughter going out with a washed up alcoholic actor, he did eventually accept the situation, knowing that at least if she was with me no-one else would dare to fuck her about. I now knew all the main players in Putney, some only on nodding terms, but enough to guarantee our safety and security. What I wasn't safe and secure from, though, was the local Police.

One evening in The Rat, Melanie and I were having drinks with some friends, when suddenly people started leaving the pub. Apparently something was going on outside so we followed to investigate. The whole of The Upper Richmond Road had been taped off by the police on either side of my flat. I ran to the police cordon and could plainly see uniforms entering my building with dogs. There was even a helicopter hovering above. I tried to duck under the tape but was physically stopped by a policewoman, but when I told her that I was the resident at this address, she radioed ahead and I was escorted to my front door. I couldn't believe what I was seeing. There were armed police everywhere.

Once inside, I could see my flat being torn apart. All my drawers had been emptied and all my clothes were being systematically searched by officers in gloves. I just stood open-mouthed as I was handed a piece of paper, which I was told was a warrant. I had no fucking idea what they were looking for and when I politely asked, I was met with a stony silence. Then all of a sudden they all left en masse, cleared the cordons, jumped back into their many vehicles and fucked off! I just stood in my wrecked living room in shock! About an hour later I started phoning all the local police stations in the area, but none of them would give me any information whatsoever. No one would even admit to ever having been at my address that night.

A few days later, as I was leaving the flat, I noticed a police car on the opposite side of the road. They were also there the next day. This was not paranoia and I was definitely being monitored. The consensus in the pub was that certain people I'd had as guests in my flat were known to the police as very highly dangerous individuals with connections to organised crime. I'd known that some of my new friends had sometimes sailed a little bit close to the wind, but had no idea that I was fraternising with the local fucking Mafia. I started to think about moving.

I was starting to get some freelance paid production work at last. I did a mad track for a duo who always dressed in Edwardian clothes called "Peter Cushing's Hair" that was great fun to make. These lads were fanatical fans of Mr Cushing; especially his hair, which they said took on a life of its own whenever he had to fight a vampire in one of his classic Hammer movies. I spent hours watching these films to get some Van Helsing vocal samples, and they were right, his hair should've had its own Equity card. I also produced an album for an Australian band called Nightfall, except the band only consisted of one person. His idea being that, once the record was finished, he would then audition musicians and get them to learn the album.

I then worked with an acapella vocal group called Peace By Peace who were fantastic, but wanted complete control of every aspect of their career, including who they would sign to. They thought that record companies would be lining up, but they weren't. I certainly wasn't earning a fortune from all these artists, but the work was good and I was enjoying it. Melanie was fantastic at making the tea and sandwiches during the day and even more so at un-corking the vino in the evening.

One afternoon I met up with a friend for a drink in pub by the river. He (John Jaques) was the manager of the local off-license, so I'd gotten to know him quite well. John was also a musician of sorts and was beginning to set up his own midi studio at home. After a few ales we were beginning to get a tad loud and our heated conversation about creating music was overheard by a young lady and her boyfriend who were sitting at the next table. Without any introduction, the lady in question came over to me and said she was a songwriter who was looking for somewhere local to record. I gave her my telephone number and then she and her other half left the pub. I thought no more about it, but a couple of days later she called.

Her name was Jude Spiro and she was an English teacher at a local primary school. She was, I suspected, in her mid-30s, very attractive in a Jewish sort of way, and horny as hell. She played me some of her compositions, which were mostly ballads about love, and I agreed to work with her on some of her arrangements. After a few sessions in the studio Jude started hanging out socially, and more often than not would end up popping down to the off-license to acquire a couple of bottles of wine. She was great to talk to but very easily impressed in my opinion, as she thought my guitar and piano playing was amazing.

I loved all the new female attention though, and even though I had a 19 year old girlfriend, which should've been enough to massage my already inflated ego, I thought having another one couldn't do me any harm.

Keeping Melanie out of the picture was never a problem, as she was often working late at The Rat in the evenings, but if it ever got tricky, I would just tell her that I was working with a client. Melanie was far from stupid though, and although she suspected that I was being a naughty boy, I didn't care. I just wanted to have as much fun as possible. Don't get me wrong, I really liked Mel, but I was not in love with her. I didn't know what that meant anymore, so to have promised her a future beyond The Rat & Parrot and the flat just wasn't on the agenda.

I never, ever threw it in her face though, and as far as anyone local was concerned, Melanie was my girlfriend. Jude, on the other hand, was a grown-up woman who, I thought, was under no illusions as to what I was up to. She knew I was being a 'Bad Boy' (which I'm sure was part of the attraction) and even though she knew that I was full of shit, still wanted to be a part of my increasingly crazy world.

Jude Spiro…2015: "I met Gary in the Dukes Head in Putney, where I was having a quiet drink with my partner of twelve years. Needless to say, it did not take long for Gary to whisk me away and before I knew it, we were making mad passionate love under the mixing desk in his living room. It does not take much imagination to work out that I left the man in my life and became completely embroiled in Gary's mad, crazy and deliciously exciting world…one where we would stay up all night, make music, sing Bob Marley tunes to Gary's guitar and generally have a totally divine, decadent time.

We had such fun, laughed a lot, and when you are told by a man that he wants you to be the mother of his children, any resistance to his charms simply melted away. I was in love. Days of joyful delirium turned to weeks. Some days we didn't even get out of bed, and if we did, it was only to collect delivery of an Indian or Chinese takeaway.

Gary did a lot for charity and one of his fundraising events was a concert at Pizza Express in Dean Street, Soho, in support of Crusaid, dedicated to helping people affected by HIV and AIDS. He called in a lot of favours from his artist and musician friends and I was thoroughly looking forward to actually going out. Dressed to kill, I turned up with Gary, so proud to be the woman on his arm, soaking up the atmosphere of the intimate basement venue.

We were sitting together, hand in hand, drinking wine and chatting to the other guests around the table, when suddenly, everything stopped. At the top of the staircase, making her way down to the event was an absolutely beautiful woman. She was tall, slender, and elegant, with long, flowing auburn tresses and was wearing a sheath of tight white silk. Everyone in the room was transfixed, men and woman alike. (It was Karen Krystel.)

With a flashing smile, she strode straight over to Gary, murmured hello, then proceeded to sit on his lap and kissed him for what seemed to be at least ten minutes without coming up for air. While this was going on, Gary's hand remained firmly entwined in mine and he refused to let go. When the kiss was finally finished, she walked away, without even a glance in my direction and went over to talk to some other people on the next table. Gary looked at me and said "Isn't she lovely?" So, taken aback and in a state of surreal shock, I replied "Yes she is". The rest of the evening continued as if nothing out of the ordinary had occurred, and I'm sure that as far as Gary was concerned, nothing had. I was determined to keep my composure, which I did, then finally, towards the end of the evening, made an excuse to leave the table for a moment, in order to quietly book a taxi to take me home. I stood at the door waiting for the car to arrive, when breathlessly, Gary rushed up the stairs and asked me what on earth was I doing. I told him. "Please don't leave," he pleaded. "You know how much I love you!"

"I know Gary, and I love you too, but aren't you going home with her?"

"Yes Jude, I am, but I want you both to stay the night with me."

I stroked his cheek, kissed him and left — alone. I remember crying all the way home. Goodness knows what the driver must have thought. Somehow, I didn't care. I knew that was it. Life had been a party and now it was over. However, my grief didn't last long. It can't with Gary. One learns that life with him is the most wonderful adventure, undefined by conventional reality. I look back on that time now and can only smile. Gary and I have remained friends ever since. Even if we do not see each other often, I know that he will always be there for me and I love him very much, although I am not planning any sleepovers."

I can't remember why I was in Stringfellows that night, but I am definitely glad that I was 'cos as soon as I walked through the doors, Peter (Stringfellow) grabbed me telling me that he had someone whom I should meet. Sitting at the end of the bar and sipping on a vodka martini was an elderly black guy in a white tuxedo who looked like he should've been in a casino. "You won't believe who this guy is," said Peter as we walked towards him. "You are going to freak!" The thing I loved about Peter Stringfellow was his enthusiasm for introducing like-minded people to each other, so I pretty much already knew that I wasn't going to be introduced to some old football player. "Gary Shail...this is Al Cleveland."

At first I wasn't sure if I had heard him right. Did he say Al Cleveland? Yes he fucking did say Al Cleveland. If this is who I thought it was then I really was about to meet one of my heroes. I just prayed that he wasn't an arsehole.

Alfred William Cleveland had co-written two of my favourite Tamla Motown songs of all time, the 1967 "I Second That Emotion" for Smokey Robinson & the Miracles and 1971's "What's Going On"- performed by Marvin Gaye. Even if he'd only written those two songs he would've be forever enshrined in the Motown hall of fame, but Al Cleveland had also written hit songs for The Four Tops, Dionne Warwick, David Ruffin, Donny Hathaway and even Jean Pitney.

"I'm glad you popped in tonight," said Peter, "Al's working with me on a little project and you have your own recording studio, don't you?"

22

**"If you don't release this record Berry, I ain't gonna record
shit for you again."**

Marvin Gaye

Somehow Peter Stringfellow had commissioned Al Cleveland to write a song for the club. I have no idea how or why, but if Al was involved, then there had to be some money to be made.

Al and I spent the rest of the evening drinking Vodka martinis and chatting about the project. I had so many questions I wanted to ask him, but tried to remain cool and professional as I'd very quickly realised from our conversation that he was over in England on his own, without any musical contacts at all. I asked him if he'd already written the song for Peter and he said that he had a suitcase full of lyrics with him, some of which could be adjusted for the project. At one stage Peter announced over the club PA system that Al Cleveland the legendary Motown songwriter was in the house, so after that Al was bombarded with Vodka martinis for the rest of the night. He always ordered one for me as well though, and by the end of the night we were both slaughtered and hugging each other like old friends.

The following day Al turned up to my flat carrying an old bag and a bottle of vodka. It was lucky I had an elevator, as Al was very slow on his feet and would've never have climbed the stairs without help. He told me later that he suffered with bad circulation (whatever that was) but I suspected that it was something a bit more serious as he took handfuls of pills almost hourly.

As we were working on some ideas in my little studio, I asked him where he was staying whilst in London. He told me that at present he was in a hotel in Bayswater, but if all went well with the Stringfellow project, he'd think about renting something more permanent. I told him he could stay with me if he wanted to and then we could work day and night. He jumped at the chance, so I ordered a cab and we went back to his hotel to pick up his stuff.

The next few days were some of the happiest of my life. Al and I never stopped laughing. The song we were supposed to be writing for Peter was going to be called "Stringfellow Girlz", and we decided to make it as politically incorrect as we could. Girlz, Necklace of Pearls, Ass, Backstage pass, Tips, Massive...you get the picture. Once we had a basic backing track recorded, I booked Sparkside studios for three days and we headed off to Brixton.

Everyone at Sparkside wanted to meet Al and contribute to the track. Eaton Blake booked us an engineer I hadn't worked with before called Andy 'McEdit' Gierus, who was also an incredible guitarist. Andy had been a member of Dennis Bovell's Dub Band touring the world with Linton Kwesi Johnson, playing reggae, but Andy was a master of all styles and when I learnt that Steely Dan was his favourite band, I knew we would get on.

Al had a contact in London for a female singer that he wanted to use, and once a deal had been struck with her manager; we started laying down the vocals. The whole of the recording process over the next three days was an utter joy and the track sounded polished and 'clubby' (if that really is a word). We eventually decided to tone down the innuendo somewhat, but it was still very cheeky and naughty enough to go with the Stringfellow brand. When we eventually played it to Peter he seemed delighted and played it constantly at the club, but when Al gave him the final bill, Peter nearly choked on his champagne.

Whilst Al was staying with me I told him all about the police raid on my flat and how I was now being watched by the police on a daily basis. To prove my point, I told him to look over the balcony, and yes...there they were. Al told me of his times back in the 1960's when the police would batter you just for being black and trying to use a public toilet, so I felt a little bit of a twat for complaining about a couple of wooden-tops parked outside my house. But still, Al agreed that I should move out as soon as possible and picked up the telephone to call someone else he knew in London.

By the end of the week, I had packed up my clothes and recording studio, stuffed it all into the back of Melanie's car, put the keys through the letter box on my way out and moved into a luxury flat in Bayswater. The flat was in a development on The Hyde Park Estate called 'The Quadrangle', just a short walk from Marble Arch and close to all the Middle Eastern restaurants on the Edgware Road. The flat had three bedrooms and was fully furnished with a beautiful fitted kitchen and a luxurious bathroom with a Jacuzzi. Al would have the master bedroom, I would have the other one, and the spare would become our studio. Al had enjoyed working in London and writing with me so much, he'd decided to stay in town for the foreseeable future and write some more songs. I was definitely up for that.

Mornings would normally start with a large Bloody Mary, followed by another one and then we would start working in the studio. I'd originally only had a Korg M1 keyboard to compose on, but found it limiting for some of the piano arrangements needed, so Al and I went shopping and bought a full-sized Yamaha electronic piano from a shop in Denmark Street. Maurey Richards and I had previously invested in an extremely expensive piece of hardware called an MV30. Manufactured by Roland, this machine was brilliant and easy to use. The sampled sounds were great and could be manipulated beyond recognition. I could also save up to 64 songs on it and over a 1000 sounds onto a floppy disk. It also came with its own flight-case so was portable enough to transport down to Brixton, where I could just plug it in to the mixing desk, and run everything I'd previously recorded live.

The way Al Cleveland wrote lyrics was interesting and genius. He could make mundane daily activities (like taking out the trash) seem like the most important thing in the world. Al could use just three words to get his point across where others would use ten. I asked him one day what he thought made a good songwriter and he said that "if muthafuckers don't get it then the muthafuckers ain't lived it". It made perfect sense to me.

Of course I asked Al about "What's Going On" and the story that Marvin Gaye had threatened to leave Motown, never to record with them again, unless they released the album. I couldn't believe that anyone who'd ever listened to it could ever not like it. It was and is regarded as a totally sublime masterpiece, so I wanted to know why Berry Gordy had been so against releasing it, and Al said... "Muthafucker didn't get it."

Although Al had written songs for one the most successful Motown albums of all time, he made very little money from it. I asked him how much he'd been originally paid, and he told me that Berry Gordy had given him a Cadillac. I didn't think he was joking.

We rarely ventured out of the flat during the day, unless it was to get some fresh mussels from a brilliant fishmonger just off the Edgware Road, which Al taught me to cook. He'd throw them all in a big pot, splash over some hot Tabasco sauce, add a dash of Brandy and a nob of butter, then put the lid on until all the mussels opened up and drowned in the hot buttery sauce. He served them up in a bowl with hot crusty bread and butter and they were fucking delicious. Most of the time, though, we lived on Chinese Takeaways and vodka.

Of course we did have visitors on occasion. Melanie often came over after her shifts at the pub, and Jude Spiro was also a regular, although I did try to make sure that they were not visiting at the same time. One evening, though, I had gone out for some reason (probably to The Rat) and when I got home, Al had a visitor.

I'd been out on the piss one night and when I got home Al was sitting in the living room with a young black guy who was wearing more gold than Fort Knox. "Hey Gary" said Al. "I got us a little treat." There on the black onyx coffee table were three little white rocks, which I knew was freebase cocaine (Crack). This was how street coke looked once all the impurities had been removed using ammonia and baking soda. Al then handed young Midas a bunch of £20 notes, which he then stuffed into his sock and left. Al then started trying to cut and chop the little rocks so that he could line it up to snort. When I told him what this was, and how you were supposed to smoke it and not snort it, he said, "fuck man...where we gonna get a muthafucking pipe at this time of night?" Fucking priceless.

All of a sudden, and completely out of the blue, I was offered an acting role in a movie to be shot in Paris. It was a French/Anglo production and I would be playing a racist thug. I would have to be away for at least a week, and although I wasn't that thrilled about doing it, I felt that I couldn't turn it down. I had been living on Al's meagre royalty payments and even though he'd assured me that it was cool, considering I'd never billed him for any of the work I'd done to date, I still wanted to be able to contribute to the household in some way, if only to buy the vodka once in a while.

My flight to Paris was booked from Heathrow at 4.00pm and I missed it. I had been in Sparkside studios with Al the night before and we hadn't finished recording until the early hours of the morning. I arranged for Melanie to pick me up from the flat the following day at 12-ish, thinking it would give us plenty of time to get to the airport and check in, but the traffic getting out of London was horrendous and I missed the flight. Because the ticket had been pre-booked by the film company the check-in people had a contact number, so I phoned the production guys in France to let them know what happened and another ticket was arranged for the evening flight. I went to the bar.

There were hardly any passengers on that flight, so I asked the trolley-dolly if I could go into the cockpit. She asked the pilot and he said no problem. I was very pissed by now but he still let me sit in the co-pilot's seat and have a go at flying the plane. When we reached France the pilot said I might as well stay for the landing into Charles de Gaulle. Can you imagine that happening today?

I don't really remember much about making that film and I have never seen it, but I do remember Paris as being wonderful, especially in the mornings. I was staying above a little café on Le Rue de Rivoli, within walking distance of the Seine, who did a fabulous continental breakfast. On my first morning before being picked up for filming, I'd noticed that all the French postmen in the café were drinking brandy with their breakfast. This seemed to me like a wonderful custom, so I ordered a large one. These posties though were just finishing work, whereas I'd not even started my day yet.

As I say, I don't remember a great deal about making that film. What I do remember, though, is having a Mohican haircut with a swastika tattooed on my forehead standing in a Crombie coat and Dr Marten Boots in the middle of a busy Parisienne street in rush hour. As I was waiting for the shot to be set up, the actor Richard E Grant casually walked past and said "Hello Gary, busy as usual I see," and then walked off.

Back in London, Al Cleveland informed me that we would be moving once again. The flat we'd were in was only a temporary let, but now his estate agent friend found us something a bit more permanent. I remember being a bit upset at this news as I was now getting used to my new luxurious surroundings, but when Al told me what our new address was going to be, I was not so upset anymore.

Our new address was now 35 Cholmondeley (pronounced Chummley) House, Baker Street, Marylebone, London, W1. Situated on the top floor, with beautiful views over Regents Park and a living room that you could land a light aircraft in, it was spectacular. I do believe the taps in the bathroom were actually gold plated and the kitchen was a chef's wet dream come true. Soon the Christmas season would be upon us, and I couldn't wait to spend this time of year in a place like this. Al had already decided to stay in England for Christmas, which I thought was absolutely brilliant. I wanted very much to show him how the British did it and now I had a bit of cash I would be able to do it in style.

We went a bit crazy with the food shopping, I seem to remember. There was a fantastic family-run butcher's shop called The Ginger Pig that was only a short walk away from the flat. We bought a turkey, a goose, two ducks and a leg of lamb, just to be on the safe side. We also bought a whole salmon and a huge bag of prawns for the starters, and a massive black forest gateau for afters. It was ridiculous really, as we hadn't invited anyone over for Christmas day at all.

The period between Christmas and New Year was spent writing and drinking. I knew that Al was not a well man and I knew that he was struggling sometimes with his health. I also knew that he was giving himself injections, but I never asked him what for. Al refused to slow down! He was a bit lethargic in the mornings, but come the evening, he'd put on his jewellery and tuxedo and we'd be off clubbing to Stringfellows or Tramps.

Al attracted woman of all ages and whenever we went out we were never short of female company. Trouble was, a lot of them were hookers. We would be sitting in the club with some very attractive woman who, after powdering their noses with Al's cocaine in the ladies rest-room, would give the impression that they were actually interested in him. I would always try and warn Al, but he really didn't care, saying that it was only money, and on more than one occasion we would be sharing our cab home with a bevy of expensive beauties on the make. I never indulged; I hasten to add, as I was always too terrified that one of these professional night-crawlers would steal all of Al's jewellery whilst he was asleep.

Al and Jude Spiro

23

"There is no such thing as accident; it is fate misnamed"
- Napoleon Bonaparte

New Year's Eve 1994 should be a date that is permanently etched on my brain, but it isn't and I even had to check that it was 1994 and not 1993, and even now I'm not so sure. When you have been told that you are very lucky to be alive on more than one occasion, it is hard to get all worked up about something that could've happened but didn't. I could've died but didn't is such a boring story I think...But anyway...

It was New Year's Eve 1994 and I was going out. Melanie was working at The Rat & Parrot where her dad, Paul, had organised a knees-up that I'd promised Mel I would attend. Al decided to stay on at the flat, but I'd promised him I'd be back before midnight to see in the New Year and to put the champagne on ice. I caught the number 74 bus from Baker Street down to Putney and had a relatively sober evening. Melanie was busy behind the bar, but it was great to see the old crowd again and it was a great party.

I'd planned to get the bus back to Baker Street at precisely 11.15, knowing that this would get me back to the flat just before midnight. At 11.10 I wished everyone a Happy New Year and made for the door. As I was leaving, my good friend Tall Chris was just entering the pub and refused to let me leave without having at least one drink with him. As Chris and I were bantering, I saw my bus and thought about running to catch it, but I didn't, and followed Chris back into the pub.

I told Chris I had to be back before midnight if possible, and he said he'd organise a cab and accompany me to Baker Street to continue the party. A cab was ordered and we hit the bar, downing at least four large whiskies each before leaving the pub and getting into the Ford Sierra Cosworth car that was now waiting outside. I sat in the front passenger seat and Tall Chris stretched out in the back.

As soon as we started the journey, I knew something was wrong. The cab driver was definitely on something, but I didn't want to broach the subject whilst he was driving at a speed that bordered on warp factor six. I swear we nearly took off whilst crossing Putney Bridge, and as he veered left into The Fulham Palace Road towards Hammersmith, he showed no sign of slowing down whatsoever. But then, we came to a set of traffic lights that were red.

We were told four things later that night, which had probably saved our lives. One: the black taxi we had ploughed into at full speed ran on diesel, which apparently isn't inflammable, two: I had my seat-belt on, three: we were drunk and never saw it coming, and four: it had happened directly opposite The Charing Cross Hospital. Oh how lucky were we then.

What was weird is that I don't remember any sound at all. Everything was so quiet and calm. I do remember thinking I would just get out of the car and stretch my legs, trouble was, I couldn't see or feel my legs at all, let alone stretch them.

The police were at the scene within minutes, closely followed by the fire services and an ambulance. I vaguely remember some New Year's Eve revellers trying to free us from the wreckage, but it was hopeless as the two vehicles were now intertwined into a mass of unrecognizable metal that Chris and I were now very much a part of. I didn't know at the time if anyone had been in the back of the taxi that we'd hit, but if there had been I didn't care for their chances, as most of the taxi was now sitting on my lap. I managed to turn my head to the right to see if our driver was okay, but he was now sitting on the side of the road with his head in his hands being questioned by a police officer. He must have seen what was about to happen and at the last split-second turned the wheel to avoid the taxi, thus driving me head on into it.

I was covered in lots of blood which I assumed was from cuts sustained when the windscreen shattered on impact, but it wasn't my blood, it was Chris's blood. Poor Chris had not been wearing a seat-belt and been smashed against the back seats at very high velocity, breaking his arm in numerous places and causing some severe facial injuries. One of the bones in his arm shattered through the skin, which was where most of the blood was coming from, and his hand looked like a mangled red mess. I asked quietly how he was doing back there and he really did say, "Oh you know Gaz, I've had better days." We started laughing.

In fact we couldn't stop laughing. Even though I couldn't move my legs at all, I could still just about turn my head enough to look at Chris who I thought now looked like Bart Simpson, for some strange reason. It took the firemen nearly two hours to eventually free us, as carefully as possible, from the wreckage. No one yet knew the extent of our injuries, so before we were put into the ambulance, we were immobilised with head, neck and chest braces as well as splints for our arms and legs. Chris kept shouting out to me for reassurance, and I kept shouting back to reassure myself, and eventually we were both put into the back of the ambulance where we met the taxi driver, who was now being treated for back injuries. We later found out that our driver had been treated for a sprained wrist.

Once in hospital, things started to move quickly. We were both put into the same recovery room, where our clothes were cut from our bodies, which caused another bout of hysterical laughter. I said I would be putting a bill in for my extremely expensive Johnson trousers and Chris said that, if possible, could his C&A shirt be saved as it had cost him a small fortune. Of course all this joking was to mask the real fear we could be permanently injured in some way, but the humour certainly helped us through the next few hours, whilst X-rays and other examinations were performed. I was still in no pain though, which worried me even more. The doctor explained that my body had gone into a complete state of shock and even if I was in pain he couldn't give me anything for it, as I still had alcohol in my system. We were put in a room, immobilized yet again, and then left for the night.

About four hours later, I made a vow to God that I would never, ever complain about having a slight headache ever again. Where the seat-belt had locked on impact, saving me from almost certain death, it had broken everything in its path, including my left collar bone, my sternum, four ribs on my right side and fracturing my hip into the bargain. My left ankle had also been fractured, but apart from that I was fine. Chris, on the other hand, would need surgery to rebuild his shattered arm and would carry the scars from this operation for the rest of his life. His facial injuries were all only superficial, thank fuck, and looked a lot worse than they actually were. Once we'd been patched up, we were put on a recovery ward.

Unbeknown to us there was a complete search and rescue operation going on back in Putney. The last thing anyone had known was that Gary and Tall Chris had gotten into a cab heading into London, and had completely disappeared. Melanie and Chris's girlfriend, Vanessa, had been on the phone all night to Al in Baker Street, but he didn't know anything either. In the meantime Chris and I were happily enjoying the morphine drip we'd now been allowed to have. Eventually the hospital contacted The Rat & Parrot and the search was called off.

After two days of complete pain and utter boredom, I decided I would leave the Charing Cross Hospital. The doctor's pain relief medication was nowhere near as good as what I could lay my hands on, so with Melanie's help I managed to drag my battered and bruised body to her car and gently eased myself into the front seat. Tall Chris would have to spend at least a week in hospital, as his injuries had been much worse than mine, but considering what could have been, we thought it was a small price to pay.

The drive back to Baker Street was hysterical and painful. Mel had to drive at about 10 miles an hour as the slightest bump in the road made me yelp like a wounded dog, which then made me laugh, which then made me yelp even more. Al had been notified I was coming home, and arranged for a private nurse to be there for when I arrived. As soon as I was in the flat, the nurse asked me to pull down my pants, and I said something along the lines of "but we've only just met" and then she stuck a hypodermic into my butt and I slept for two days.

Even though I was wearing a neck-brace and a sling, Al and I continued to write and record. My ribs, though, would have to heal in their own good time, but with the daily shots of morphine mixed with Al's superb vodka martinis the pain wasn't too bad. After a couple of weeks I was able to laugh again without fear of collapse and fit enough to get back into the studio.

The girl Al used on the Stringfellow's track was brought back in to record all the vocals for the new stuff, which he then wanted to take back to the States to secure a new publishing deal, which I would also have to sign. A meeting was set up with a music lawyer, who I thought was charging far too much for doing far too little, but as I wasn't paying for it yet, I let Al deal with all the boring stuff and kept my gob shut about any fears I might've had. After all, I was living rent-free in one of the most desirable areas of London, with no bills to pay and a fully stocked bar, so the last thing I wanted was to ruin it all with any pessimistic thoughts. No…I wanted to enjoy all this for as long as possible.

Al had a friend who lived in London who was a Lady. When I say Lady, I mean that she was married to a 'Lord of the Realm' type of Lady, and she was as mad as a box of frogs. I cannot for the life of me remember who the fuck her husband was, but he obviously had a few bob, as Lady whateverthefuckhernamewas would often turn up to the flat in a chauffeur driven Bentley smelling of lavender water and hashish, which she smoked in a little china pipe. I really liked her.

One afternoon, whilst Al and I were jamming in the studio, she asked if I'd ever produced music for anyone other than Alfred as she had a friend who was looking for a producer. Obviously, I didn't know it at the time, but my decision to follow up on this information would have lasting consequences for me for the next ten years. But first, I was off to LA.

Al decided to return to Pittsburgh, Pennsylvania, for a couple of weeks, and the plan was that we would then meet up in Los Angeles (with the new tapes) to do some re-mixing, have a few meetings and eat Mexican food. I was going to stay with my friends Dondi Bastone and his English born wife, Jane, who lived in Hollywood. I'd worked with Dondi at The Edinburgh Festival and we'd stayed in touch ever since. The night before my trip I'd been working at Sparkside again, but this time I was determined not to miss the flight.

Melanie got me to the airport with plenty of time to spare. As I was only going to be in America for a short time I packed light, with only a couple of pairs of jeans, a few T-shirts and a bandanna, as I still had my mohican hairstyle from doing the French film. The journey would be in two stages. First I'd have to fly to Seattle, and then catch a connecting flight on to LA, where I would catch a cab for the final journey to Dondi and Jane's.

Once I was in the departure lounge I met a bloke in the champagne bar who was making the same trip as me. We got chatting over a bottle of Veuve Clicquot with complimentary nuts and I learned that he was a rep for a computer company based in Houston, Texas. He'd been in England, promoting something or other, and was now on his way back home where he had a house in the Hollywood Hills. The name of the company he worked for was called Enron.

After another bottle of plonk (or was it two?) my new friend asked how I was flying, and when I told him that I was in economy, he said that he could get me upgraded to first class as he was a frequent flyer and very well known to the airline. I couldn't believe my luck. The flight was a joy. I'd never flown first class before, and couldn't believe the food and service. The champagne never stopped flowing and by the time we were approaching Seattle, we were both pissed as farts. As I only had hand-luggage, I would only have to stagger through arrivals to the next departure lounge, where I would then meet (as arranged) my new bestest buddy before boarding the next the flight to LA. All was going as planned... until I met the dog.

I was totally not sober as I walked towards the security guards at the arrivals gate. As I was about to retrieve my passport from my bag, a beautiful German Shepherd dog jumped on me, quickly followed by his gun-wielding handler who was now on his walkie-talkie calling for back-up. Suddenly, and without warning, I was quickly frog-marched to a little anti room where I was asked to remove all of my clothes. As I took my shoes and socks off, a Police officer thoroughly searched them before asking for my shirt, jeans and bandanna, which were also searched. As

I stood naked as the day I was born, a young policeman with terrible acne stood so close to me that I could actually smell the fucker's beef-jerky he'd had for lunch. Then they found what they were looking for.

Inside the ticket pocket of my Levis was a tiny amount of weed. I'd bought a fiver's worth the night before at the studio, and the tiniest amount had obviously fallen out of the bag and was now sitting as evidence on the table. I couldn't help laughing, as you would've had to have been a very small ant to have got high on this. These fuckers were taking it seriously though, and there was a real fear that I was going to be put back onto the next plane heading for England. After a few minutes of deliberation, the decision was made that it had been an unintentional accident and I was not an international drug smuggler. I was allowed (after my haul was confiscated) to board my flight to LA. As I was going through departure, one of the police officers said, "In future Mr Shail, whenever you visit America, I suggest you wash your jeans."

It was great to see Dondi again and also to finally meet his wife Jane, whom he'd never stopped talking about whilst in Edinburgh. They'd recently had their first child, a beautiful baby girl they'd named Ella, after the legendary jazz singer Ella Fitzgerald. Dondi was a huge fan of many styles of music and acquired, over many years, an incredible record collection of rarities and peculiarities that he was only too happy to play for me. He also had one of the best collections of rare vintage whisky, which he wasn't so happy about letting me play with, but I was respectful of this, and stuck to his cheap stuff.

Dondi had given up acting to concentrate on a new career as a Music Supervisor for the movie industry and was about to start on a new film called *Get Shorty*, which was very exciting. I told him about my collaboration with Al Cleveland and we had a jolly time catching up with all the news from all our mutual friends back in England.

LA just seemed to me to be filled with Mexican restaurants and tyre shops, but it was fun driving around town and observing the 'Downtown Homies', who Dondi begged me not to talk too under any circumstances. Apparently LA was on a gang flash alert, which meant that if anyone flashed their headlights at you at night you should ignore it, because if you flashed back then you were targeted and shot to death at the next traffic lights. This was a new gang initiation process and already innocent people had been blasted to death whilst just trying to be polite. It was interesting to see such deprivation in a city that prided and publicised itself as luxurious and civilized. In this part of town kids were shooting each other over a dollar, whereas only a short drive away in Bel-Air millions were being spent on a new sprinkler system for Barbra Streisand's garden. I don't think much has changed.

One morning I got up early before everyone else, and asked a neighbour where the local liquor store was. He pointed up the road and said it was about six blocks away. It was a lovely sunny LA morning, so in my cut-downs and bandanna I started walking. After about half an hour, with no liquor store in sight, I started to wonder if I'd made the wrong decision.

As I was pondering this thought, a cop car pulled up beside me and gave me a quick blast of the siren, which nearly gave me a fucking heart attack. The seriously armed cops wanted to know what the fuck and where the hell I was going. I replied in my best privately educated English accent that I was looking for a convenience store and if it was any further could they perchance give me a lift. "Oh…you're Australian! Get in." The lovely policemen then drove me to buy a bottle of champagne and orange juice from the store which was about another five miles away; they then drove me all the way back to Dondi's house, where I woke everyone up with a Bucks Fizz.

I had loved seeing Dondi, Jayne and Ella, but now my little holiday was over and it was time to get back to why I was there in the first place. I telephoned Al in Pittsburgh to make the arrangements to meet, but he was not well enough to travel. It was a real shame, as I had really been looking forward to spending some time with him in LA, but we both thought that we could always come back at a later date, and said that we'd meet back at the flat in London later on the following week. It was the last time I would ever speak to Al.

Alfred W Cleveland died in Las Vegas on August 14th, 1996, of chronic heart disease, and I only found out about it once Wikipedia had been invented. It was never reported in the press, and not even Motown made a statement. Over the years I have watched many of the documentaries about Motown and Black American soul music, but not once has his name ever been mentioned and it's almost like someone wanted him air-brushed from history.

I wish I'd talked with Al more about his early life on the road doing the "Chitlin' Circuit"* but Al lived in the moment, and I think that the past held little joy for him. Yes, he was irresponsible with his health, useless with money and should've known better, but he was also one of the funniest, most generous and talented men I have ever had the pleasure to meet. He should've been a very wealthy man, but bitterness wasn't in his vocabulary and he always looked to the future. He was my mentor… and I got it Muthafucker!

*The "Chitlin' Circuit" is the collective name given to the string of performance venues throughout the eastern, southern, and upper mid-west areas of the United States that were safe and acceptable for African American musicians, comedians, and other entertainers to perform in during the age of racial segregation in the United States

24

"Advertising is Legalized Lying"   - H.G.Wells

Lady Whateverthefuckhernamewas put me in touch with a songwriter called Barry Kirsch. I spoke with Barry briefly on the phone about his project, and arranged to meet at Sparkside studios in Brixton to discuss it further. I arrived late for the meeting, but Eaton Blake and the rest of the staff made Barry comfortable in the downstairs office, and when I eventually arrived, Barry had already been acclimatized into my working environment. I needn't have worried though, because Barry Kirsch always felt very at home wherever music was created.

Barry had written a song called "Chasing Dreams" that had originally been intended for a singer called Leo Sayer*, who for some reason backed out of the project. I was disappointed at this news, as I'd always loved Leo Sayer's voice when I was a kid, and my mum had always been a huge fan. Barry and I felt that the lyrics would also suit a female singer though, so I got a friend, who'd been staying with Al and I for a while at the flat, to sing it. Her name was Krysten Cummings and she was like a firework ready to ignite. I nick-named her 'Snipper'.

The recording engineer for the project was Andy McEdit Gierus who must've thought (as I had) that Snipper was a superstar just waiting to happen, and they would eventually team up to record some amazing music together in the late 90's. Snipper was a great little actress too, going on to appear in many West End and Broadway shows, including *Rent*, for which she was nominated for a Laurence Olivier Award for best actress. At this point, though, she had only just started her career. So Barry Kirsch and I had been very lucky to get her.

The "Chasing Dreams" production was one of the most ambitious undertakings I'd had to date and it was going to be expensive. The finance was coming from a Greek/Cypriot millionaire, who was connected (by family I think) to the Stakis family, who'd made their fortune from the hotel chain they owned. With this knowledge I did a great deal with the studio and off we went.

The track sounded fantastic, and Barry even had a little launch party at his house in Brockley to play it to an assembled mix of Barry's musician friends and family. Then Barry hit me with a bombshell. The promised finance had fallen through. Even though I'd never for once blamed Barry, it still left me in an awkward position with the studio, who'd let me have the time on reputation alone. By now though, Eaton Blake knew me well enough to know that I would've never have defaulted on purpose, and we just had to put it down to experience.

---

*Leo Sayer is a British-born singer-songwriter musician and entertainer whose singing career has spanned four decades. Sayer launched his career in the UK in the early 1970's and became a top singles and album act on both sides of the Atlantic during the 1970's.

To make it up to me in some way, Barry asked if I'd consider writing a little piece of music for a TV commercial he had the contract for. If it did well, it would also be used for a national TV campaign and could earn me enough money to pay the bill. The contract was for a new chain of chicken restaurants called Nando's. It would be my very first Jingle.

Obviously I wouldn't be able to afford to continue living in Baker Street, and I certainly was not going back to Putney, so Melanie came to the rescue (yet again) and rented us a little house in her home town of Woking. She'd wanted to give up working for her dad at the pub and found a nice little job working for an events company that would cover the rent. It was the first time we'd actually lived together as a proper couple and it was nice. I had my music equipment, a local off-license and a Chinese takeaway, so what more did I need?

The music for Nando's had taken all of ten minutes to write, and after I'd stored it into my little MV30 I took the rest of the week off. I was bored shitless in Woking and started to drink heavily again just to get rid of the hours whilst Mel was at work. I was back in touch with Maurey Richards and we spent hours drunk-talking on the phone planning our next musical venture. These little chats kept me relatively sane but I missed London terribly.

Barry Kirsch

I never gave much thought to the jingle writing idea, but then suddenly Barry Kirsch was back on the line and I was booked into a London recording studio called Crocodile to master the Nando's commercial. I was actually really nervous about that first session at Crocodile. I was walking into completely unknown territory as far as I was concerned, and didn't know what to expect.

The studio was fantastic and, compared to what I'd been used to, very high tech. The staff were also nothing like anything I'd been used to and I was being treated like a proper client, which I suppose in a way I was. I'm sure Barry could sense my nerves, but after a glass of wine (or two) I started to relax a bit and began to take control.

The house engineer was a very handsome young man called Matthew Faddy who knew Barry Kirsch well. Barry had obviously worked with Matt on previous advertising projects, and they were like a well-oiled machine. My Little MV30 machine was wired up to the mixing desk, and I pressed play.

It sounded fantastic through the studio monitors, and Matt and Barry were ridiculously complimentary about my music, which I later found out is what they always did when listening to someone else's compositions, and once it had been synced up to the film it all fitted beautifully. We spent the rest of the evening adding little sound effects and that was it. I'd written the music for my first TV commercial.

The Nando's commercial was actually very funny. It was to advertise a particularly hot and spicy new range of chicken called 'Real Hot'. It was so hot in fact, that you had to put the toilet paper in the refrigerator overnight, so that in the morning when you went for your morning ablution...well I'm sure you get the joke.

After that very first session at Crocodile recording studios with Barry and Matt a real sense of purpose and self-belief swept over me. This was definitely a job that I could do, and do well. I understood film making and how music was essential to the texture, mood and tone of any movie, even if the movie was only 30 sec long. This way of making music was exciting and experimental. I wanted to do more. Barry Kirsch also wanted me to do more.

Barry rang almost every day and I always looked forward to him calling. He was so enthusiastic about projects that it was almost impossible not to get enthusiastic too. He wanted to write music for anything and everything, but could only do so much on his own. At this moment in time he was busy writing and recording the music score for a British heist movie called *The Steal*. He was recording and editing the whole thing at his house in Brockley with another musician called Adrian Sutton. Adrian was not only a complete computer-geek; he was also a classically trained Violinist and Cellist, as well as being a fine Pianist.

One of the first projects I was given was to produce a charity record for The Children's Heart Foundation. There was no money in it for me whatsoever, but Barry said it was a good thing for me to do, as it would get me known at the studio and raise my profile. Barry was brilliant at making me do stuff for nothing but he was always right and it did raise my profile.

I was starting to spend more and more time recording in London, and on some nights I would fall fast asleep on the train going back to Woking and wake up in Maidstone. Melanie, as usual, would always come and pick me up, but it was becoming very clear that I would have to move back to London if I was going to do this job. Maurey Richards came up with the solution.

Maurey and Craig had recently moved into a new flat in Balham, SW12. They had rented the top floor in a building that had once been an old cinema back in the 1920's and the flat below was available. I borrowed £1000 from Craig for the deposit and moved in within the week. This is when I should've made the split with Melanie, but I just didn't have the heart to break hers. Melanie was so excited to be actually moving in with me, I just couldn't do it. So once we were in, we started decorating.

The new flat was amazing and a joy to decorate from scratch. We had to buy everything of course, including carpets and curtains, as well as knives and forks. But with no real money it would have to be done on the cheap. In the mid 1990's there were still second-hand furniture shops that hadn't yet become trendy vintage shops, and they were still (at this time) selling beautiful 1930's, 40's, and 50s furniture at reasonable prices. A shop such as this just happened to be on Bedford Hill- which was directly opposite my flat.

The living room in my flat was the largest open space in the entire building, so I didn't want to clutter it. I painted the walls dark red and had dark blue carpets fitted throughout. I bought a huge chandelier and put it on a dimmer switch (which gave the effect of candlelight) and I bought a faux leather 1930's three-piece suit in bottle green. It wasn't the most comfortable sofa in the world, but fuck did it look good. The curtains were the most expensive item on the list, as I had to have them hand made by a local seamstress. The three sash windows were fucking huge and the curtains in Tesco just didn't fit.

The kitchen was all late 1950's, early 60's. I bought a beautiful powder-blue kitchenette which I restored back to its former glory, and I matched the same blue with some old knives and forks that I found in an old shoe box in the shop. There were two bedrooms, with one en-suite. I turned the smaller of the two into a walk-in wardrobe-come recording studio, and I let Melanie decorate the boudoir. To actually get to our front door you would have to climb a black wrought iron spiral staircase, which pissed off the postman but gave the building great character and looked fantastic.

Living in Balham was wonderful. The local fruit and vegetable market was so close I could actually open my living room window, shout to the veg man below, and he would throw me up 3lbs of King Edwards, an onion and six bananas. All the local butchers were Halal, which never bothered me at all, as Mohamed's legs of lamb were half the price of Tesco's legs of lamb and tasted just as good. In fact, the only time I can remember having to go to Tesco's was if I really did have to have some bacon or a pork sausage, but it didn't happen that often. Also, directly next door was a fantastic greasy spoon I that did breakfast and lunch, so the only time we ever really cooked was on a Sunday.

Sundays were all-day events in the Shail/Richards household, with friends coming and going throughout the day and always bringing something to the party. When it was Maurey's turn to do a Sunday he would always make his secret southern fried chicken and potato salad, which took all morning to prepare, whilst drinking Bloody Mary's and smoking hashish (that was his secret I think). Charles Augins always turned up with his special homemade crab-cakes, and Miquel Brown always brought the salads. The local off-licence was close enough to throw a rock through the window of, so we never ran out of vodka and wine. Yes, living in Balham was brilliant.

The other great thing about Balham was that it was only half an hour on the tube train into central London, and the other great thing about Balham was that I'd met a very sexy school teacher called Maria, who lived in the flats opposite. I think Maria and I knew we were going to have an affair from the moment we met at a cocktail party in Tooting Bec. We were in the garden, smoking, when we started chatting about music and art—as you do. She was very knowledgeable about both subjects and very funny with some of her appraisals, which I laughed out loud at. It's always polite, I think, to laugh when a lady is trying to be funny, but Maria really was funny, and when she told me that she lived opposite me in Balham and I should pop over for a little drinky-poo, I knew it was only going to be a matter of time before I would have to start lying to Melanie again.

Barry Kirsch rented a little front office space in Soho. The actual address was No 2 Meard Street, which in French, is number two Shit Street, which I totally loved, and I started spending more and more time there. The office was sub-let from an old advertising stalwart called Terry Howard, who was a total and utter reprobate. He liked drinking in the morning, taking cocaine in the afternoon, and shagging hookers in the evening, and I really liked him a lot.

Terry had been an advertising legend in his time, but now the new-bloods were snapping at his heels, and Terry had more or less retired from agency life. Terry now spent his entire time organising a Summer Ball where all the advertising agencies would get together, give each other awards, and get horribly drunk. In fact, the first year I went to the ball I won an award for the Nando's advert. Terry Howard obviously liked me too.

Barry also had a business partner called Nick Harris, who was supposed to be dealing with all of the office stuff- such as invoices and databases. Nick delegated all these responsibilities to an aspiring young author called Nikki, whilst Nick played Tomb Raider on his new computer. I really liked Nick too.

The third person who was there at the very beginning was Adrian Sutton, the computer-geek from Brockley. Adrian was the serious one, and really didn't approve of the team's lifestyles I think, but he seldom came up to the office unless it was to install yet another computer, so I very rarely had anything to do with him.

As we had no recording studio of our own yet, we hired studio time if and when we needed it. Some days, I would be in two different studios on opposite sides of town for two different clients, but I loved working in Soho so much that I would've worked all night if possible. Socially, it was brilliant too. Meard Street is a tiny little link road between Dean Street and Wardour Street. The office was right next door to what was once Billy's Nightclub, the first place that Rusty Egan and Steve Strange started back in 1979. It was then, in the 1980's, the famous Comedy Store, where the likes of Rik Mayall and Ade Edmonson changed British humour forever, and now in the 90's it was a late-night pick-up joint frequented by idiot tourists who paid £100 for a bottle of spumanti and the glimpse of a girl's tit. Yes, we were right in the middle of dream town where everything went, and usually did.

We all used to have lunch together regularly in many of the local restaurants in Soho, but the one we always ended up back at in the evening was Zilli Bar in Dean Street. Zilli's was owned by a chef called Aldo Zilli and did the best Italian food in town. Aldo was a showman as well as being a fine chef, and he got to know his regular customers on first name terms, becoming friends in the process, and therefore securing enduring and loyal patronage. It was a proud moment for me when Aldo Zilli actually started using my name in the restaurant, instead of being just known as Barry's friend.

Lunchtime was usually spent in one of the many pubs in the area. The nearest, I suppose, was The Ship on Wardour Street, where I could run a bar-tab, and the other was The Dog & Duck on the corner of Bateman and Frith Street. On Fridays (if not working) we would start at one or the other until the early evening, and then move onto Zilli's until closing time at around 11. Some nights I never got home at all though.

Quite often I would miss the train home (on purpose) and end up staying at the office, which I now had a set of keys to. Zilli's was always packed with the advertising glitterati talking bollox, making deals, drinking wine, and buying drugs. Cocaine was definitely the advertising industry's drug of choice as, after one line of coke, one could talk with great enthusiasm about a commercial for cat food all night long without taking a breath.

Some of our regular clients became good friends, and would try to educate me on how the advertising industry actually worked. At the end of the day, no matter how good a musician I thought I was, I was still only a supplier and quite low down in the chain. I quickly learnt that to get new clients would mostly depend on flattery and bullshit, and knowing where to get decent cocaine.

Barry Kirsch was the master of flattery. He could look at the worst piece of crap ever, and with a completely straight face turn to the prospective client and say that it was the most wonderful piece of work he'd ever seen. He would then hand this rubbish over to me to write music to. I didn't care though, as Barry was a visionary with huge aspirations for this new company, so he had more important things on his mind. I started to spend lots of time with Barry.

One day I called a meeting with Barry and Nick to discuss my future within the company, which at this moment was called Natural Sound. I was working almost daily by now and although I was getting paid by the jobs I was producing, I was not getting a regular salary.

I reasoned I could go anywhere as a freelance writer/producer, but would obviously rather stay with a new company and help it build. It was a huge gamble on my part, as we were now getting demo tapes daily from plenty of other musicians who were far better than me and also wanted to get into advertising. It paid off to a certain degree, as Barry and Nick put me on a £500 a month retainer to keep me at Natural Sound. It was fantastic, as my rent was now covered and anything else I made on top of that was now my Soho Lifestyle Money.

It was coming to the end of 1996 when Barry suggested renting a French Chateau for Christmas and the New Year somewhere in the south. Melanie and I would be travelling from London on the Eurostar to Lille, accompanied by one of our regular and favourite clients, a lovely old geezer called John Williams. At Lille, Barry and one of his girlfriends would then pick us up in a hired car to drive us all through the French countryside to this wonderful Chateau for the festivities. We should've packed thermals.

We met John Williams at the station and already the weather warnings for France were in place. They were not good. The whole of France, including where we were going, was under a thick blanket of snow, and we were completely unprepared. When we got to Lille it was like a ghost town, and as we stood outside the station waiting for Barry we all wondered if we should've stayed at The Dog & Duck.

Eventually Barry and his mad girlfriend arrived, and we headed off into a blizzard. How the fuck we found this ramshackle old house we were going to be staying in is beyond me, but find it we did, and once the bedrooms had been allocated, we set about trying to get the iced-up plumbing system to work. With the heating on and a roaring fire in the hearth, we settled in to start having our Wonderful French Christmas Adventure. I can hardly remember a damn thing. What I do remember though, is John Williams getting so pissed on New Year's Eve that he fell over in the men's room, hitting his head onto the toilet bowl on the way down, and me having to drive him, covered in blood, to the hospital about 20miles away in an old Citroen 2CV in a fucking snow storm.

Natural Sound was going from strength to strength and we were becoming known in Soho as purveyors of fine music, as well as being purveyors of fine narcotics. It became very clear that almost all of the people I was working with (or for) were taking cocaine. Trouble was, it wasn't regulated at all, so the quality and availability varied from week to week. Come Friday evening in Zilli's, if a dealer was in the restaurant, it was like feeding time at the zoo. There was always a cue of people waiting for someone to vacate the little downstairs toilet, and a hell of a lot of people seemed to be suffering from head colds, considering the amount of nose wiping that was going on in the place. It seemed logical to me that someone needed to take control of the situation.

Obviously I was not going to become a drug dealer, although I would've certainly made an absolute fortune in Soho in the mid 90's if I had, but I already knew of one who, with a little bit of help, could expand his little business to include some of the contacts I now had in Soho. It would be an exclusive service to the advertising industry only. Within six months, my little dealer friend stopped being a painter and decorator, swapped his overalls for a Paul Smith suit, had all his teeth capped, and started driving a Jaguar.

Barry Kirsch had lots of contacts/clients in The Middle East, and on some occasions one of these contacts/clients would be over in London to oversee one of the projects that never seemed to be registered on the books. Barry always made a fuss of these guys though, and quite often someone would be sent down to Old Compton Street to buy a box of ridiculously expensive cigars for the mysterious Arab sitting in the office. I never questioned anything as I'd quickly learnt that after the job was finished and the client happy, I would be given a large wad of cash in an envelope which nobody knew about.

All of Barry's fussing and flattery finally paid off though, as he'd managed to secure private investment to enable us to finance our very own recording studio in Soho, and when it was finally revealed where our new studio home was going to be, I very nearly spat out my wine. Trident Studios was a legendary place where albums such as Bowies *The Rise and Fall of Ziggy Stardust* had been recorded, as well as a host of other zillion selling records. Other artists recorded at Trident included the Bee Gees, Carly Simon, Chris de Burgh, Genesis, Brand X, James Taylor, Joan Armatrading, Joe Cocker, Kiss, Lou Reed, Peter Gabriel, Marc Almond, Soft Cell, Queen, the Rolling Stones, Thin Lizzy, Tina Turner, T-Rex, and my old mate John Entwistle. Situated at 17, St Anne's Court, it would be the perfect location for Natural Sound.

As a standard recording studio Trident was just about workable, but as this was going to be a studio primarily for the advertising industry, it would not only have to sound the part, it would have to look the part too. With this in mind, a mad Scottish designer called Rex was hired, who then went to work with a brief that concentrated on the word Natural.

Rex started with his team of builders by completely ripping out everything, including the floors, and then started building again from scratch. An incredible hand-cut stone floor was installed for the reception area and offices, whilst beautiful dark green carpet was laid in the split-level main studio. The space was actually quite small, but every inch of the place was utilized to its full potential giving it a much more open-plan feel.

I said from quite early on that we should have living breathing plants in the studio, as I'd read somewhere that they reduced stress and gave people a sense of well-being. The subject of plant care was then put on the agenda, where it was discussed which type of plants didn't need a lot of water or natural light. It was decided to get Cactuses, which I thought was a ridiculous idea until I saw them. Some of these plants were three to four feet in height and cost hundreds of pounds each. A few of them were actually poisonous, which meant that they would have to be well out of reach in case we put a client into cosmic shock. A false glass wall was created to house the plants which only had to be watered about once a year. With the studio lights dimmed they cast beautiful shadows across the walls—which was an added bonus, as we didn't want anything, including clocks, on the walls anyway.

The reception area was the only place that had any natural light at all, so Rex made the most of it with vibrant orange colours and a fake zebra skin receptionist desk with matching sofa. A water cooler with a tea and coffee machine was installed in this area, as well as a fridge for the wine and champagne that we planned to stock for the clients, and us. When it was all finished, after about five or six months, we moved in. Now all we needed was some staff.

We never had to advertise for staff, as Barry, Nick and I already knew we probably wouldn't be tolerated by normal job seeking human beings. No...what we needed, above experience, were girls or guys who were a fucking good laugh, prepared to go the extra mile (one of Barry's conditions, whatever that meant), able to use a computer spread-sheet, and be young and funky. Over the past year we'd got to know a pretty young waitress at Zilli's called Lyndsey Bartlett who was originally from Manchester and was brilliant. She'd studied Media Studies at university and was one of the happiest and most cheerful people in Soho. Barry hired her as the studio manager.

Next to be hired was a fantastically sarcastic and cynical woman called Rose Gunn. Barry worked with her before and assured us that she took no prisoners when it came to dealing with clients. She also had a Filofax full of session musicians she knew personally, which would definitely come in handy. Barry hired her as the office manager. The final piece of the jigsaw came in the form of young lady called Maya Hart. Maya had studied at the Camberwell College of Arts and was extremely attractive and stylish in an unconventional sort of way, but again, a real good laugh and someone you just wanted to spend time with. Barry hired her as the marketing manager. None of these job titles meant a damn thing though, as each project would bring its own set of unique problems to the table, so whatever your job title was it didn't mean you wouldn't be the one making the tea or posting the mail in the morning.

With the office staff sorted, we would now have to find the creative team who would create the product (music) to be able to afford the staff we'd just hired We always knew right from the beginning we wanted Matthew Faddy from Crocodile Studios to work with us. He had a unique set of skills and done nothing else except create music at Crocodile since leaving school. It would be a massive wrench for Matt to leave, but he knew this would be a step-up for his career, and he would also get the chance to compose as well as engineer. Also, the money was better.

Natural Sound had two working studios. The main room where Matt and I lived had all the sofas and expensive-looking equipment for the benefit of the clients, and the second, where Adrian Sutton would now live, was a smaller very high-tech programming suite, where complex orchestral arrangements using a bank of sampled sounds could be created. We also had an extensive music library of pre-recorded tracks covering almost every genre, in case a client couldn't afford tailor made-to-measure music. We covered ourselves for every musical eventuality. With our new Natural Sound logo, letter heads, and personal business cards, we were ready to rock and roll.

Word soon got out that we were the new kids on the block, and after a couple of boozy launch parties, and a few expensive lunches, the work started to pour in. One of our first accounts was for The Dixons Store Group. This company owned all the main electrical outlet stores including Curry's, PC World and, of course, Dixons. Whenever the Dixons people needed something, everything else went on the back-burner until theirs was finished. They were definitely our most important clients and took precedent over anything else that we happened to be doing at the time. Sometimes, and this happened a lot with clients, they would want three different styles of music for one commercial, so that their clients could have a choice. Whenever that happened, Adrian, Matthew and I would compose one each in a different style, not caring which composition was eventually chosen as long as the company got the job. Either way all three of us got paid, but only the writer would get the P.R.S. royalty cheques*.

*Performing rights royalties are paid to a songwriter, composer or publisher whenever their music is played or performed in any public space or place.

I was starting to spend more and more time away from the flat in Balham. Quite often I would be out with Barry until the early hours and end up back at his, or if I got lucky (which happened a hell of a lot), end up back in the Meard St Office (which we'd kept on) with a young lady and a takeaway bottle of wine for the night. Either way, I knew what I was doing was wrong and not fair on Melanie at all. I would have to tell her that it was over between us. I justified this decision to anyone who'd listen, that I was doing Mel a big favour as she was so young and had the whole of her life ahead of her. Where, in fact, all I really wanted was to enjoy my new Soho lifestyle without any ties to my past.

No one in my new world had any idea I'd once been an actor, and I wanted to keep it that way. Of course this notion would not last, but for now, it was just wonderful to be able to completely re-invent myself into a new person and start my life again from scratch. Melanie did not take it well. I'd wished that she'd thrown crockery at me or at least given me a slap, but she was just very deeply upset. She had been through a lot with me over the last three years, and when she finally left I really did miss her. She was such a loving and loyal person and I still think of her often and wish her love and happiness.

With Melanie out of the picture, I felt no guilt about popping across the road to my school teacher friend Maria for a bit of afternoon delight once in a while. I also felt no guilt at renting out one of my bedrooms to a 5ft 11inch Swedish blonde girl called Zara either.

Zara was the bi-sexual girlfriend of Diana Raymond, whom I'd produced some tracks for whilst in Putney. Zara had nowhere to live and Diana asked me if she could crash at mine for a while, whilst she looked for a London place of her own. She was great fun to have around, and felt nothing about wandering the flat in only her tiny white panties first thing in the morning—which was nice.

One night I came home late to find a white Rolls Royce with a policeman's helmet displayed on the back shelf parked outside the flat. When I entered the living room I found Zara entertaining the owner of the Roller, who was busy lining up cocaine on my coffee table. He seemed friendly enough though, and even went across to the off-license to buy a bottle of champagne. Once he was gone, Zara whispered in my ear loudly that he was Dave Courtney*, like I was supposed to know who that was.

*David Courtney (born 17 February 1959) is an English self-proclaimed former gangster who has become both an author and celebrity-gangster figure. Author Bernard O'Mahoney and the former member of the Richardson gang Frankie Fraser have accused Courtney of embellishing and fabricating his criminal record and position in the underworld; however, Courtney has denied overstating his past.

Natural Sound became my life completely and utterly, and I had started to become a well- known face around Soho. The landlord at The Ship on Wardour Street became a great friend and gave me a £100 tab limit, which I got a receipt for at the end of each week. I would then hand this little document over to Nick as expenses, and then he would reimburse me with the cash. I also had a little box room at The Ship that I could hang clothes in for meetings, as I didn't want to ever attend two or three appointments in a day wearing the same suit twice. I was now not only looking through the windows of the guitar shops on Denmark Street, I was on first name terms with the owners, who were now only too glad to give me a discount when I bought three or four guitars in one go.

25

"I like being single, I'm always there when I need me"

I was still drinking on a daily basis, but then again so was everybody else, so I gave it no thought whatsoever. Yes, I was always a bit shaky first thing in the morning, but I always kept a quarter bottle of vodka in the bathroom medicine cabinet for this very reason. I would get up, take a shower, have a ciggie and drink the vodka in one go just as I was about to leave the flat. This would enable me to deal with the morning rush hour until I got off the train in Leicester Square. I would then walk through Chinatown up to Old Compton Street, where I would purchase a small bottle of Russian Vodka from a brilliant little specialist wine merchants, before walking up Wardour Street to the studio. This amount of alcohol was just enough to get me through the morning until 11.00am when The Ship opened, where I would have my first double Jack Daniels of the day. It would take me precisely 29 seconds to get to the bar of The Ship: 3 seconds to knock back the Jack (which was already waiting for me) and be back in the studio in less than a minute. I know, 'cos I'd timed it to the second. If I had clients in at that time, as far as they were concerned I had only just popped out to the loo.

I loved being in the studio with Matthew Faddy. We were definitely on the same wavelength when it came to writing music. It didn't matter if we were writing for a chocolate biscuit or a new super-car on the market, the energy and enthusiasm always remained the same.

Quite often, if the budget allowed, we would hire in musicians and singers, and of course it was always better if you knew them well, as then we wouldn't have to go through all the politeness bollox. We started to put together a regular stable of reliable singers, musicians and voice-over performers that we used time and time again. Rose Gunn brought in David and Carrie Grant, whom I'd last seen praising God in The Kensington Temple. They were originally only hired for a series of PC World commercials, but they were so good that we used them for anything and everything. Andy McEdit was also a regular player at Natural Sound. I loved it when he was required, as it meant that I could now pretend that I was in Steely Dan for the day. On one of these occasions I'd been commissioned to write a jingle for a new luxury hotel in Dubai called The Jumeirah Beach Hotel.

I never actually met the client for The Jumeirah job, but we had quite an in-depth conversation over the ISDN telephone line*, discussing possible lyrics and musical styles.

---

*ISDN. Integrated Services Digital Network, an international communications standard for sending voice, video, and data over digital telephone lines or normal telephone wires. ISDN supports data transfer rates of 64 Kbps (64,000 bits per second).

I suggested that because of the Dubai weather conditions, which were always hot, the track should have a hot and steamy feel. As an example, I asked the client if he'd ever heard "On the beach" by Chris Rea or "Aja" by Steely Dan. "Can you do that?" asked the client, and off we went. When I eventually got to Dubai a few years later, I visited the Jumeirah and was ecstatic to hear my tune being played on a loop in the hotel's elevators.

Ems Hope 2015: "So there I am at my usual hangout Zilli's in Dean St. At lunchtime, of course. It's the mid 90's and I go to Zilli's for lunch and then again at 5.30 every day. I'm with my ex-boyfriend, a car photographer, and we've already polished of a bottle (or two) of Pinot Grigio. It's then that I spot Mr G Shail. He's laughing with friends and is gorgeous and intriguing. I ask the ex if he knows who he is. Turns out they are acquaintances and Mr Shail comes over to join us. I didn't go back to work that afternoon and spent the next XXX hours and many more with the guy I nicknamed 'Spikey'. He had the look of a Punk Rocker circa 1980 and had the most infectious laugh I had ever known...even to this day. It's up to him to tell his readers of the kind of stuff we got up to, but let's just say there were always large quantities of illegal highs and copious amounts of alcohol. We'd often end up back at mine, a sprawling party pad in Little Venice, and literally laugh our socks and other items of clothing off.

Knowing lots of people, as I worked in advertising and of course Gary worked with the rich, glamorous and infamous, we socialised with them all. We became inseparable—joined at the hip, but never a threat to others. But there was one lady that we definitely could get enough of. A brash, beautiful, half-American, with a voice and accent that could cut metal. We mimicked her name with her raw accent and soon dear Wendy became 'Wendddaaayyy' with a drop octave slant on the dayyyyy. Somehow Gary and I ended up agreeing to work on a project with her. What a disaster. Mr Shail as producer, me as project director and Wenddayyy, the client. As a hardened TVC producer she wasn't going to let us screw her around. It didn't go well. After a usual night in Zilli's on a hot summer's eve, knowing we had to take it easy and be responsible, we decided to buy just one more G and go back and party in Little Venice. I can't remember what time we eventually got to sleep but it was a huge mistake that we did, as when we eventually came to (Wake up is too generous here) we were desperately late for the big day back in Soho. Not knowing who we are or even where we were, we somehow got out of the door at 8:50 for the 9am meeting with Wennndddayyyy and jumped in a cab. Only 20 minutes late—which is pretty good in Ad Land, she was livid.

We were still fucked from the night before and found the whole thing utterly hysterical. She didn't, and might've fired us on the spot, but I can't actually remember. We did eventually get our money, but I'm not sure if we ever spoke to her again.

This is one of many brilliant, crazy and ever so slightly debauched events I enjoyed with Mr Shail. There were thousands and I could write my own book. But, until a few years ago, I couldn't remember a single thing."

Natural Sound won an award for something or other in the Middle East and the awards ceremony was to be held in Beirut, of all places. I'd written the music for the commercial, so there was never any question that I would not be going. I didn't give a fuck who took the credit (Barry normally did anyway), but I'd always wanted to visit the Middle East and Beirut in particular always held a fascination for me, ever since Terry Waite's release by Hezbollah in 1991. Beirut seemed to me to be a mysterious and dangerous place to visit, so when Barry said we'd need to apply for visas, I went shopping for a bullet-proof vest.

Even though Barry and I knew we were going on an all-expenses Middle Eastern piss-up, we still arranged a few business meetings with some fledgling new Ad Agencies to warrant the expenditure. Beirut had been at relative peace for a few years now, so it was ripe to start selling useless crap to. McDonalds and Burger King (as always) were quick off the mark and were already there, so we thought we could definitely get some of the action and set up a subsidiary office. If we installed an ISDN unit in Beirut we wouldn't necessarily ever have to go back, as we could now send the music over a telephone line. It would take a couple of years, but Barry Kirsch actually made this happen, until Hezbollah and the Israelis had another barney and started blowing the shit out of each other again.

The flight out was interesting. Most people on the plane were holiday makers heading to Cyprus, but when they all got off at Larnaca International and we took off heading on to Beirut, the remaining passengers (who all looked like Saddam Hussein, including the women) got out their cigarettes and started smoking. It was dark when we landed in Beirut, but I could still see the glints of the machine guns carried by airport security as we passed through arrivals. We were picked up by some guys outside who Barry kissed and hugged like long lost brothers, so with my recently learned 'wa 'alaykum as-salām' we got in the car and we headed off into the darkness.

I can't for the life of me remember the name of our hotel, but it was spectacular. On arrival our luggage was taken to our rooms and we went to the bar to meet our hosts. After a couple of hours drinking Arak (the traditional alcoholic beverage in Lebanon), I staggered off to find my hotel room and crash. At about five in the morning I was awoken by an amazing sound that was definitely not coming from my room. Through my Arak hangover I managed to negotiate how to open the curtains and the view took my breath away.

The hotel had been built on the side of a mountain and the strange and wonderful sounds were the pre-dawn prayers being sung (Fajr) from some far away

Mosque. This was like nothing I had ever seen before and to think that I was here because of a 30sec long piece of crappy music made me feel sad. Did this ancient and traditional world really need McDonalds and Burger King?

We had a couple of days before the Awards ceremony, so we took a drive north up the Mediterranean coast to a place called Byblos, which was credited as being the oldest continuously inhabited city in the world. We were welcomed as family and spent the entire day eating some of the tastiest and freshest fish that I'd ever had. You could actually see the boat coming in to port laden with fish that were then brought up to the restaurant still flapping, before being immersed in hot olive oil and on the table ready to eat within minutes. Lunch took all day to eat, and I loved every fucking minute of it. If it hadn't been for the fact that Lebanon was and is such an unstable place to live, I think I would've quite happily stayed there forever.

The awards ceremony was, as expected, a long and boring drawn-out affair filled with very long thank-you speeches and mucho back-slapping. When it seemed safe enough to leave without causing any offence, Barry and I were taken to one of the downtown nightclubs for some après award winners' entertainment. We had our important meeting the following morning with our new Beirut contact so I didn't want to get slaughtered and got a cab back to the hotel. Barry said that he was going to stay on at the club for a while, but would see me bright and early the next morning for breakfast.

I was having breakfast in the bar but there was no sign of Barry. I called up to his room from the hotel switchboard but there was no answer. All of a sudden the car arrived that was supposed to be taking us into the city for our one and only important meeting, so I went to Barry's room and gently knocked on the door. Still no answer. I was now starting to get worried. What if he'd been kidnapped like Terry Waite and shackled to a radiator. As I was pondering how to raise the ransom money, I heard a noise coming from the room and it sounded female. I knocked on the door again. Very slowly the door opened and there was Barry wrapped in a sheet looking like he'd just returned from a Toga Party asking what I wanted. I looked over Barry's shoulder and could just see the outline of somebody lying on his bed. "Barry we have the meeting this morning and the fucking car is here," I said, "Oh Gaz you can deal with it can't you?" said Barry, "Okay. But where shall I say you are?" said I, "Tell them I'm in a meeting," said Barry.'

Natural Sound was still going from strength to strength. Some of the agencies that we worked for would ask us for recommendations when it came to using a voice-over artist, so we would then have to go to one of the V/O agencies in London and use their guys. I thought we could cut out the middle-men and form our own voice-over agency. That way we could offer our clients a complete package and negotiate a better price for all concerned. I was very enthusiastic about this, and so was Barry Kirsch.

I'd met, on a social level (at Zilli's), a very attractive Irish lady called Bernadette who worked as a voice-over agent for The Noel Gay Agency. She was very ambitious, so I told her that if she could work in conjunction with Natural Sound and bring her voice-over client list with her, we would finance it for a percentage, give her an office and use her clients for all our commercials. I remember there being a bit of a hoo-har when she made the move, and I got a few actors slagging me off for being so ruthless, but I could definitely see the way things were going in the advertising industry when it came to the talent. The days when actors could earn thousands for doing adverts or just saying a few V/O lines were coming to a close. I knew lots of actors who were out of work that would be quite happy to say anything for fifty quid and a sausage roll, so why pay more? We called the new voice-over agency Natural Voice.

We had the office in Meard Street completely refurbished by Rex our studio designer, and Bernadette and her assistant Caroline moved in. I remember Terry Howard in the back office being very happy about this, as he now had two very attractive and funky females to ogle at during the day.

I hadn't been single for this long in my entire life and it felt strange not having to justify or lie about my actions to anyone. I got in touch with the love of my life, Cate Latto, thinking that now I had some money in the bank, this would be the perfect time to declare my devotion, and maybe have a proper relationship. Cate had some wonderful news of her own to share with me though, she was pregnant. Bollox.

Barry Kirsch came back into the office, after an obviously boozy lunch, and immediately called a company meeting. He'd been out with his old friend Ken Russell to Zilli's and secured Natural Sound the contract to write and produce the music for Ken's forthcoming movie project *Treasure Island*. Barry had previously worked with Ken on a TV film called *The Prisoner of Honour*, which starred Richard Dreyfuss and Oliver Reed and Barry won an Emmy Award for the music. Knowing a little bit about Ken's previous film work, I didn't think his version of *Treasure Island* was going to be what Robert Louis Stevenson had in mind when he wrote it somehow. And I was not wrong.

Ken Russell was going through his "I don't need any money to make to make a movie" phase at this point in his long and illustrious career, and unfortunately this movie was one of them. The film's casting was as bizarre as the script, with Ken's third wife Hetty Baines playing the title role of Long Jane Silver as Marilyn Monroe and Michael Elphick playing Billy Bones like a demented pirate. My old mate Charles Augins somehow ended up in all this glorious mess playing an extremely camp Blind Pugh.

As there was very little money to write and produce the music, we actually couldn't afford to hire our own studios, so whilst Adrian Sutton did all the orchestrations in his spare time, I hired Sparkside studios in Brixton to write and record the original songs. It was actually brilliant fun to do as I'd always wanted to write a song for Marilyn Monroe, and Hetty's impersonation was spot on. It was also great to see Michael Elphick again who, like me, was only doing this job because it meant working with the great and crazy Ken Russell.

Once the film was eventually all cut together, we were invited to a preview at a little screening theatre in Soho. As the final credits rolled and the lights came up, there was a stunned silence. The only member of Natural Sound to get a music writing credit was Adrian Sutton and I remember being slightly peeved by this at the time, but in retrospect, he was welcome to it.

Some of our regular clients became really good friends, which was brilliant as the production meetings could be done in the pub over a pint without all the bullshit that was normally spouted at these events. I once sat in a production meeting for four hours discussing the colours of M&Ms and very nearly screamed "Who Fucking Cares!" I also went to meetings where the meeting was to discuss when the next meeting was. No wonder cocaine was so popular.

One of my favourite clients was a bloke called Ross Cameron who ran a production company called Tangent TV. They were based in Dean Street and kept me busy for years. Our production meetings would normally last for about five minutes and then it would be the pub, followed by a long boozy lunch in Zilli's. Ross had a producer/partner called Tamzin Locise, who was mad as a March Hare, but totally efficient in her job. We would meet at least once a day for a drink and a chat even when we weren't working on a project, and Tamzin became my sister in crime. There was always something vaguely familiar about Tams that I just couldn't put my finger on though.

Many years previously, back in Hendon High, there had been a young lad that had also become an actor who had appeared in a movie spin-off from a successful TV series called *Please Sir*, playing the part of a gypsy lad called Nobbler. His name was Nicky Locise. I asked Tamzin if they were related in some way. It was her brother. I must have seen Tamzin running around as a five year old whilst playing with Nicky as a child. It made us even closer. As I still didn't have a proper girlfriend at this time, and Tams was unattached, we became like a couple (without the sexual side of things to ruin the friendship) and had a fantastic time in each other's company. Many years later, once Tamzin left the advertising industry, I found out that she had changed her life completely, becoming a Yoga Master and Nutritionist and marrying my old band mate Joe Mcgann. Strange world.

There are so many great studio stories that I could tell about the total and utter nonsense talked and the waste of time and money spent discussing whether or not a Bassoon sounded as sad as a flute, or if a Saxophone had the same political impact as a fucking spanner, so here are a couple of examples of what Matt Faddy and I had to endure on a daily basis.

Matthew Faddy

One day we were given the brief for a fantastic commercial for Johnny Walkers Whisky. The film was for cinema and must've cost an absolute fortune. The pretext for the film was a masked ball where everyone is dressed in baroque costumes, looking like they were guests at Elton John's wedding. Suddenly a suave-looking man appears at the ornate bay windows in evening dress, and seeing that he is not dressed appropriately, improvises by stripping off, retrieving a fig leaf from a bush and placing it strategically over his man bits before casually strolling through the astounded party goers to the bar. Once there, he orders a large Johnny Walkers with the voice-over tag line 'Expect the Unexpected'.

We had about three or four meetings to discuss the music and I suggested mixing together old classical baroque music with up to date hip-hop. I managed to get some very old vinyl records from a specialist shop in Berwick Street and brought in a Technics deck to scratch them on. We created a fantastic musical bed of sound and overlaid the scratching. It sounded wicked. I played the composition to the Creatives', who all started high-fiving each other saying it was in the bag. Or so they thought. The only person who wasn't high-fiving was the actual Johnny Walker client who thought it was absolute shite and wanted Status Quos "Whatever You Want" instead. Why the fuck hadn't anybody asked the man with the cheque book what he had wanted in the fucking first place?

On another occasion, we had a client from Sky Sports who wanted something uplifting and housey for some late night sports show. As soon as he told us that he was "a bit of a musician himself", I knew we would be having trouble and I wouldn't be able to look at Matt for the rest of the day. Matthew Faddy was a terrible giggler and he knew that I would be testing this client on his musical knowledge and ability at some point during the session. It only took a few seconds before it started.

When doing a house track most people start with the bass drum, and this we did. The computer was running and I beat out four duh duh duh duh's, before the client made his first musical remark. "Hmmm do you think that's the right bass drum?" he said. Matthew was already starting to convulse. "Oh really," said I, "I tell you what, why don't we give you all the bass drums in our library and you can choose one." With that, Matt loaded up about 200 bass drum sounds, which our client then spent the afternoon choosing from. I went to the pub and told him to call me on my mobile once he was happy.

Once we had eventually finished the track and started mixing, he started again. "Don't you think that the bass is too loud and the guitar could come up a bit?" I said that it was a rare thing to have a client who was so knowledgeable about recording music and asked him to come up to the desk to show me what he meant. Matthew was going red with suppressed mirth by now, knowing what was coming next. The client started to move the faders on the desk whilst looking at me and saying "I think you'll find that it sits better in the mix like this," I readily agreed with him knowing that it didn't matter what he did with the faders as they were not controlling the track at all, Matt was. He went away happy, though, thinking he had contributed to the production, and soon came back with another job.

We were not the only music makers in the building in St Anne's Court. On the ground floor was another company called Moving Shadow which was run by a producer called Rob Playford*. Rob had a client called Goldie who was a drum & bass DJ and recording artist and they'd had some underground hits. If ever I was bored and not busy I would often pop down to their studio for the afternoon just to hang out and meet the interesting people that Goldie always seemed to have following him around. On one occasion I had a very long and drawn out conversation with an extremely tiny young lady called Bjork, who I tried unsuccessfully to get into our studio to do a voice-over for PC World. On another time I was sitting on Rob Playford's sofa when David Bowie casually put his head 'round the door to say hello. Asking Bjork to do a V/O was one thing, but asking Bowie to sing the PC World jingle would've been the advertising coup of the century. Can you imagine it! "Where in the world... PC World". It doesn't really work on paper, but just imagine it in your head!

I didn't ask him.

*In 1994 Playford began working with the drum & bass artist Goldie on tracks written using his Rufige Kru alias. The result was Goldie's Timeless album, produced and engineered by Playford and released in 1995 on the better-funded FFRR Records. Lauded by critics, the album was one of the first drum & bass titles to achieve mainstream success, going on to be one of the best-selling drum & bass albums of its time.

26

"Fame changes a lot of things...but it can't change a light-bulb"
Gilder Radner

In 1997 *Quadrophenia*, without warning and very unexpectedly, scootered back into my life with a phone call one morning from some geezer who wanted to take me for lunch. This bloke worked for an independent film company charged with the re-release of Quad back on to the nation's cinema screens and wanted to know if I'd be prepared to help promote it. An event had been planned in Brighton, where it was hoped that the original cast would attend, watch a screening of the film, then sign autographs at an after show party. A specially commissioned train (not the 5:15) would ferry us from London Victoria with a host of TV crews and journalists asking us for our recollections of making the film which apparently had now become iconic. There was no fee involved (well I certainly didn't get one!) but there was some sponsorship to be had. I said that as long as everybody else was doing it, I could take as many guests as I wanted, and as Jack Daniels sponsored me, I was in.

A couple of my work mates (including Barry Kirsch) knew I'd once had a brief taste of fame back in my youth, but I don't think that what happened next had quite prepared them (or me) for this. The News of the World ran an article entitled 'Where Are They Now?' and they'd come to Natural Sound to interview me and take pictures.

Barry and the girls in the office were brilliant. Once I was sat in the studio with the journalist and the photographer they kept coming in with tea and calling me Mr Shail. False telephone messages were relayed, giving the impression that I was controlling the whole of the advertising industry from the sofa. "Mr Shail we have Charles Saatchi on the line, shall I tell him to call you back?" It had the desired effect. On the following Sunday, the 'Where Are They Now' article said I was now the multi-millionaire owner of one of the most powerful and influential music companies in the world.

The News of the World were renown for writing absolute bollox about people, so it seemed only reasonable to give them absolute bollox to start with. That way, whatever bollox they wrote, well at least it would be the bollox that I had given them. Made perfect sense to me.

The last time I'd been in Brighton I'd had to stay in one of the cheapest hotels in town, this time it would be different. We booked most of the suites at The Grand and put it all on the Natural Sound Credit Card. I loved Barry Kirsch's style. We treated the whole event as a work outing and took everyone, including Goldie from downstairs. It was quite an incredible experience. Jack Daniels had given me a crate of booze for the train journey and wanted me to wear a jacket with their motif on, but it was shite, so I gave it to a fan at the station. Everybody on the train was slaughtered well before we pulled into Brighton station, and the crowds that greeted us were overwhelming but pleased to see us. We were being photographed by so many people it was blinding and the police had to hold the crowds back at one point. We were bemused, and really had no idea that *Quadrophenia* had become so popular since we'd made it.

My little re-brush with fame certainly didn't make me want to go back to acting; in fact, it just reinforced my belief of just how fickle fame was. And when I heard that my former agent Sharon Hamper had been arrested and charged with fraud, I knew I'd made the right decision to quit whilst I thought I was ahead. I hadn't seen Sharon for a few years now, but I was still very sad to hear of her downfall brought about when Caroline Quentin* found out that she was owed £421,000 that Sharon had spent on a house. Sharon Hamper was eventually banned from running an employment business for 10 years and her agency went into liquidation, owing clients (including me) almost a million pounds.

I have been asked about this over the years by people who have no idea how the entertainment business was run in the 70's and 80's. This is when agents and casting directors really were agents and casting directors. These days, it seems that anyone with a Facebook or Twitter account can profess to be one or the other without knowing the first thing about either profession. But back then, people like Sharon Hamper really did create stars from nothing. When she'd first taken on Caroline Quentin (whom I'd been to school with, by the way), she was only appearing in a fringe production at The Old Red Lion Pub before she found the success that would enable her to sue the agent that made it all possible for her in the first place. In fact, if it wasn't for Sharon Hamper, I wouldn't be writing this fucking book.

One day, I got a call out of the blue from an agent at London Management who wanted to take me out for lunch to discuss a particular client of hers who wanted to write music for advertising. I already knew without listening to him that I wasn't going to hire him, but the agent sounded cute on the phone, so I arranged to meet her in Zilli's.

Her name was Jacquie and she was astoundingly beautiful. So much so, that I really didn't hear anything she said at that first lunch meeting at all. I just wanted to see her again. I couldn't get her out of my mind for the whole of the week. So, on the pretext of further discussions about her client's musical ambitions (which I knew were going nowhere), I took Jacquie back to Zilli's for dinner. Jacquie had become an agent by default. She'd been working as a P/A for an old school theatrical agent at London Management when he'd suddenly died of a heart attack, leaving Jacquie temporarily in the driving seat.

---

*Caroline Quentin (born Caroline Jones; 11 July 1960) is an English actress. Quentin became known for her television appearances: portraying Dorothy in *Men Behaving Badly* (1992–1998), Maddie Magellan in *Jonathan Creek* (1997–2000), and DCI Janine Lewis in *Blue Murder* (2003-2009).

Obviously as a P/A she'd learnt enough about being an agent to keep the ball rolling, and it was decided that she was good and ready enough to take the job on permanently, therefore becoming one of the most powerful and influential theatrical agents in London. I didn't give a fuck about all of that, as all I could think about was how I was going to get this gorgeous girl to go out with me. Over the past couple of years I had dated some very lovely ladies who'd all had jobs within the advertising industry. Most were secretaries or Personal Assistants who would flock to Zilli Bar religiously at 5:30pm for their first, but certainly not their last, large glass of Pinot Grigio.

With Jacquie things were different. I didn't have to pretend to be interested in what she talked about. Jacquie not only looked after actors, she was also one of the first agents to take on Chefs and comedy writers. She actually thought these people were the future of TV entertainment and she was not wrong. Within a year, she'd secured TV shows and book deals for people who could now show you how to boil an egg with a sexy wink and had fast- moving sketch shows commissioned with catch-phrases like "Does My Bum Look Big In This" that entered the psyche of Great Britain's conscientious, making all concerned household names and very, very, rich.

I think I actually began to fall in love with Jacquie. It wasn't difficult, as she was actually quite vulnerable and sweet under the hard-edged business image she tried to portray in The Groucho Club we frequented some evenings. One night I was sat at the bar of the Groucho abusing Jacquie's bar-tab, when Kathy Burke* came in. She was with a well-known TV comedy actor called Harry Enfield, who was a bit of a star at the time. Kathy saw me and shouted at the top of her voice…YOU CUNT!!! It was, if you knew Kathy Burke, meant as a term of endearment.

Jacquie owned a flat in Greenwich above a chemists' on the high street that was for rent. She also owned the flat downstairs, so instead of us actually living together, I rented the upstairs flat for £500 a month- which Nick at Natural Sound paid to Jacquie direct. I'd become bored with Balham and it was time for a move anyway. I now had a proper new girlfriend so no more popping over to Maria's for afternoon delight or watching Zara prancing around the living room in just her panties and socks. No…This was going to be an adult relationship based on trust and respect. We were being sensible with not moving in together quickly and it was actually very sexy having your girlfriend living just downstairs.

*Katherine Lucy Bridget Burke (born 13 June 1964) is an English actress, comedian, playwright, and theatre director. She won Best Actress at the 1997 Cannes Film Festival for her performance in the Gary Oldman film *Nil by Mouth*.

I would, of course, Miss Maurey Richards. We'd been through some emotional roller-coaster rides together over the past few years and a lot of them ended up as songs. Maurey had now quit the Platters and had started a new career in musical theatre where he'd found a new family of friends. He'd joined the cast of *Starlight Express* and had to learn how to roller-skate and sing at the same time. I went to see the show and it was brilliant. Now Maurey had a new life and so did I. We both knew that we would definitely work together again at some point, but I think we just needed a complete break from each other for a while.

Jacquie drove into work every day, so now we travelled into town together in the mornings and if I didn't have a late session at the studio, we would drive home together too. Most evenings, though, were spent in Zilli's or The Groucho Club, which was only two doors away. Jacquie's job didn't finish at 5:30pm like most did: quite often she would have to meet one of her clients socially to discuss business over a few glasses of bubbly. I would always be introduced but never encouraged to get involved with the agent/client conversation. I was really glad about that, as being from a theatrical background myself, I knew how important having a good agent was to these people who certainly didn't need or want my opinion. It was never a good idea to put me (after a few drinks) in a room full of celebrity chefs or TV presenters anyway, so Jacquie never did.

In that first couple of years Jacquie and I did quite a bit of travelling that was always connected to business in some way. There was a yearly event in Ireland for the advertising industry held in a tiny little fishing village called Kinsale that I'd been to a couple of times. It was supposed to be a long weekend of meeting and getting to know potential new clients, where in fact it was just one monumental piss-up from morning 'till night. The seafood restaurants in Kinsale were world famous, but my stomach obviously hadn't been informed of this fact when I got poisoned by a very vindictive prawn and spent the whole night redecorating the bathroom with the entire contents of my belly.

On another occasion, Jacquie and I travelled to Greece for the opening of a new play in a little theatre in Thessaloniki. Whilst Jacquie dealt with the business side of things, I did all the touristy stuff and ate Calamari and Kleftiko. The Edinburgh Comedy Festival was also a yearly event with Jacquie, where she would be expected to spot the next big comedy star on the scene and then hopefully secure them some TV work. The first year I went I only remembered one comic who made me laugh out loud, his name was Johnny Vegas*.

Things were going well for Jacquie and I at this point and we'd decided to buy a little two bedroomed cottage in Greenwich which I absolutely adored. Greenwich was going through a complete rejuvenation at this stage, with the promise of riverside cafes, new luxury hotel complexes and beautiful landscaped gardens with waterfalls.

*Michael Joseph Pennington, Sr., better known as Johnny Vegas (born 5 September 1970) is an English actor and comedian, known for his angry rants, surreal humour, portly figure and high husky voice.

Of course none of this actually happened, but the promises were enough to send the local house prices through the roof. We had bought this little cottage just at the right time and for the first time in years, I felt at home.

Jacquie and I decided to get engaged. Well actually, Jacquie decided that we would get engaged, so I bought her a beautiful little diamond and sapphire ring and presented her with it one night outside Zilli's. She was obviously not impressed with my choice, as she spent £3000 on a replacement which she then told everyone that I had bought for her. As long as she was happy, I didn't care. It wasn't that I didn't have any money of my own though. My PRS cheques were starting to come in and they were amazing.

One morning a cheque arrived and I was pleasantly surprised that it was for £1100. It had come just at the right time, so I wanted to get it in the bank as soon as possible. I went into Greenwich town centre to deposit the cheque. When I handed it over to the young teller and collected the receipt I was even more pleasantly surprised to find out that I had miss-read the cheque and it was actually for £11,000.

We also bought a new Triumph Spitfire convertible sports car in the classic Old English off-white colour that had the worst steering of any car that I'd ever been in. But it looked great with the top down and had a great stereo system, so we put up with it. We even bought a dog.

This was a happy time for me. I had a lovely home with some money in the bank, a lovely professional fiancé whom I adored, a lovely job where I didn't really have to answer to anybody and a lovely drink dependency problem that was not going to get any better. I went back to the doctors.

27

"My doctor told me to stop drinking....Then he told me to stop laughing."

My doctor in Greenwich was a very funny man, who I suspected drank more than me. He wanted to know what I did for a living and when I told him I was a musician he laughed and said I was in the perfect profession. He said that as long as I didn't have any suicidal thoughts or was planning on working with heavy machinery, try and cut down and maybe substitute vodka for wine. I didn't have the heart to tell him that I was drinking copious amounts of both on a daily basis. I did try for a while not to drink in the mornings, but by 11am I was a physical and mental wreck. No...giving up drinking would have to wait for now, as I had far more important things to deal with. Of course I didn't, but the thought of a life without alcohol was too boring to contemplate.

Soho was always fun in the summer months, when everyone who was not actually working could just sit outside one of the many bars or cafes to watch the world go by. Old Compton Street was immensely popular with London's gay community and became the home of many bars, restaurants and sex shops like Clonezone. It was a fun place to be as long as you weren't a radical anti-gay terrorist with murder and mayhem in mind.

It was Friday April the 30th, 1999, at the beginning of a bank holiday weekend when we heard the blast. It was 6.30 in the evening and we'd all finished early for the day and were drinking wine with some of our regular clients on the roof. All of a sudden it felt like all of the air had been sucked out of the atmosphere and the entire building shook. Then we heard the sirens.

By the time I'd got down the stairs and onto the street it was beginning to resemble a war zone. People were beginning to stagger up the street towards me covered in blood and debris and by the time I got down to Old Compton Street it was total pandemonium. There were people lying everywhere with severe injuries and burns. People were stripping off tablecloths to wrap around the bleeding victims, of what I later found out was caused by a nail-bomb strategically placed in The Admiral Duncan Pub, which was a well-known gay hangout at the time. It was a very worrying event, as only a week before, another bomb had gone off in Brixton that was suspected as being a race-hate crime. If this bomb had been planted by the same people then they were now targeting gays as well as immigrants in London. The death toll that day was three innocent people, including a 4 months pregnant woman and countless life-changing injuries, including amputations.

The arsehole responsible, a 23 year old loner called David Copeland, was quickly caught within a month of the explosion and stated at his trial that he was a Nazi sympathizer and believed in the master race. The jury found him guilty and he received six life sentences. I don't think that the shock of that day ever really set in.

Anyone of us could've been in that street and outside that pub on that terrible evening.

Something was going on at Natural Sound that I didn't know about. One day I came in a bit later than usual and Rose Gunn quickly grabbed me and took straight to the pub. She told me to sit down and have a large Jack Daniels before breaking the monumental news that Barry Kirsch had been fired. I very nearly spat my drink back in her face. How the fuck could anyone fire Barry? It was his fucking company for fuck's sake. Apparently the shareholders, led by Barry's former protégé Adrian Sutton, had given him a vote of no confidence (whatever that meant) and he was out. I was stunned beyond belief and obviously worried about my friend Barry, who I knew would not be taking this news very well at all. Yes, Barry did like to party, and yes, he did try to arrange work visas for the odd Russian hooker or two, but that was part of Barry's charm. He created this business from scratch, and I would've forgiven any of his misdemeanours just to watch him in full flow. Natural Sound was Barry Kirsch and it would never survive without him, in my opinion.

Adrian Sutton was one of the finest musician/composers that I'd ever worked with, but he was about as much fun as a finding half a worm in an apple. Once Barry had gone I knew that it was only a matter of time before I would be next. It really did feel like the end of an era, so when Adrian told me I now had to answer to him, it made my decision to quit very easy. I don't think anyone was surprised, but it was still very hard to leave a place that I'd thought I'd helped create. Financially it couldn't have come at a worst time though, as Jacquie had found us a palatial new home she wanted us to buy.

When Jacquie first showed me this house, in a little hamlet called Ladywell situated on the outskirts of Lewisham, I took one look at the kitchen and said yes. It was my dream kitchen. The rest of the house wasn't too shabby either. It had three huge bedrooms, two sitting rooms, a self-contained granny-flat and a basement that would fit the recording studio I'd already planned on installing. It also had a garden that you could fit an Olympic sized swimming pool in. I don't remember asking how much the house was, as Jacquie was now holding the purse strings, and I was unemployed.

Of course Jacquie still went to her office every day, but now I had absolutely nothing to do except drink and wait for her to get home in the evening. I did make a vain attempt at building a studio in the basement, but found no joy in writing music anymore, and the more I drank, the less chance I had of writing anything worthwhile anyway. Some days I didn't even bother to get dressed in the morning, and by the time Jacquie got home I would be passed out in the back garden which I'd promised Jacquie to dig over the night before. I was back in the circle of despair, and I knew that this time it wasn't going to end well.

On the morning of 11 September, 2001, 19 hijackers took control of four commercial passenger jets flying out of airports on the east coast of the United States. Two of the aircraft were deliberately flown into the main two towers (the

Twin Towers) of the World Trade Centre in New York, with a third hitting the Pentagon in Virginia. I had just retrieved a bottle of vodka from the fridge when the telephone rang. It was my friend Milton Jaghai who told me to turn the TV on. As I stood incredulously in front of the screen, the second plane hit. I opened the bottle.

"They tried to make me go to rehab, I said: "No, No, No"
Amy Winehouse

As far as I was concerned, we were now at war. I could see no way out of it. If I'd been the President of The United States, I surely wouldn't be putting up with this kind of outrageous behaviour. Surely he must know, or have a pretty good idea who had master-minded such an audacious and cowardly attack on over 3,000 innocent office workers who were probably only just enjoying their first coffee of the day, before looking out of the window and seeing a fucking 747 heading straight towards them. Yes...Bush would have to retaliate with every weapon at his disposal. I drank another slug of vodka and waited for an announcement. It never came.

There was a knock on the door. It was lovely to see two of my oldest friends again. Mark Wingett and Trevor Laird had been constant in my life ever since we'd made *Quadrophenia* together almost 21 years previously. Trevor (thanks to me) was now being managed by Jacquie, and Mark and I had always had a good, if somewhat argumentative relationship over the years. Mark also had to battle some demons in his past, but he had successfully embraced the 12-Step Programme over time and seemed to be doing well. I didn't even see the ambulance.

I think I managed to finish the Vodka before I was gently led to the white van and then driven on to the Lewisham Hospital, where I was put in an anti-room for observation. There wasn't much they could do. I was hysterical with laughter, and Mark tried to keep me calm until I somehow managed to convince him that I needed some fresh air, and then ran full pelt to the nearest off-license for another half-bottle of vodka before returning to the hospital and Mark. I wasn't fooling anyone though.

Unbeknownst to me, Jacquie and Mark had already decided that I would not be going home that night. A couple of friends of Mark turned up in a Range Rover and I was gently coerced into the back seat where I passed out. I woke up outside a stately home a few hours later and was introduced to what was going to be my home for the next six weeks. This was Clouds House, where apparently I would be offered a well-structured treatment programme for me to learn about myself in relation to addiction, my vulnerability to relapse and how I could sustain recovery by working with a 12-step abstinence based philosophy. This was going to be interesting, I thought.

The first thing they did was give me some drugs. Chlordiazepoxide (try saying that after a drink) or Librium—as it was commonly known—was administered immediately to help me through withdrawal. I'd had withdrawals before, so I sat patiently in my shared room waiting for it to happen. I wish I could say that this, (as I spent that first night on Librium awaiting the demons that were gathering in their hordes to fling their slings and arrows at me) would be a defining moment. But it wasn't. I just thought that there must be a decent pub in this part of Wiltshire that did a good roast.

The first morning was horrendous! I had a fucking hangover the size of a Spielberg production and it was too fucking early to do anything but stare at the door which I was sure would be opened at any minute by Nurse Ratched*. And there she was.

"Morning, and how are you feeling this morning?" "Yes good morning, well apart from the fact that at this time yesterday I was happily standing in my pyjamas drinking Stolichnaya from the bottle in my kitchen waiting for the world to end, I'm not doing too bad I suppose."

"Oh that's good, breakfast in five."

After a cheap breakfast of cereal and toast it was time for my first group session. These gatherings, I later discovered, were all based around the philosophy of Alcoholics Anonymous and the 12-step system of recovery. Basically, it was just drunks and drug addicts telling each other terrible stories of how their once perfect lives had been totally fucked up by a gin & tonic, or three, resulting in the loss of their loved ones, jobs and self-respect. After the first half an hour of listening to some of these quite remarkable tales of woe, I needed a drink.

With no way of getting out of this place anytime soon, I settled for another dose of Librium and took stock of my situation. The rules were strict. There were no newspapers allowed and the only literature on offer was books on recovery and the Bible. Mobile telephones were confiscated on admittance and you were only allowed to use the pay-phone once a day. The house was in the middle of nowhere in the wilds of Wiltshire with the nearest village a good hike away, where the local pub allegedly had pictures of the Clouds House inmates pinned to the wall. I did not believe this for one minute though, and vowed to visit this boozer as soon as I'd worked out my escape plan to see if it was true.

After a couple of long days and nights, I was deemed sober enough to join in with some of the activities, and one of these was to write a diary of events that led up to you being in here.

I wrote a song called 'Daze Like This'.

*The character of Nurse Ratched won the actress Louise Fletcher an Academy Award for the 1975 movie *One Flew over the Cuckoo's Nest*. About a mental asylum.

Daze like this when the world gets so busy
Spinning like a top full speed it makes me dizzy
I wish I had a break I'd slow it right down
Plan a great escape and I'd escape from this town
But where can you go where your mind doesn't follow
Running from yourself is such a hard pill to swallow
I guess I'll have to stay and turn the bad into good
Wish I could get away...If only I could.

The finished song actually has four or five verses and I recorded it for a project I was working on in 2007. If you want to hear the song in its entirety, just put my name into Youtube and you can see the video for yourselves.

By the third or fourth day I'd had enough of this place. I spoke to one of the administration people to enquire about leaving and she told me there were no refunds. I hadn't even mentioned money, but I was curious to know how much all this was costing. When she told me it was £6,000 for the six week programme, I nearly spat my Librium at her. For £6,000 I could've sobered up in fucking Barbados!

I had now made it my mission to get out of this place as soon as possible, but I would need a telephone, and as I was only allowed to use the house phone once a day, I would need to locate a mobile to put my plan into action. There was a very young cleaner who came in every morning who I'd made friends with. He was always listening to his Walkman whilst doing his chores and we'd got chatting about music. I waited until no one was in ear-shot and basically told him that if I could use his mobile for one minute, I would mail him a cheque for £200 to an address of his choice, which I was sure would come in handy over the Christmas period that was fast approaching. He wrote down his address and handed me his Nokia.

If there was one phone number that was forever etched in my memory, it was for an African bloke called Moses who ran a cab service in Soho that I'd been a customer of for years. Moses once carried me up three flights of stairs to put me to bed in the past, as well as getting me out of some tricky situations when it came to overlapping girlfriends, so I knew he was the man for a job like this. "Gary my good friend...how good to hear from you…where and when?"

By my reckoning it would take Moses about five or six hours to get out of Central London and get to Wiltshire, but now that I knew he was on his way, I could already taste that pint of beer that I'd fantasized about over the past week. I packed my few belongings and sat in a bay window overlooking the beautiful snow covered grounds of Clouds House, waiting.

It was really quite funny that nobody believed I was leaving. One by one the other inmates approached me with concern etched across their faces. They really did think I was having some kind of delusional breakdown and fabricated a rescue story to hide myself from the truth. Yes… I wasn't just hiding from the truth: I was running like hell from the truth. If there was one thing I'd learnt whilst in this place, was that I was a class A Alcoholic. There was absolutely no question about it. I didn't drink for pleasure, I drank for survival.

Some of the people I'd met in Clouds talked about reaching a 'Rock-Bottom-Moment' in their lives, and this meant that they could then start to rebuild themselves without the need for drugs or alcohol. I got it with the drugs bit. I'd already decided to quit taking drugs around my 40th birthday, but drink? Would I never be able to taste a Jack Daniels again without having to drink the whole fucking bottle? Would I never be able to just have one glass of red wine with a meal in the evening without stashing a back-up bottle in the basement? Of course I could, I would just have to try harder.

As I sat alone pondering these questions, I saw a little black dot on the horizon snaking its way through the snow towards the house. I picked up my bag, thanked everyone for all their kindness, and went outside to meet Moses. As I was putting my bag into the boot of the car, Moses looked up at the house, smiled broadly and said, "Mr Gary, was it a good party?"

The village pub had been a lot closer to Clouds than I'd thought. As Moses waited for me outside in the car, I went in and ordered a pint of lager with a whisky chaser. As I was waiting for my order I glanced around the walls. No...my picture wasn't there.

Needless to say, I was not welcomed home with open arms. Jacquie thought that I could've at least tried to stop drinking for six weeks, and to be honest I think I could've done it if I'd been in the right frame of mind. What I'd objected too was being committed (to what I thought was an asylum) without any discussion whatsoever. I knew that Jacquie only had my best interests at heart, but I took it as a complete affront to how I'd decided to live my life. What a fucking arsehole I was.

If I'd not been such an egotistical twat I could've done the six weeks in rehab, got my little medal for being a good boy and still would've been home in time for Christmas. But now I couldn't drink anything without getting a disapproving look of utter disappointment with a tad of loathing thrown in for good measure. I started spending more and more time in the basement, where I could drink without the fear of getting daggers thrown at me.

One drunken afternoon whilst Jacquie was at work, I decided to visit a local pub to play pool. I got into an argument with some local lads who obviously didn't appreciate my witty banter and boyish good looks. As I was staggering out into the street, a few of these gentlemen followed me outside, and to cut a long story short, beat the fucking crap out of me!

I came to in St Thomas Hospital the following morning surrounded by machines that bleeped. My assailants had obviously been practising their new line-dancing routines on my face, as I now had a jaw that was broken in three places and a shattered eye socket. It was explained that surgery was required, so I was wheeled into the operating theatre, where three steel pins were inserted to hold my face together. After the operation, screws were fitted into my upper and lower jaw attached to heavy elastic bands to stop me from opening my mouth. I wouldn't be

I'd complained to my surgeon, (who'd been the man responsible for inserting the metal in my face) that I now had a constant ache just above my cheek bone but could feel nothing below my bottom lip. He explained that I'd received extensive nerve damage during the attack and because of my age, the nerve endings may never knit back together. So I would have that numb feeling possibly for the rest of my life, as for the ache in my upper jaw—that, I would just have to deal with. The surgeon told me talk to my GP about pain management and prescribed pain relief, and after one brief examination, he prescribed Codeine. Chronic pain is defined as pain that has lasted longer than three to six months, though some theorists and researchers have placed the transition from acute to chronic pain at 12 months.

There was little evidence for treating most types of chronic pain with opioids, but I took them anyway. They worked to a certain degree, but the best and most reliable pain relief was alcohol. That all changed when I met Hetty Baines*. Since my disastrous spell in rehab, I had made no real attempts to stop drinking at all, and now I had the perfect excuse. I don't know why, but Hetty was the first person I actually really talked to about my feelings. We had a lot in common and spent the evening swapping stage-school stories and talking about the theatre. She was so funny and vivacious and sweet and vulnerable all at the same time that I found it easy to be honest with Hetty about my drinking and constant pain problems, not thinking for one brief moment that my admissions could possibly lead to Hetty and I becoming an item. But they did.

Hetty had a young son, the result of her marriage to the enigmatic Ken Russell, and lived in a smart two bedroomed flat in a complex on the river just south of Battersea Bridge. I could get a bus direct from Catford to Victoria, then catch another bus to Chelsea and be with Hetty within the hour. Some evenings she would get a sitter and come over to my little penthouse for the night. She would always leave early enough to be home for when her son woke up though, to give him breakfast and then drive him to school. This was the most important thing in the morning, but quite often Hetty would come straight back after dropping him off and spend the day with me. If we weren't together, we were on the phone. I had never been a telephone person, but I could talk to Hetty for hours. She definitely made getting up in the morning worthwhile, so when she suggested that we spend even more time together and move some of my belongings into her place, I happily said yes. I didn't know that this would be the start of a lifelong journey into self-discovery, recovery and madness though.

*During her career Hetty has received three best actress nominations for her performances; in 1991 as Rita in Henrik Ibsen's *Little Eyolf* (Off-West End Awards), in 1992 as Maddy in Michael Wall's *Women Laughing* (Manchester Evening News Awards) and as Marilyn Monroe in Marilyn Bowering's *Anyone Can See I Love You* (Sony and Prix Italia Awards).

Hetty knew plenty of alcoholics in the Battersea and Chelsea area, so setting up my first Alcoholics Anonymous meeting was as easy as pushing a button on her phone.

I was going to be picked up by two AA members, who would then drive me to my first proper sober meeting where I could just sit and observe. I wore a very smart jacket and tie and polished my shoes. After all, this meeting was in Chelsea, so who knew whom I might end up bumping in to before the night was through. The church was packed full of actors and minor TV celebs who were all smiling and greeting each other warmly. There were some very familiar faces amongst the throng that I'd always suspected had a drink problem, but there were others who you would've never have guessed it was possible. I relaxed, knowing that I was definitely in the right fucking meeting and took my seat.

Alcoholics Anonymous (AA) is an international mutual aid fellowship founded in 1935 (two years after the end of prohibition in the United States in December 1933) by Bill Wilson and Dr Bob Smith in Akron, Ohio. AA states that its primary purpose is to help alcoholics "to stay sober and help other alcoholics achieve sobriety". With other early members, Bill Wilson and Bob Smith developed AA's Twelve Step program of spiritual and character development. AA's initial Twelve Traditions were introduced in 1946 to help the fellowship be stable and unified while disengaged from "outside issues" and influences. The Traditions recommend that members and groups remain anonymous in public media, altruistically helping other alcoholics and avoiding affiliations with any other organization. The Traditions also recommend that those representing AA avoid dogma and coercive hierarchies. Subsequent fellowships such as Narcotics Anonymous have adopted and adapted the Twelve Steps and the Twelve Traditions to their respective primary purposes.

The one thing I got out of that first meeting in that church in Chelsea was that I was not the only one who thought the same way as I did. I heard at least twenty people talk that night that I could definitely relate too. Even the bloke who said he nearly had a relapse when his Porsche got nicked had a point. Yes, this was an asylum full of guests that could come and go as they pleased. They wanted, and in some cases needed to be here, and I could feel the positivity emulating from each and every one of these hopeless cases. When I finally had to speak it was only to say my first name followed by the immortal 'And I Am An Alcoholic.' I then had to say how long I'd been sober for, and when I said about 24 hours, I got a fucking round of applause.

It was suggested at that first meeting that I try and do two things. 1, go to 90 meetings in 90 days, and 2, read a book that was known in alcoholic circles as The Big Book. This was the life stories of the founder members of AA and, although written in the thirties, still packed one hell of a punch. I read it in one sitting wondering how two old American drunkards from the 1930's could possibly know that much about me. I started going to meetings. Lots of them!

Over the next few weeks I had some very bad days and nights. Even though I was in a safe place at Hetty's and no one actually knew I was there anyway, I still had the paranoia that came with the withdrawal symptoms that I'd been told to expect but were normal. Hetty was wonderful, staying up with me until first light, wrapping me in cold towels and making sure I ate. Whilst there, I attended every meeting in the Chelsea area, and sometimes I would go to two or three in a day, Hetty even came with me on occasion and encouraged me to share with the other attendees, which I found extremely difficult to do as I didn't know how.

I kept hearing the same old story of how a once wonderful and promising life had been ruined and wrecked by alcohol. How wives and girlfriends had been discarded, houses re-possessed, careers lost and bank accounts drained. Yes I could relate to all these things, but what about all the fun? I'd had an absolute fucking ball of a life! Yes, of course there had been heartbreak and tears, I had made a lot of money and lost a lot of money, I'd had nice places to live and not so nice places to live and I certainly couldn't complain about the women that had been in my life. So, all in all, things weren't as bad as they seemed. I kept remembering the old joke which goes like this: "I spent most of my money on wine woman and song, and the rest I wasted".

I quickly realized that to get any sort of perspective I would have to attend meetings where my fellow alcoholics didn't drive Porsches and live in riverside pads. I started going to meetings nearer to home. Even though I loved being with Hetty in Battersea, I always made a point of returning to my little Catford flat once in a while to give us both a break.

The AA meetings in this part of London were slightly different to what I'd been used to. For instance, people were more reticent to talk about themselves and the biscuits served were Rich Tea and not chocolate Hob Nobs. Also the quality of booze drank seemed to vary considerably, depending on which post-code you were in. Some of these people were raiding the gas meter for a few pennies to buy a litre of super-strong cider, which would do the job equally as well as a bottle of Stolichnaya. I could've saved myself an absolute fortune had I known this fact, but I made a note of this for future reference, as already, I was thinking about drinking again.

When the first relapse came, it wasn't the hell that I'd heard about, and it was such a relief to stop the pain in my jaw that I felt no guilt at all. Of course I lied to Hetty, but now I knew that to keep this pretence up would be almost impossible. Once back at Hetty's, my drinking would now have to be planned like a military operation. One night Hetty and I had been invited to a dinner party in a restaurant in Chelsea. I knew I'd never be able to get through it on orange juice alone, so I bought half a bottle of vodka, went to the restaurant in question during the day and stashed it in the toilet cistern. At the party in the evening as far as anyone was concerned I was on mineral water and completely sober. Hetty was so proud of me.

Of course it was a slippery slope I was on, and once Hetty eventually discovered I was back on the booze, it was only a matter of time before things came to a head. I think the final straw came when I let George the budgie out of his cage to give him some exercise and he nearly flew out of the window. She still hasn't forgiven me for that.

Hetty Baines

29

"Life and death are balanced on the edge of a razor."
Homer

My oldest and 'bestest' buddy from Hendon (Milton Jaghai) had been back in touch. I hadn't seen him for quite a while, but with all good friends it didn't matter. I'd known Milton since I was four years old and his family and mine were intrinsically linked by history and love. We were only ten days apart in age, so when he told me that he'd been diagnosed with stomach cancer and it wasn't looking good, we had a good laugh about how I would now be able to lay claim to his record collection and cricket bat once he was gone.

Milton told me he'd split from his wife Kim (whom he'd been with since high school), which I thought was a real shame, as they now had two beautiful daughters which made the news of his illness even harder to bear, it seemed. We talked and laughed over old times and promised to see each other once his next treatment period was over. I decided to try once again to get sober.

The next piece of terrible news came from another dear friend one morning whilst I was trying to clean out a toaster in the kitchen with a bread knife. It was Trevor Laird on the line telling me to sit down as he had some bad news to tell me. John Entwhistle was dead. John had died in a fashion any self-respecting rock legend would be proud of: from a heart condition brought on by taking cocaine during a night of debauchery with a Las Vegas stripper. I was actually quite happy about this, but equally as sad, as I'd always imagined John would've eventually retired to Quarwood to shoot trespassers off his land with a blunderbuss from a top floor window whilst quaffing a large brandy from a vintage glass. I decided to put off getting sober for another day.

As the old saying goes, bad news always comes in threes, so when my good friend from Soho Ems Hope rang to inform me that Michael Elphick collapsed and died from a heart attack at his house complicated by his drinking problem, I had somehow been expecting it. I had known Elphick since I was 12 years old, and worked with him on numerous occasions ever since. I'd seen him only a few months previously in Soho, and we'd spent an afternoon drinking together in The Groucho Club, where he told me he was unhappy about being cast in a show called *Eastenders*. The character he was playing was going to be revealed as a paedophile in up-coming episodes, and he thought it was awful. I totally agreed with him. The trouble with shows like this was that some viewers couldn't differentiate between fact and fiction, so all of his past acting achievements could quite easily be forgotten for the sake of a sensational plot twist in a Soap.

He was very depressed about this it seemed to me, and was obviously back on the booze, even though he'd been given some very clear warnings that if he didn't stop, it could kill him. I actually asked Elphick, knowing this information, why he continued to drink, and he said…"because it makes me happy". I knew exactly what he meant.

As rehab and AA had been totally unsuccessful for me, I decided a new doctor was needed. There was an alcohol advisory clinic advertised in a town not far from me, so I called to make an appointment. I explained to the doctor that I had tried everything, but couldn't stop drinking, and he told me of a treatment that wasn't widely known about or used, because of the dangers involved. They were tablets called Disulfiram or better known as Antabuse, and it was explained to me how the drug worked.

Treatment with Disulfiram could only start once at least 24 hours had passed since I'd had my last drink of alcohol. If I took this medicine and drank alcohol at the same time there could be a dangerous build-up of a chemical from the alcohol in the body. This could then lead to a severe and sometimes fatal reaction known as a disulfiram–alcohol reaction. If you didn't actually die, you would definitely wish that you had, promised the doctor.

This medication was not cheap though, but if it could actually stop me from drinking, then it would be worth it. My only problem would be not drinking for the 24 hours before taking the first tablet.

I started taking the medication three days later, once I'd had one last blow-out with a really expensive bottle of scotch and some good quality Belgium beer. The following day I spent asleep, followed by a night of listening to some Bob Marley, and then the following morning I opened the packet of pills and ate three. I didn't know if it was all just psychological but the fuckers actually worked. As long as I took that magic little white pill first thing in the morning, I knew I wouldn't drink for the rest of the day. There was no will power involved and no praying to a God who I suspected was far too busy fucking up the world than listen to my pathetic problems. No...I was responsible for my predicament...and I would sort it out using science. After all, if you broke your leg or arm, no amount of praying would fix that, would it?

The first few weeks were difficult though, as I couldn't get the thought out of my head that it might all be just psychological and that these pills might just be placebo. I just had to know. One morning after breakfast I decided I would find out if these tablets were real or not. I went down to the corner shop and bought a miniature bottle of Jack Daniels, which I placed onto the kitchen table before staring at it for about an hour. I thought about pouring it down the sink more than once, but I just had to find out once and for all if it really was just all in my mind. I opened the little bottle, took a deep breath, and knocked it back in one!

It only took about two minutes before I wished that I'd poured it down the sink. I started to convulse violently before my entire body felt like it was on fire. My eyes felt like they were bleeding and when I looked at my bloated face in the bathroom mirror, I could see that they actually were. I looked like Dracula just after he'd finished his dinner. I thought about phoning an ambulance, but what would I say? I wrapped myself into a duvet and spent the rest of the day thanking myself for not trying out this stupid experiment with a bottle of vodka.

Things were looking up, and although I was alone, I was relatively happy. With most of my savings now gone, and not too keen on dealing with the benefits system, I needed a job. I always knew that one day Maurey Richards and I would work together again; I just didn't think it would be like this though!

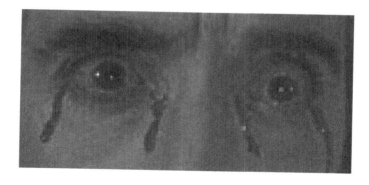

30

"The wise musicians are those who play what they can master"
Duke Ellington

Maurey Richards turned up at my flat one afternoon with a request that I knew could put my entire recovery into jeopardy. After his brief stint as a West End performer, he'd decided to go back to what he thought he did best: playing live. Maurey had secured a gig at a little coffee house on The Old Brompton Road called The Troubadour that had once been a very famous live music venue back in the 50's and 60's. The new owners wanted to re-vamp the place and re-launch the Troubadour as a venue for live music once again.

Maurey had a new band that would be playing jazz standards and they needed a sound engineer for a gig planned for the following weekend. The money wasn't brilliant, and I suspected it was coming out of Maurey's own pocket, but I had nothing else on the cards, so I agreed to do it.

The club was in the basement of the coffee house and had a 120 capacity with a tiny stage and an even tinier dressing room to the side. I'd arrived at the club early to get acquainted with the equipment that was available and to meet Maurey and his new band. That first show was a complete and utter shambles. The thing about jazz musicians is that they seem to think they can play any old bollox, and as long as they start and finish at the same time, anything goes. I always hated this kind of jazz, as it was always so predictable. Song starts, singer sings, piano solo, bass solo, drum fucking solo, whatever else fucking solo, back to chorus and finish with a flourish looking pleased with yourself. Yes, it can safely be said that there weren't many jazz albums in my record collection, and although the playing was undoubtedly impressive, it was as boring as fuck. The audience for that first performance, although sparse in numbers, were very appreciative though, and Maurey and his band were booked again for the following week. (So what did I know?)

As I was clearing the stage of microphones and leads, the owner and his wife, who'd both been in the audience that night came over to tell me that the sound in the club that evening had been the best yet, and would I consider possibly doing the sound for some future gigs that were planned in the very near future. These lovely people thought I was a sound engineer and in some respects I suppose I was. After all, I'd been listening to and making music for most of my adult life, a lot of that time in recording studios where micing up a drum kit was one of the first things you learnt back in the days when musicians actually played their instruments.

I asked Simon the owner what the pay was, and he said he'd give me £10 an hour and arrange for a car to drive me home as I would be required to be at the club until closing time, which on some nights could be 3am. So if I started setting up for the show at say 6 in the evening, I could be going home with £90 per night. I told Simon and his lovely wife Susie that as long as I was paid in cash, I would be very happy to be the new resident sound engineer for the new Troubadour Club. I knew I had to stay sober to do this job, but how? I would now be surrounded by booze that would be available to me on demand. I had my little magic pills though, so it wouldn't be a problem, would it?

For the first couple of weeks, I treated the Troubadour Coffee-House and the Troubadour Club downstairs as two completely different places. At the very beginning, I started coming in during the afternoons to sort out the sound and lights. Simon (the owner) could be a bit abrasive sometimes, but he fully supported any ideas I had regarding any new equipment that I thought would be beneficial to the club. Simon knew full well that to attract any decent acts in a venue of this size, then there could be no hint of any feedback. Simon was a rhythm and blues man at heart, and with that in mind we made sure we had enough SM58 microphones to mic-up the entire band, including the drummer if needed. SM58s were the Sherman Tanks of the microphone world, as they could be thrown against a brick wall and still be working at the end of every gig.

Once mic'd, all of the sound and vocals could now be controlled completely from Gary's Hut. Gary's Hut was originally the sound booth, where the engineer would control the sound and lights, but it became much more than that to me. I treated it more like a garden shed than a sound booth. First thing I did was put a combination lock on the door with only Simon and I in possession of the numbers. I would also be using this little room to lock away things like microphones and leads. I would be responsible for their safety, so I wanted them under lock and key. You'd be surprised how many microphones can disappear each year from a venue.

After about two weeks of trial and error, I now knew the sound I could achieve in such a small space. Of course it always sounded better when the club was full, but some nights I would be mixing the sound for a singer-songwriter with just a guitar and only twenty people in the audience. So whoever was playing on any particular evening I would always ask for a brief sound-check, so I could see what I was letting myself in for. We've all been to a live gig where the sound is atrocious and everyone looks at the poor sound-guy, well that was never going to happen whilst I was in charge.

Most of the artists were over the moon about this as they all had the same horror stories about bad sound men who didn't give a toss and just turned the mic on and then fucked off for a fag! I never wanted anyone to ever say that of me, so I always did my very best to give the performers the sound that they wanted, even if they didn't know it. If a band or solo performer wanted a great sounding little gig to showcase their talents, then you could definitely do a lot worse than play at The Troubadour.

I also started using the lights. It was a very old system but I'd learnt on something similar when I was at Nucleus Drama Club as a boy, so it was great fun getting it all to work properly again.

I also re-arranged all the Fresnel lanterns and spots and bought new multi-coloured gels to jazz things up a bit. The bands and singer-songwriters loved it. I could now give each song it's very own lighting cues and fades. It's much more dramatic if the lights fade to black at the end of a song, in my book.

Maurey Richard's band was getting better every week. They started to funk things up (I said funk) and did some far less self-indulgent new arrangements. The drummer was fucking incredible, not only for his drumming, but because he could hardly stand three minutes before doing a show. His name was Paul, and he was an alcoholic.

One night no one could find Paul the drummer. He was eventually found lying paralytic under a bunch of coats in the dressing room. When Maurey woke him to do the gig he told everyone that they were complete and utter cunts and to fuck off. He then went out and played one of the best shows ever. When Paul was sober he was one of the nicest guys on the planet, but after just one vodka he'd turn into a total tosser until he drank himself into a coma, completely forgetting who he'd insulted the night before. This was just the kind of person I needed to be around. I told Paul in complete confidence about my own battle with the bottle but told him empathetically that I was not going to even attempt to make him stop drinking, but if he ever needed someone to talk to who knew exactly what he was going through, I would be around. Paul treated me differently after that and we became very close friends.

Another very interesting thing about working at a restaurant was the un-spoken hierarchy that existed amongst the waiting staff. I found all the politics, intrigues and tantrums wildly exciting as sometimes it almost felt like an arguing family unit, and I never even wondered or cared what their lives away from The Troubadour were like. That all changed one day when one of the waitresses came downstairs and asked if I had some time to chat about an idea that she had about putting on a one woman show starring her. Her name was Celine Hispiche.

Celine was a poet in the original sense of the word, and funnily enough, much like a real Troubadour*. She had stories to tell, and whether real or imaginary, told her fantastical tales to her customers whilst delivering lattes and croissants with a smile and a curtsey. She was nothing like any of the other waitresses I'd seen strutting about, so when she came to talk to me one afternoon whilst I was doing something or other in the club downstairs, I was intrigued!

Celine had noticed that I was now putting on shows and not just performances. She wanted to know if I could put on a show just for her that would include shit loads of music cues, costume changes and lighting effects. It was such a strange idea as she had absolutely nothing to show to me on paper. Of course I wanted to do it.

---

*A French medieval lyric poet composing and singing in Provençal in the 11th to 13th centuries, especially on the theme of courtly love.

The show was going to be called Celine the Mysterious. We started working on an idea that was quite frankly ridiculous. Everything Celine did was off the cuff, and she could change her remarkably agile mind at any given time. It scared the shit out of me because as the producer, which I supposed I now was, I had absolutely no idea what Celine would get up to next. Her show made no sense to me whatsoever. I can honestly say being on stage with Mark (Brain Damage) Wingett was a far less scary thought. Celine was so focused and committed though, that I bought into it entirely. We had no time at all to actually rehearse anything at the club, but a date was set anyway for 'Celine the Mysterious' and she started designing the bloody poster.

The show would consist of monologues, a dance routine and a potted history of vaudeville, amongst other things that might be thrown in at the last minute. As I was busy engineering a gig in the evening, Celine would rush into my little hut and blurt out yet another mad idea whilst I was trying to focus on my fucking job. I had to sit her down one evening and tell her in no uncertain terms that she was doing my fucking brain in, and we needed to fucking rehearse. I decided that if Celine could coincide her shifts in the I with mine in the club, then we would both have our days free, and even though we would both be totally knackered, we could actually map out her show and perhaps stop me from actually possibly having a fucking heart attack.

As Celine lived absolutely nowhere near me, I decided she should move into my little flat for the duration. Now...I know what you must be thinking, but there really was no other option, and anyway, Paul the alcoholic drummer was spending a lot of time at the flat anyway and I just didn't see Celine in that way at all. I had become very fond of Celine the bleeding mysterious by now, and I never wanted to risk our blossoming friendship with some kind of misplaced pass. If I'd been back on the booze though, then this story could've had a completely different ending. My little white magic pills were working just fine, thank you, and it had been at least three months since my last drink. I could even watch Paul down his half bottle of vodka in the morning without getting the urge and the memory of drinking whilst on Antabuse and the effects it had had were still very fresh in my mind.

When the big night came we had one technical rehearsal for the sound and lights, and then a dress rehearsal where everything went totally tits-up, and then we waited for the audience to take their seats. Unbeknownst to me, Celine had been very busy in the café upstairs, telling anybody and everybody about her show and telling them all to come. And come they did. The place was packed to the rafters. In fact it was a complete sell-out with a risk of us getting a visit from the fire department for breaking the 120 capacity rule.

As I sat in my little hut preparing all the sound and lighting cues, I felt a wave of excitement I hadn't felt in years, and I was so thankful to Celine for giving me this kind of feeling once again. There is nothing like complete and utter terror to focus the mind. Celine would be performing so close to the audience, that if she faltered even for a second, they would all know. She was flawless though and received two standing ovations. Even I had to admit that Celine the Bloody Mysterious was fantastic. I left my little hut.., and joined in with the applause!

Celine the Mysterious

I hate working! Now by that remark I certainly don't mean that I am lazy, far from it, it's just that if left to my own devices I will get far more done than if I am told to do something. I have always been this way. I truly believe I am unemployable. That doesn't mean that I shouldn't be hired, just don't expect me to clock on at a certain time, answer to a supervisor, or hand in a Curriculum Vitae... because it is not going to happen.

I enjoyed my few months at The Troubadour immensely, and watching the club quickly grow into a vibrant music venue that could easily hold its own against more established places like The Rock Garden. It had been a pure joy. But for me the pleasure had been embryonic. Of course the Troubadour Club had existed way before I happened to fall down its hallowed steps, it's just that I truly believed that I had seriously shifted it up a gear and given it some order. Maybe this was all just in my pickled mind, but I never, not even for one tiny minute, ever thought of myself as a member of the Troubadour staff. Even the Troubadour staff didn't think of me as being a member of the Troubadour staff. I'd been asked personally by the owners Simon and Susie to sort out the sound and lights, and this I had most certainly done. Yes I had been paid well to do it, and quite frankly, now that it had all been set up, a first year sound engineering student could've done this job in his sleep. The dynamics of my position within the company had begun to change.

One afternoon, whilst I was changing batteries, sorting out leads, and generally doing my maintenance chores, a very young bespectacled lad who looked like he had a pineapple shoved up his arse introduced himself to me as the new 'Club Manager'.

He then told me that now the sound and lights had been sorted, I would only be required to come in, when requested, to do whatever it was that I did in the evening. I would also be required to sign up to P.A.Y.E...whatever that was...and be paid accordingly. I stopped what I was doing immediately, picked up my jacket, and left. I didn't even bother to say goodbye.

Actually, thinking about it now, Simon and Susie taught me a very valuable lesson in life. Never let the monkey know where the peanut is hidden. Or to make an even clearer analogy, don't let the Muggles know the Magic. Before I left The Troubadour, I could've quite easily re-routed all the cables to the mixing desk, took out all the batteries from the direct injection boxes and re-programmed the lighting board. I could've quite easily leave the place as I'd found it, if I'd been that kind of guy, but I'm not, thank fuck, and I wish The Troubadour well. I have many great friends who have since played there, and they all want to play there again.

So now I was out of work yet again, and without the booze to relieve the boredom, all I had for entertainment was to watch the American and British Armed Forces bomb the shit out of Baghdad. It was 2003 and, according to U.S. President George W. Bush and British Prime Minister Tony Blair, the coalition mission was to disarm Iraq of weapons of mass destruction, to end Saddam Hussein's support for terrorism, and to free the Iraqi people. Well we all know how that all turned out, don't we?

Actually, for the first few weeks I was quite productive. A lot of the ramblings I'd scribbled down whilst inebriated weren't as incoherent as I first thought they were, and after a bit of editing, made absolute sense, even if only to me. I started writing all the lyrics down long-hand, and after a couple of weeks I'd filled a large note book with enough lyrics for an album. I'd also included the song written during my very brief stint in rehab called "Daze Like This", and then I began to write the music.

A lot of the music didn't work for the themes I had in mind, but nothing went to waste, and on one occasion I came up with a song that reminded me of my young niece, who was still very young at the time. She was always dancing and was very balletic; I put the song on to CD and mailed it to my sister who on hearing it said that it had made her cry. I wasn't quite sure if that was meant as a compliment or not.

My best mate Milton Jaghai was not very well. He'd been in and out of hospital and had to completely give up work. I knew that this was not going down well, but I told him that as long as it meant that he could now get some intensive treatment to sort out the Bastard Cancer once and for all, it would be worth it. Of course I'd told Milton about my own problems, but they all just sounded pathetic compared to his. Nevertheless, after I'd explained my predicament, Milton phoned me every evening to see how I was doing. He would spend all fucking day thinking up a joke just to make me laugh. We hadn't talked this much in years, but that didn't matter. We never discussed his illness and that was intentional, as I think just talking and laughing with me gave him the break that he needed from all the medical jargon that now filled his days. I could hear the pain in his voice though, and on more than one occasion I had to lie and say the kettle was boiling, just so I could go to the bathroom to wipe away the tears. He told me he would soon have to go back into hospital for yet another operation, and I told him that I would help out in the theatre, just to make sure that the surgeon didn't balls it up. They were great conversations that lasted for hours, often well into the early hours of the morning, and they helped me enormously. Does that sound weird?

Milton was not the only one concerned for my health. My younger sister also called me every day just to chat and keep me up to date with the family news. We'd always fought like cat and dog when we were kids, and as there was only two years' difference in our ages, sometimes she'd win the battles. My mother also started writing me letters, just so I'd have something nice to expect through the letterbox in the morning. I treasured them and would read them over and over again throughout the day. They never showed it, but I knew they were all worried sick.

31

"Only a fool trips on what is behind him"

November the 10th, 2003, is a day that I remember for all the wrong reasons. Yes it was my 44th birthday and guess what I did? Yes you've guessed it, I had a drink!

I had been told by the alcohol advisory doctor that I could no longer take my magic pills anymore as they could be destroying my liver. I almost laughed out loud as that's what I thought I'd been doing quite well for myself in the first fucking place—thank you very much.

Apparently I would be able to resume taking them after a month's rest, but for now, I would have to go back to good old fashioned will-power to get me through. Well, will-fucking-power and me hadn't been on speaking terms for months now, and I knew that once we'd been re-acquainted, he'd want revenge. And the revenge he took was dastardly.

After the news that I could no longer take the pills for at least a month, I went into minor despair. A month may as well have been a year, as I knew I might not even make the day…or even an hour. Actually I made it until the end of that week before my brain informed me that is was my birthday and I should celebrate with a little drinky-poo…or ten. I didn't have a lot of money, but I'd remembered what someone told me at an AA meeting in Lewisham, about the cheap and cheerful Kick-Ass Cider that could be purchased for just a few of the Queens pennies at almost any shop in Catford. I didn't have to search far to find some of this delectable nectar, as there was a little shop owned by a certain Mr Patel that was situated almost at the bottom of my stairs.

Of course I'd been in Mr Patel's shop before, normally to buy my cigarettes and a pint of milk, but I had no idea of the hidden treasures to be found at the back of the place secretly hidden behind the pre-packed sandwich section. This was literally an alcoholic's wet-dream, with huge bottles of instant cure going for a tenth of the price of the stuff I was used to drinking. I picked up a very large bottle of something called 'White Kill You' and headed to the counter.

I started off by drinking this disgusting liquid in half measures, but very quickly discovered that the only way to keep it down for more than a second was to drink it in quantity. I started drinking pints of the stuff, knowing that Mr Patel didn't close until late, but also more importantly that he opened very early to do the morning papers, so as long as I could manoeuvre the stairs without breaking my neck, I should be able to stay pissed for 24 hours a day.

I didn't want to sober up for long enough to face what I was doing to myself, and anytime the guilt and shame started to creep up on me, I just drank another bottle until I passed out and the whole routine would start again. How the fuck could this stuff even be legal?!!

I must've been like this for at least ten days with no communication with anyone except an increasingly concerned Mr Patel, who obviously didn't want a death in his shop, when in a very brief moment of clarity I heard the phone ringing. I held my breath... and answered it. I hadn't been into central London for many months, but on one of the last occasions I'd heard on the Soho grapevine that Barry Kirsch, my old boss from Natural Sound, had cashed in his chips and moved to Dubai. I also knew that Matt Faddy, my old writing partner, had, at a later date, flown out to join him, taking his family with him as well. I have no doubts whatsoever that, had I been well enough, Barry would've asked me to join them. But I wasn't, so he didn't.

In one of my very rare moments of lucidity I'd had a day of writing letters, lots of them. I'd had this ridiculous notion that I could return to the world of acting and the theatre and I'd be welcomed, not with open arms perhaps, but at least with a warm hug. I bought a book from W.H Smith called Contacts. This book was basically just a directory full of all the theatrical agents and casting directors in Great Britain. I started with the names that I knew, and then moved on to a few that I didn't but were based in the London area. I know I wrote to at least fifty, and didn't get a reply from a single one. I wish I could say I was surprised, but I wasn't. I had been out of the game for at least a decade now, and the industry I'd once been a part of was changing beyond recognition.

With my final remaining stamp, I wrote a long letter to my good friend Matt, who as I've said was now working and residing with Barry Kirsch in Dubai. Anyway I digress...the phone was ringing.... I lifted the receiver...Hello...

It was Barry Kirsch! "Hello Gaz...how the devil are you?" Now. I have spent quite a while thinking of a way to describe Barry's voice, and the best I could come up with, is that it is like hot honey sliding off of a lizard's back. It was so good to hear that creamy voice after so long.

I didn't want to go into any details as to recent events, as I didn't want to spoil either of our days, so I probably just said Bazzaaa! Barry Kirsch had now formed a new company called B.K.P. (Barry Kirsch Productions) and they'd been commissioned to write and produce an entire album of original music for a company called Tetra Pak that now had business interests in Dubai.

Tetra Pak's new Dubai management apparently were young go-getters with an eye to the future, and their brilliant idea was to mix the musical styles of The Middle East with those of The West, put the finished product on to a CD, and then package it all into a hand-carved wooden box to give to all of their representatives around the world. Nice!

Barry told me that a production meeting had been held, and when the subject of who should be the producer for such a mammoth task only one name came up, and that was Gary Shail. It was such a joy to know that Bazza hadn't lost his touch when it came to flattery and utter bullshit. There was only one problem as far as they were concerned, and that was that the entire project needed to be written, played, produced and packaged within a month. WHAT!

Once I'd completely sobered up and got up off the floor, Barry continued. Could I be in Dubai by the beginning of the following week and start work immediately? I didn't even have time or the inclination to think about whether it could be done or not, so I just said yes! After all, Steven Spielberg was hardly searching his Dinosaur Skinned Filofax for Gary Shail's phone number, was he? And swapping the beautiful panoramic views of Catford for a beach in Dubai didn't seem like any sort of option. My Emirates Airline ticket would be waiting for me at Heathrow Airport, Terminal 4 the following Friday. It was now Sunday.

My preparations for my trip and the task ahead were simple. Sober the fuck up, and fast! There was a public swimming pool about two miles away in Lewisham that opened at 6am, so I would start by running the two miles, then swimming two miles (didn't want to push it). Follow up with a local breakfast, then a brisk walk home. I would then spend the rest of the day working on pre-production for the album. I hadn't run or swam anywhere in years, but I did have a couple of things going in my favour, a certificate for swimming a width when I was eight, and a pair of Adidas trainers.

That first Monday morning was crazy. I'd set an alarm for 5 a.m. as I didn't want to give myself any chance of backing out. I also knew I would need some sort of alcohol to keep me alive for at least the first ten minutes of my run, hopefully after that, the adrenaline would kick in to carry me for the rest of the way. I settled on a quarter bottle of cheap brandy which I mixed with my Tesco's own brand coffee and eked it out over three cups, before heading out into the cold and wet November morning.

By the time I'd got to the bottom of the stairs and out of the front door, Mr Patel was already lifting up the shutters of his shop, getting ready to start sorting out the morning papers. The look on Mr Patel's face was hysterical. It was about 5.30am and there I was standing in the dark doing star-jumps and stretches. "Good morning Mr Patel, and what a fine morning it is," I said (it was actually spitting with ice cold rain). He must've thought I'd finally lost it completely, but still had the good manners not to phone the local asylum.

I started running, slowly at first, but quickly picking up pace as I passed the Broadway Theatre at Rushey Green. It was Panto season in Catford, and as I passed this beautiful Gothic building, I glanced at the posters for Cinderella and said a quiet prayer for all of those poor actors who would be slapping on their grease-paint ready for yet another thankless task later on that evening.

It took me less than 45 minutes to get to the swimming pool, and it was shut. I nearly died. During my run it had still been dark, but now the dawn was beginning to break with the rush hour traffic angrily barking like wild hyenas surrounding their prey. I felt like a complete twat! Why the fuck hadn't I checked the times properly, why hadn't I worn some socks, why hadn't I brought some bus fare money, why hadn't I bought half a bottle of cheap brandy and why the fuck was I standing outside The Lewisham Swimming Pool shouting at myself?

It was now raining steadily and hard, and as I stood soaked and dejected I pondered that age old question for the meaning of life, the universe, and bloody everything.

And the answer wasn't fucking 42*. By the time I'd dragged my wet and cold carcass back along Lewisham High Street, back up Catford hill, past the theatre and up to my flat. I was totally and utterly sober!

Yes, I don't get it either!

*42 (forty-two) is the natural number that succeeds 41 and precedes 43. The number has received considerable attention in popular culture resulting from its central appearance in The Hitchhiker's Guide to the Galaxy as the "Answer to The Ultimate Question of Life, the Universe, and Everything"

32

"Illness is a road without signposts"

I only had three full days to sort myself out. I was terrified of course, but not about the actual job, as I knew I would be in my comfort zone once I was in the studio. What made me anxious were the thoughts that I was having about never coming back to England, if given the chance. I knew that Barry and Matt really would welcome me with open arms once I was there, but I would have to re-think my life completely... yet again.

One of the first things I did was pack my bags. I'd already been told that I wouldn't be needing my mohair Crombie coat on the Equator and packing anything thicker than a linen suit would be a waste of space. The idea of completely starting again from scratch kept me awake at night, which was fine, as I spent the next few nights recording some basic grooves and beats that I thought might come in handy once I was in the Dubai studio.

Everything in my brain started to work again. I wouldn't have any real time for any second thoughts once I started recording. I had to write, record and deliver exactly 73 minutes of music, which doesn't sound like a lot but it bloody well is. Also, as sole producer, I would not be asking for any opinions from anyone. You could quite easily waste hours asking whether or not somebody likes something, so I wouldn't be asking. I'd already been assured by Barry that although I wouldn't be able to work with Matt, as he'd be too busy doing all the day to day commercial stuff, I would be working with two other engineers who were both more than capable to handle the work load. This was an important job for Barry's new company, so I knew he would've vetted them personally. All I had to do now was some personal shit.

Once my immediate family had been told of my plans, I think they were just so relieved that I wasn't phoning with more bad news. They had been so supportive over the past few months, especially my two sisters, who'd even attempted to actually see me one afternoon when I was particularly bad. It must've been horrible to see their big brother in such a state, but they never showed it on their faces, and they just did practical things like the washing up and hoovered the flat. I'd pretended that everything was fine of course, but I could see the disappointment in their eyes when they thought I wasn't looking, and when they'd both left I'd buried my head in my hands and wept. Then I drank.

Next on the agenda was sorting out my bloody passport, which had long since run out and needed replacing. Obviously I wouldn't have the time to send off for it and wait for the postman, so I went down to Petit-France and queued up all day. Once that had been sorted, and with my bags packed, there was only one more vital thing I had left to do.

Visiting my old friend Milton Jaghai in The Royal Free Hospital was never going to be easy, but I am an optimistic chap, if the truth be known, so I was hoping that the news would be good. The walk from Belsize Park up through the leafy streets of Hampstead Village to the hospital had been pleasant and refreshing; with just enough sunshine to take the edge off the November chill. I'd lived here in the early 80's, so it was interesting to see how many characteristics of the old Hampstead remained, and I was happy to see that it hadn't changed that much. The wonderful thing about this part of London is that you can't just buy a property and turn it into a fucking fried chicken shop, no matter how much money you have.

The Royal Free Hospital actually has real showbiz connections. For instance, the new gardens had recently been opened by Sir Elton John, obviously because of his close association with his fund-raising activities for HIV and Aids charities, and the fact that The Royal Free was the first hospital in the UK to appoint a consultant in HIV medicine. Also, the out-patients centre was opened in 1992 by the actor Sir Ian McKellen and is named after the actor Ian Charleson. The hospital is also credited for making significant advances in the fields of liver medicine and transplantation, so this I thought would probably my next port of call if I didn't stop drinking.

Over the years I had gotten used to visiting people in hospital, usually children with life- threatening illnesses or burns where I had perfected the art of disassociation and distance, but with Milton it was a totally different emotion I felt when entering his room. At this point in my life, I'd never had anyone close to me who'd had a life-threatening illness, and for it to be Milton was beyond my comprehension. He'd been one of the fittest out of all of us. A great sprinter, due to his extremely long legs, a keen martial artist who'd kicked my arse on more than one occasion, and an able tennis player too. He didn't smoke, drank in moderation, and in all the years I'd known him, I never once saw him take drugs. Yet there he was clinging to life, whilst I could've probably jumped out of the top floor window of the hospital and landed safely onto Elton John's wig that he'd left unattended in the garden. Who said life was fair?

We spent the afternoon laughing and joking as usual. I told him all about my time at the Troubadour Club, and my aspirations to now become a Bedouin Tribesman in the deserts of Arabia, where men were men, and cute looking camels ran scared. We spoke at length about our children, and how proud we were that they were so independent and happy in their young lives with no criminal convictions to their names...yet! We spoke about the great parties we'd had at both our parents' houses over the years, and the great music that we'd danced to. We spoke about the women in our lives and the joy and the pain that they'd given us, but most importantly… we talked about the future.

All of a sudden the door of Milton's room opened and his parents Fredrick and Avis were here, and although I'd always been treated as part of the family, I somehow felt that it was the right moment to leave. This wasn't going to be some long drawn out goodbye, just a 'see ya' in a few weeks when I get back' kinda thing and we'd go for a few beers. I hugged the family quickly, gave Milton the thumbs-up, and I left the room with a smile on my face. It wasn't on my face for very long. The walk back to Belsize Park Tube Station was far from pleasant.

33

**"We in the UAE have no such word as 'impossible',
it does not exist in our lexicon."
HH Sheikh Mohammed bin Rashid Al Maktoum**

The Emirates flight to Dubai was comfortable and peaceful, and although Barry only booked me onto economy, it was still the best 'cheapy flight' I'd ever been on. Even though I knew I'd be spending most, if not all, of this trip in the studio, I'd still bought an Arabic phrase book, just in case I came into contact with any of the locals or needed to buy something from a shop. The feeling of relief at being airborne and away from London was incredible and liberating, and as I reclined in my window seat, I took stock of my situation.

The last thirty years of my life had been incredible for many reasons. When I first started acting as a child, I thought I'd been the luckiest boy on earth, but that luck probably wouldn't last. So to get the part of Spider in *Quadrophenia* so soon after leaving collage just seemed ridiculous. Of course, I had no idea that the film would be regarded as one of the classics of the 20th century years later (how could I?), but somehow my lucky streak remained with me. Almost everything I touched turned to gold and had given me a lifestyle most kids of that age would've killed for. I'd met some incredible and talented people, who (unlike me) deserved the accolades and praise heaped upon them.

Even whenever I'd been on stage, I'd half expected someone waiting in the wings to take me back to Hendon High where I would be canned by Mr Thompson for being a little upstart and trying to get ahead of his station. I'd worked with some of the biggest names in show business, with many becoming good friends in the process, and I'd been loved by many women who were all well out of my league. I had a son who, thank fuck, took after his mother and was incredibly handsome, I'd travelled to places well off the beaten track, and I'd survived anything and everything that had been thrown at me, even at warp speed. Could this be why I repeatedly pressed the self-destruct button? Was I subconsciously feeling guilty at having such a great time...all of the time? And is that why I drank so much?

It couldn't be that easy, surely? Could you imagine spending thousands of pounds on therapy only for the psychiatrist to tell you that you are fucked up due to having a good time? No... there had to be more to this than that. After all, I'd given up trying to fool people that I could act almost a decade previously and embarked on a completely new career. But even that had been a lucky break. If I hadn't been in Stringfellows that night, I wouldn't have met Al Cleveland, then I wouldn't have met Lady Whatthefuckishername, then I wouldn't have met Barry Kirsch, and then I wouldn't be sitting on this plane. If this was all down to circumstances and fate, then, I reasoned, the blame fell on the pair of coloured socks I'd been given detention for all those years ago. If I hadn't worn them at school that day, I wouldn't have met Marcus Kimber, then I wouldn't have got into drama school...and on it goes. How far would I have digress back to find someone to blame, I wondered. I ordered an orange juice.

Dubai International Airport could be a holiday destination in itself. You could probably book into one of the many hotels within the complex and never get sand on your feet-ever. It is a glittering palace of gold, silver and white marble that completely attacks the senses with its ostentatiousness and grandeur, and after living above a kebab shop in Catford for the last fifteen months or so, it was just what I needed to experience. As I was coming up the escalator towards passport control, I could already see Matt Faddy on the upper level waving to me from behind the glass. With my passport and visiting visa stamped, I made the final short journey towards the doors that would, once opened, mean that I had finally managed to arrive somewhere on time and sober. I hadn't drunk any alcohol on the flight out and was feeling incredibly pleased with myself, if the truth be known. As the doors slid effortlessly open, I was hit by a rush of hot air that almost took my breath away.

Waiting outside for me was Barry Kirsch, Matt Faddy and an incredibly attractive long legged blue eyed blonde called Polly Gotseva, who before I'd even been introduced, knew was Barry's new girlfriend. It was so good to see them all that I was speechless. I think I was actually in shock, as everything had happened so fucking fast over the last week, I just couldn't get my bearings at all. It took quite a while for my eyes to re-adjust to the brightness of everything that surrounded me, and I think it amused them all somewhat to see Gary Shail with nothing to say. It really was an amazing but alien feeling.

Our first stop was for dinner at a Chinese restaurant at the Dubai Marina which was still under construction, as was everything else in Dubai, it seemed. Everywhere you looked, something was being built skyward. Huge metal skeletons as high as the eye could see dotted the landscape, all awaiting the white marble skins that seemed to be Dubai's trademark in decor, and I wondered where all the workers were. Apparently they were all transported in from little shanty towns situated on the outskirts of the city at sundown, where they lived ten to a shack in appalling conditions whilst earning a pittance, which they then sent back to their even more impoverished families back home in India. It was cheap labour on an unimaginable scale. The veneer of this city of gold and silver was easily pierced, it seemed.

Everyone had alcohol with their dinner except me. I so wish I could say this was an easy thing for me to handle, but it wasn't. In fact, this was the hardest it had ever been, as I just wanted to relax with a cold beer or a glass of chilled white wine and catch up with my old friends. I was determined to do this job sober though, and I knew if I started drinking at this early stage, I'd have no chance of making the deadline, or even the end of the week.

It had been arranged that I would be spending the duration of my stay at Barry and Polly's place, which was about a fifteen minute drive from BKP Studios. As I would normally be working throughout the night on the album, it meant I would have the house to myself during the day to sleep and review the previous night's work. Barry's house was a beautiful Spanish style villa which Polly had furnished immaculately with comfy sofas and middle- eastern type cushions, and it felt like a proper home. My room was small but comfortable enough, with just a single bed and a small chest of drawers to put my few clothes in. I was not on holiday, and had packed just enough to get me through the month in the studio. After about an hour of catching up with Barry's news, I was ready to retire to my room.

As I sat on the little single bed I saw something move out of the corner of my eye. There, on the white marble floor, was the biggest fucking ant that I'd ever seen. This ant had a face, for fuck's sake. I still had some complimentary biscuits from the flight, so I broke one in half and put it on the floor beside him. The fucker actually picked it up, gave me a wink, and carried it off. I just hoped my new clients would be just as easily pleased.

The following morning I awoke to an empty house and the sounds of bird song. I walked bleary-eyed out onto the veranda in my boxers to be confronted by a sea of colour that I was not expecting in the slightest. It was only a small garden, but filled with such an array of plants and blooms that it looked more like an English garden, and certainly not something to be found in the middle of the desert. They were all European hybrids though, and had to have been imported, as the beautiful scarlet red roses that I was looking at surely couldn't have grown here naturally in the UAE, I thought. It already seemed that nothing was impossible to achieve in this oil-rich country. It was only mid-morning, but already hot enough for me to be uncomfortable even in just my pants, so after a quick ciggy, I jumped into a cool shower before dressing, and then waited patiently for Polly, who I'd been told would be picking me up at around 11ish.

She was right on time and looked stunning in her black Ray-Ban sunglasses as she told me in her Eastern-European accent all about the new company, and what they hoped to achieve. She said she'd heard all about me, which worried me somewhat, as I couldn't be sure what old bollox Barry had made up, but I knew how much he loved me, so I knew it couldn't be all that bad. Polly was now a director of BKP, as was Matt, but I didn't dare ask her how she and Barry met as I was pretty sure I'd find out sooner or later. When I did eventually find out, I was relieved to hear it had been in a café where she'd been working; and not in some Beirut nightclub at three in the morning. I liked Polly.

I'd long stopped being impressed or amazed at Barry Kirsch's sheer determination and ambition years ago, so to see his new studio set-up and offices came as no surprise whatsoever. How the fuck he could leave a country with next to nothing, and in only a few short months create the biggest, and at that time, the only advertising music company in the UAE, had obviously been on his agenda all along, and I couldn't help thinking that if Barry had been allowed to continue to manage Natural Sound in his sometimes unconventional style, then it could've been a successful world-wide company by now. It was never in Barry's nature to gloat, but I knew he knew he'd been proved right all along. It was a joyous thing to see.

Barry had many friends and contacts in the Middle East, some of whom I'd known from the Natural Sound days, and they remained loyal to him, so work was flying in from all over the region. There were two main studios in the building that had both been furnished with the latest state of the art recording equipment. Pro-Tools* was now industry standard, and both studios had this facility, which meant that the recording compatibility between the two would never be a problem. A third studio was still under construction, and this I was told would be where I would be working, although I would eventually work in all three over the course of the month. On my first day, before I'd played a note, we had a board meeting.

If there was one thing that I fucking hated more than anything, it was having meetings to discuss music. The board meeting was attended by Barry, Matt, Polly and the company accountant, a lovely quiet Indian chap named Itty, who insisted on calling me Mr Gary. Even though I'd worked with Barry and Matt for years, I still felt incredibly nervous at having to put my ideas into words, as I still didn't have a fucking clue what the actual brief was. The Middle East meets the West was all I had to go on, but that could've meant anything. I needed some sort of starting point. Next on the agenda was money. I hadn't given how much I was going to be paid for this project any thought at all, but was not surprised in the slightest when Barry informed me that the budget wasn't big, and I would have to watch what I spent carefully. No change there then, I thought. Personally, I would be paid 1000 Dirhams for the job, which worked out to about £150, so after I'd stopped pissing myself laughing and picked myself up off the floor, I explained that for that derisory sum, I'd want complete production control and credit for the project. I wanted my name all over this album.

Barry had two freelance writers/engineer, that although were not strictly employees, submitted lots of recorded snippets of music that I spent the first afternoon listening to. Some of these short recordings were fantastic and funky, and with a bit of expansion and editing could be the perfect way to start the project, I thought. If I could get all the western influenced music out of the way first, then I could then get the Middle Eastern musicians to try and improvise over the top, and then mix the two together. It was a simplistic plan but usually the best ones are, I think. So that's what we did.

As there was no musicians' union or, at that point, any agencies for players at all in Dubai, I'd have to rely on the guys and gals that Barry had used in the past for the ethnic stuff. A list was drawn up of reliable players, and I started to get them in one at a time.

---

*Fundamentally, Pro Tools, like all digital audio workstation software, is similar to a multi-track tape recorder and mixer, with additional features that can only be performed in the digital domain. It supports 16-bit, 24-bit, 32-bit, and 64-bit float audio at sample rates up to 192 kHz, and can handle WAV, AIFF, AIFC, mp3, WMA, and SDII audio files and QuickTime video files. It features time code, tempo maps, elastic audio, automation, and surround sound capabilities.

Some of the instruments they played I'd never heard of, such as the Oud, which looked like a medieval Lute but was played with a plectrum, another was the Swar Mandal, played by an Indian lad (who looked like he was only twelve years old) whilst sitting on the floor cross-legged, hitting the instrument with little sticks. I got in a local violin player called Khaled Ghadri who improvised over a drum & bass groove, and an Arabic flute player called Bert (not his real name) who didn't want to leave the studio 'cos he was having such a good time.

Grahame (my engineer and co-writer) and I played almost everything else. We borrowed influences from almost every musical genre, including jazz, funk, garage, drum & bass and pop, and once we started mixing in all the Arabic stuff, the music started to take on a life of its own. Even though I'd not planned on having any singers, I still felt that some vocal textures were needed, so we sampled some local pearl divers and an African tribal choir complete with foot stomps to add colour and depth. Barry and Matt both wanted to write something for the album, which was fantastic as it took some of the pressure off me for a while, and both their submissions, as expected, were brilliant.

There was no time for any second thoughts, so if it sounded right, it was right. During the day the studios were busy with recording adverts for luxury cars and international banks and the like, with all the professionalism and courtesy laid on for the paying clients, but come the evening when we started working, the place was filled with whoops of laughter and joy once a musical idea had come together, and after a couple of weeks everything started to take shape and it started to sound epic.

Obviously my clients from Tetra-Pak wanted to know what I was up to, but I flatly refused to play them anything until the album was mixed and finished. I'd had to meet them though and one of them, who was the boss, looked vaguely familiar. His name was Des Joseph.

Fridays in Dubai are like our Sunday used to be before greed took over and they became just like any other day in the U.K. No one does bugger-all in Dubai on a Friday except eat, drink and relax. So when Barry and Polly invited me to spend the day with them at a luxury hotel with a private beach, I jumped at the chance. I badly needed to get the music out of my head for a few hours, so with the promise of seeing, and possibly riding, a camel on the sands, off we went for the day.

Even though I'd been in Dubai for a while and staying at Barry's villa, we really hadn't had that much time to talk. Whenever we'd spoken it had normally been about the project, which I knew he was no longer worrying about. At the rate I was going, I knew I'd definitely meet the deadline and be on brief, and apart from the small matter of client approval, it was almost in the bag.

I'd never seen Barry quite like this before. Whilst in London I'd never really seen him relax or take any real time-out. Even when socializing, his mind had always seemed to be preoccupied with business, so to see him like this was remarkable. Polly obviously adored him and I could tell that Barry reciprocated, and it was like a huge weight had been lifted from his mind. The Dubai climate and lifestyle obviously suited him to a tee, and I wondered if the same effect could be applied to me.

The pain in my jaw had completely disappeared due to the constant heat, and I hadn't had to take any form of pain killer since I'd arrived. Back in the cold and damp British climate I'd been in constant pain since my operation, but since I'd been here, I'd not given it a second thought. As I lay back on the hot white sand gazing out at the perfect blue sea of the Persian Gulf, I made a mental list of all the things I'd miss about London. I couldn't think of a single one.

Of course I would miss my family I thought, but would I really? This was always the first thing anybody said whenever families were parted for any length of time, but I hadn't really been that involved with mine for years. In the last ten years or so I hadn't seen much of them at all, to be honest, and I was pretty sure that during that time they'd had no idea what I'd been doing anyway. I knew that I'd been a constant worry to my mother, who was now suffering with health problems of her own, and I'd always tried to mask my alcoholism whenever we spoke on the telephone, but now that it was out in the open, I just felt an enormous sense of guilt whenever we spoke. As the eldest son I should've been there for her, but I was the last person to be relied upon in an emergency and stayed away. If I left England for good I imagined that my entire family would breathe a huge sigh of relief.

Could I manage to stop drinking here I wondered? As an Islamic country you'd think that alcohol would be a complete no-no, but it was everywhere. Of course there were no off-licenses to speak of, but every hotel had a well-stocked bar, and there were plenty of nightclubs where, as long as you didn't fall out into the road paralytic, you could get as smashed as anywhere else in the western world. No, I would face the same problems here I thought, but at least I wouldn't have the physical pain in my face anymore, which I accredited somewhat to my alcohol intake, and at least I wouldn't be bored. It was time to talk to Barry Kirsch about my future.

Barry and Polly

276

34

"In the end, everyone leaves."

When Barry, Matt and I had been working at Natural Sound it always seemed like one big adventure and such a laugh. Yes, of course we'd taken the job seriously, but I couldn't remember a single day when we all felt we needed time off, or holidays to re-charge our batteries. It seemed very different here though. Once it had been agreed that I would be leaving the U.K to work for B.K.P in Dubai, a formal contract was drawn up which had numerous clauses stating everything from bringing the company into ill repute, to how much I would be getting paid. I started to have second thoughts.

Gone would be the long boozy lunches and pub crawls, and all the outrageous flirting and fraternising with the opposite sex would have to be a thing of the past. It was one thing to come here for a two week holiday, but to become an actual U.A.E resident meant abiding by some extremely strict Islamic rules that, if broken, could and would result in some very harsh penalties. Just walking hand in hand with someone of the opposite sex who you weren't married to was frowned upon, and being drunk in a public place away from the hotels could quite easily land you in jail, with a few lashes added into the bargain. On the other hand, you could engage the services of a prostitute quite easily, it seemed. It was an open secret that girls from all over the world flocked to Dubai to work in the bars and clubs to make easy money, and all the cab drivers knew where these girls could be found. Apparently no gay people lived here at all, with no cases of H.I.V or Aids recorded whatsoever. Gambling was illegal, and yet you could win a gold plated Rolls Royce on a scratch card, and slavery was rife.

Health and safety in the ever-expanding building trade was almost non-existent, and unions and workers' rights were concepts that simply didn't exist. Yes, the lifestyle here was no doubt amazing, but at what price I wondered? No doubt I'd soon be finding out for myself though, as I'd already decided to sign the contract and leave England for good.

The album was nearly finished, with only the mixing and the mastering to complete, so I began to relax enough to start letting people into the studio to listen to it. Of course it didn't really matter what anybody at the studio thought, but I wanted some perspective on the project which had been thrown together in such a short time, that I couldn't now tell if it was any good or not. Before Des Joseph (Tetra-Pak) and his team heard it for the very first time, I wanted everyone at B.K.P to be completely behind it in every way. If they didn't like it, then there would be absolutely no time to re-record anything, so I really was the most nervous I'd ever been about presenting a piece of music to a client.

As Des and his team sat in the studio, I felt it best not to make any comments at all about what they were about to hear, so I just pressed play and retreated to the back of the room where I spent the next 73 minutes trying almost unsuccessfully to stop my beating heart from trying to escape my body via my chest. By now I knew every beat and note that was coming next, so to watch people experiencing it for the first time was enthralling. When the last note had faded, I was exhausted. And they were ecstatic.

Des Joseph, as I'd mentioned earlier, seemed vaguely familiar somehow, but I just couldn't place where I knew him from. He'd wanted to hold a post-production party at his very smart house on Jumeirah beach for everyone concerned with the making of Infinity, which is what the album was now going to be called. As we sat chatting in his garden, with Infinity playing in the background, Des told me something that was totally astounding. He'd known all along who I was, having once also been a pupil at Hendon High in the 1970's when I was there. His mum and dad still lived in Hendon, and he'd followed my career closely ever since. He had not said anything because he didn't want me to feel under any more pressure than I already was, but he'd never had any doubts whatsoever that I could pull it off. Barry Kirsch couldn't fucking believe it, saying that only I could travel 8000 miles at a moment's notice to work on a project for someone whom I'd known since childhood without even knowing it. Yes it was astounding, but shit like this just seemed to happen to me all the bloody time.

The next few days were spent with sorting out all the CD pressings and packaging. All the musicians, composers and engineers would, at my insistence, be credited, and Barry Kirsch took the executive producer's credit as he quite rightly should've. My name was all over it. Not only as sole producer, but also as a composer and musician. On every track except Matt's I'd played something or other, plus Des Joseph had written me a special thank you message on the inner sleeve which was heart-warming and sincere. The whole project had been a resounding success, it seemed, and with this success Barry and B.K.P started planning for future album projects for me to produce once I'd sorted out my affairs back in England.

I was actually seriously considering not going back to England at all. My month's visiting visa was almost up though, so I would have to leave the country anyway, but to renew it I could just as easily fly to Tehran for the day before coming back in the evening and getting another visa stamp. As I was sitting discussing this with Barry and Polly in their living room, the phone rang. It was my sister, and the decision as to whether or not I should return was made for me. My oldest and bestest friend Milton Jaghai had passed away!

I telephoned Fred and Avis immediately but didn't know what to say. I needed to be there as quickly as possible, as for me to be celebrating in the sunshine planning my new stunning life just wasn't right. Being with Milton's family was far more important than anything I could possibly think of. Fred told me they would hold off the funeral until I could get there, so I told him that I'd be with them as soon as was humanly possible and telephoned the airport.

The night of my flight back to England, Barry threw me a party at a beautiful Indian restaurant that was attended by all the staff at B.K.P. It was a lovely evening and I even treated myself to a couple of beers and a cigar. I'd managed to complete the project on time, on budget, on brief and without needing any alcohol. I would be back within the month with the promise of an apartment of my own, complete control of which projects I chose to do, and a monthly salary. My new life seemed assured, and I couldn't wait to get back.

I landed back in England on a wet, cold and windy December morning with nothing but my passport and a bag full of fake Louis Vuitton handbags that I'd bought as Christmas presents for my sisters. I'd also bought my mum a beautiful bracelet I'd haggled for in one of the local gold souks for a fraction of the price, and a coffee-table book on the wonders of Dubai for my dad.

I would be spending the Christmas period at my parents' house, which I knew would be a bit strange, as the whole trip home was now tinged with the sadness of Milton's forthcoming funeral. I didn't even want to think about going back to my flat in Catford, as I couldn't be sure that once back there I wouldn't somehow just wake up sweating, wrapped in a duvet in the corner of the room, and all this had just been a dream. No, I would go back to the flat once Christmas was over and not give myself time to dwell on the situation of what I would be doing with all my stuff.

As I walked from Hendon Central Station I took the long way home, past my grandparents' old house where both me and my mother had both been born, past the Hendon Junior High School where all of my family except my dad had been educated, and past the little corner shop where I'd used to collect the paraffin for the heaters before we'd had central heating installed. During those cold winter evenings, I would be a walking petrol bomb as I staggered up the road with the pink highly inflammable liquid in both hands. It seems strange to think that now children aren't even allowed to climb trees or play conkers without eye protectors, but in my youth there were dangers everywhere that somehow we managed to survive without a government health and safety hand-book.

All the Christmas decorations were up in my parents' house already. For as long as I could remember this had always been my dad's job, and although my mum had always said that she had hated this time of year, we all knew that she was fibbing. All the presents had been wrapped and under the fake tree that had been retrieved from the loft for more years than I could remember, and already there were Christmas cards strung up all over the living room walls. I would be sleeping in my sister's old room, as my old little box room had now been turned into a mini museum for my dad's camera collection, where he had everything from a box Brownie to a Leica. It was good to be home.

On the day of Milton's funeral I went round to his parents' house that was already filling up with family and friends, and as I sat in Fred and Avis's living room, the memories of Milton and I doing the hustle to Barry White's "You're the First, My Last, My Everything" made me smile. The service was to be held at The Hendon Crematorium on the 22nd, just three days before Christmas, and I felt honoured and overwhelmed that Milton's family waited until I could be there. I was asked if I would be a coffin bearer with Milton's father and two brothers and I actually could not believe that I was having this conversation at all. Even now, it hadn't sunk in that I would never be seeing my old mate again.

After the service, which all my family attended, we had a party where the music and food were as fantastic as you would've expected for a Jamaican funeral. Lots of my old Hendon School friends were there, and it was interesting to see how everyone had grown into adulthood with children of their own and mortgages. I sat eating my chicken, rice, and peas with Milton's wife Kim and Jacqui Bischoff, reminiscing. We had all known each other since pre-school, and sat laughing about playing spin the bottle in Jacqui's mum Vera's back room when we couldn't have been more than ten or eleven years old. We thought we were so grown up, and the long hot summers would never end

35

"Saying goodbye is the most painful way of solving a problem"

Once Christmas and New Year were out of the way, it was time for me to return to Catford and try and not go into Mr Patel's little shop on the way. This was never going to be easy, as my brain was already once again telling me that surely one little drink couldn't hurt. I'd managed the whole Christmas and New Year period without a drink, but still my mind was sneaking up on me and whispering in my ear. I thought about going to an AA meeting, but didn't get any further than the thought; as I was sure that listening to all the Christmas relapse stories I was sure to hear would probably make me just want to go to the pub.

Of course the flat was exactly as I'd left it, and the only mail I had was a Christmas card from Oxfam asking if I had any old clothes to donate to the starving children of Africa. This made me laugh, as I could now imagine some little chap collecting water from a river dressed in my old cashmere Crombie coat and Doctor Martin boots, both items I would no longer be needing in the hot temperatures of Dubai. In fact, there was nothing here that couldn't be replaced once I was in Dubai, and the only thing worth keeping was my record collection, which somehow I'd always managed to keep a hold of throughout the years. They were all packed neatly into proper record boxes and there were lots of them. They say one can tell someone's personality from their literature and music tastes, and I wondered what this collection would say about me. I decided to trust their safety to my son, who was now 18 years old and starting to find a musical identity of his own. At the moment he was into Goth Rock and tattoos, but I was sure that at some point in the not too distant future he'd discover Bob Marley and the Clash for himself, and when he did, all he had to do was open up a box and there he'd find everything that these artists had ever recorded.

Of course I had furniture and lots of other crap that normal people would've probably put into storage for when they returned, but I'd already decided that I didn't want any form of safety net at all, and the only people I would be saying goodbye to was going to be Mr Patel and Cate Latto, who I'd always kept in touch with over the years. I'd long stopped being hopelessly in love with her, but always enjoyed our long conversations on the telephone, normally at some ungodly hour of the night when she came home pissed from a night out. She now had a young son of her own though, so the drunken late night conversations become less frequent, but still she always found time to call to see if I was alright. Apart from that, I could think of no one that would even notice that I'd gone.

I spent my last night in England on my own watching television and drinking tea. There was a news report stating that Israel was once again bombing Lebanon in retaliation for the killing of one of their soldiers in a Hezbollah missile attack on Israel's northern border. Would I ever live to see these two bordering countries reach some kind of peace agreement, I thought. Even though I was about to be living in the Middle East, Dubai seemed to be immune from all of this horrible strife and chaos. I remembered what one of the locals had told me about this observation...Even terrorists need a holiday.

The following morning, once my cab to the airport arrived, I picked up my small bag, shut the door, put my keys through the letter box, and said goodbye to absolutely no one.

Epilogue

Obviously I came back, but that is another story. I truly believe I was privileged to have lived and worked in what I consider to have been one of the golden ages of music, theatre, TV, and film. I didn't know it at the time, but I was witnessing first hand, in some cases, true genius and innovation within the entertainment and advertising world.

Yes, Glam Rock and Punk were fleeting moments, and The New Romantics probably only lasted for a weekend or two, but still we hark back to those crazy days when anything and everything seemed possible. I was walking, sometimes falling, but always laughing through a period of history that will never be repeated, and for that, I feel blessed.

Yes of course I made mistakes, but don't we all? Yes I took drugs, drank far too much, and spent some wonderful times with an array of very beautiful ladies. But to me, that was the whole point of living. You only have one life, and believe me when I say, that life is short and sometimes painful, but if you can avert your attention away from your mobile telephone for more than a minute, then there are still remarkable experiences to be enjoyed. But you have to go out there and grab them!

It would be too easy for me to criticise the state of today's music, advertising and film industries, and not a very wise thing for me to do, as I rarely have anything to do with them now. But I lose no sleep worrying about this, as they are unrecognisable to what I was privy to, and if people want to watch people watching television whilst watching television, then that's their business. And if you want to start your day by listening to people shouting at each other for shagging your sister, then who am I to criticise? I just don't let it into my life.

My days are a lot quieter these days, but I still have my moments. I get invited to talk regularly at events, and people always seem happy to see me when I attend. I am associated with many charitable organisations who I am always more than happy to speak to raise funds and awareness for. It's the nurses and doctors who are the real heroes though. But if me being at an event can raise more money for a worthy cause, then I will be there if I can.

Quadrophenia has now entered the realms of legend, with more young fans being created year after year, when they eventually discover the film for themselves. Pete Townsend's wonderful and mythic music and lyrics will never fade from memory, and if I had the words 'Here lies Spider' inscribed on my head stone, then I could do a lot worse.

I was going to have 'I Told You I Was ILL'... but Spike Milligan has already got it!!

Acknowledgements

I would like to thank everyone who contributed to this book. And special thanks go to Shelly Daniels for spellcheck and coffee.

Gary Shail Brighton 2015